NARRATING JUSTICE AND HOPE

Narrating Justice and Hope

How Good Stories Counter Crime and Harm

Edited by
Lois Presser, Jennifer Fleetwood, *and* Sveinung Sandberg

NEW YORK UNIVERSITY PRESS
New York

NEW YORK UNIVERSITY PRESS
New York
www.nyupress.org

© 2025 by New York University
All rights reserved

Please contact the Library of Congress for Cataloging-in-Publication data.

ISBN: 9781479824496 (hardback)
ISBN: 9781479824502 (paperback)
ISBN: 9781479824526 (library ebook)
ISBN: 9781479824519 (consumer ebook)

This book is printed on acid-free paper, and its binding materials are chosen for strength and durability. We strive to use environmentally responsible suppliers and materials to the greatest extent possible in publishing our books.

Manufactured in the United States of America

10 9 8 7 6 5 4 3 2 1

Also available as an ebook

The authors would like to dedicate the book to

Helen Presser, who was always hopeful

Gregory and Luisa Amenta

Solomon and Samson

Sanna Schliewe

Grace Carswell

Victor Fleetwood

Leyla Lynn-Johnson

Simone Dahle Sandberg

Tia and Ntare, whose births during the pandemic embody hopeful stories in troubled times

CONTENTS

Foreword: Stories of Hope   ix
    Shadd Maruna

Introduction: Good/Story   1
    Lois Presser, Jennifer Fleetwood, and Sveinung Sandberg

PART I: STORIES THAT DO GOOD

1. What Good Can Stories Do?   19
    Sveinung Sandberg and Sébastien Tutenges

2. "I Actually Came Out on Top!": Narratives of Formerly Incarcerated People Who Made Prison Work   41
    Vanessa Lynn

3. Fresh Home: Narratives Celebrating Freedom from Prison and the Durability of the Street Self in UK Rap Music   67
    Jennifer Fleetwood and Jonathan Ilan

4. Real Utopian Stories to Counter the Climate Apocalypse   91
    Christina Ergas

PART II: GOOD IN THE TELLING

5. Morality from the Mountaintop: Comparing Philosophical and Narrative Approaches to Increasing the Good   117
    Paul Joosse

6. "The Places I Could Go": A Good Story of Probation   140
    Fergus McNeill

7. Good Storytelling and the Fraught Promise of Intimacy   163
    Francesca Polletta, Tania DoCarmo, and Kelly Marie Ward

8. Youth Narrating the Future: Climate Change Activism as a Civil Rights Movement   186
   Robin Kundis Craig

9. The Gift of Survivor Stories: Recognizing the Political Promise of Sexual Violence Narratives   209
   Tanya Serisier

10. Mandela and Luzira Prison: A Mother-Daughter Story   231
    Charlotte Andrews-Briscoe and Molly Andrews

Acknowledgments   251

About the Contributors   253

About the Editors   255

Index   257

FOREWORD

Stories of Hope

SHADD MARUNA

My friend Gethin Jones has a good story. Actually, it is an amazing story. Well, really it is a horrible story. A terrifying story about society's disregard for human life. Most of it, anyhow. But the ending is something else.

Gethin grew up "in care"—or really without care—born to a teenage mother who was herself an orphan and unable to look after him or protect him from serious abuse. Although he reached out to social services for help, all he got from the state was punishment, getting his first criminal conviction as a child of eleven and getting locked away by age fourteen. The rest of his youth was spent spiraling between prisons, addiction, homelessness, and crime. In his last prison, some twenty years ago, he met a drug worker with lived experience of addiction, who helped him begin a process of finding forgiveness—for his mother who abused him, for the system that abandoned him, for himself most of all. He detoxed from drugs, joined a recovery community, and started a career in youth work, devoting himself to helping young people in circumstances like his. Eventually, he founded the organization Unlocking Potential, which delivers coaching and training to both prison groups and professionals all over the world.

I am not doing justice to his story here. You have to hear the story from Gethin himself. Literally. He is, after all, a professional storyteller, a motivational speaker, who draws on his lived experience in all of the work he does, regularly leaving audiences speechless, stunned, or discreetly wiping away tears. His is a tragic story, but it is the epitome of a redemptive story. It is a good story. Damn good. Not just well told, but utilized for the achievement of true good—for training social workers and prison staff to see the humanity in the people they work with, for inspiring those in prison to see the humanity in themselves.

One time he was giving his good story to a prisoner whom I will call Nick, who was serving a draconian, indeterminate sentence in a British prison. They made a real connection and Nick thanked him for giving him hope that there may be some kind of future for him. If Gethin could overcome all the things that life has thrown at him and achieved all that he has, then maybe there was hope for Nick and his fellow prisoners after all. Then Nick said a funny thing. He asked Gethin, "Do you know what the word 'hope' stands for?" Now, Gethin is in the hope business. It would be no exaggeration to say that he is kind of the living embodiment of hope. Hope is the magic formula driving his consultancy work at Unlocking Potential, and hope is the outcome he seeks to achieve in his sessions. But . . . no . . . he had to admit that he had no idea what the word "hope" stood for. The man explained that HOPE is an acronym that stands for "Hearing Other People's Experiences." Suddenly, a lightbulb went off with Gethin—as it has for everyone he has subsequently told this story to. Obviously, Gethin Jones knew that storytelling was a powerful force, the (rather open) secret behind the motivational work he does, but he had not realized that the sharing of his story was literally synonymous with giving hope.

This remarkable collection of academic essays and analyses gives me great hope. We could really use some good stories like his right about now. I mean *really* use them. With a world (barely) emerging from a global pandemic, shaken by seemingly endless wars, ravaged by the climate catastrophe, and (especially) immobilized by social and political divisions, the timing, literally, could not be better for this exquisite collection exploring the power of "good stories" like Gethin's to unite communities, to sustain social movements, and to inspire social change. Good stories are not all that the world needs right now, but it is fair to say that without them, there is little hope for change.

Some will object, of course. There is always an academic career to be made by criticizing good ideas—after all, the best ideas are complex enough to contain contradictions within them. Critics might ask, Why focus on *stories* at all? In a time when there is so much need in the world for hard facts and concrete structural change, why (on earth) focus on something as ephemeral as stories? Maybe there is a whiff of "Let them eat cake" in the idea that what is needed at this moment of economic hardship and climate chaos is a good story to make us all happier. Others will ask, Why *good*? and indeed, What *is* good? or even (somewhat remarkably), Is good any good? Maybe the world already has too many good stories; maybe good stories (or stories *of* the good at least) are at the heart of many of the problems and divisions tearing our world apart. What one side calls "good" the other side calls "evil." Who among us is to say what is good or who is good in a world as divided as ours? How dare anyone even use the word "good" in these postmodern times? Others will say something generally impenetrable about neoliberal subjects something something and responsibilization something something. To their credit, the editors and contributors to this collection engage with these critiques of narrative in the chapters that follow. They acknowledge that stories can do great harm as well as good, that even the best stories are not the solution to every problem.

I have to say, though, I have never met anyone in prison who has any truck at all with such concerns. To people in prison, there is nothing fluffy or neoliberal about hope. Hope (and the lack thereof) is not just a big thing in prison, it may be the only thing. What is the difference between the person who gives up on life and overdoses on the cell floor, and the person who survives prison and proves to all the doubters that she can succeed without drugs, without stealing? Anyone inside will tell you that the first person lost hope and the second one found it. We may dismiss that ("Not very scientific, is it? How do you even measure this thing called hope?"). Yet, if you keep talking to those inside, you might even meet a guy like Nick who will tell you exactly where to find that hope: the power of good stories. That is real enough for me.

Introduction

Good/Story

LOIS PRESSER, JENNIFER FLEETWOOD, AND SVEINUNG SANDBERG

Well, darkness has a hunger that's insatiable
And lightness has a call that's hard to hear
—Indigo Girls, "Closer to Fine"

The moment in which we live teems with harms and hardships, both current and looming: war, genocide, mismanaged global health crises, climate crises, political repression, mass migration and malignant neglect of refugees, persistent racism, economic exploitation, inequality, mass incarceration, and surveillance. This volume tells stories that have emerged in the shadow of such troubles. While narratives inspire and legitimize actions and arrangements that cause suffering and injustice, including the aforementioned problems, our focus in this book is on how narratives can also do good. By "good stories," we mean stories and storytelling that contribute to comfort, safety, and support and reduce suffering. Drawing on research across a variety of harms, the book asks, How do people create good stories even as they face hardship and danger? What kinds of narratives can make harms and threats thereof endurable? What kinds of narratives might effectively produce social change? What does it take to tell good stories? What are some pitfalls in trying to tell good stories? What are good stories, anyway?

This introduction describes the thinking that launched the book and the research that grounds it, and summarizes the book's chapters, with an emphasis on the support that they can provide those in difficult circumstances and the suggestions that they might offer researchers for framing cultural studies of adversity. We begin with caveats about embracing stories and storytelling as good.

Caveats

We have been warned against undue scholarly devotion to stories. Most germane to this volume, it is said that one should not put too much stock in the progressive potential of stories. Hence, Keen (2007) contends, based on available research evidence, that the capacity of narrative fiction to induce empathy has been overstated. In fact, the capacity of fictional stories to stimulate and support tribalism and fascism ought not be overlooked. In terms of nonfiction, or people's "own" stories, Fernandes (2017) raises concerns about "how the messy and inchoate experiences of everyday life are marshalled into compact and portable narratives that can be deployed by states and nonprofit organizations toward instrumental ends" (13). Stories, Fernandes observes, are being "guided by utilitarian logics and forms of liberal and neoliberal subject-making" (163). For example, advocacy groups have given undocumented students brought to the United States as children "scripts to follow that emphasized their achievements, assimilation into American society, and rejection of their home culture" (105).

"Story-critical narratology" warns of the dangers of stories, including "the focusing on individual experience instead of macro-level or complex phenomena" (Mäkelä 2018: 175) and points out that online storytelling is flattening life's complexity. Atkinson (1997) calls out researchers' ideas of "redemption through narrative" (335)—the idea that storytelling is healing *per se*. Strawson (2004) objects both to the view that we know ourselves mainly through the narratives we construct, and to the view that it is virtuous to know ourselves in that way. He maintains that narrativity can discourage people from living in the moment: "It is in the sphere of ethics more of an affliction or a bad habit than a prerequisite of a good life" (450).

The criticisms above remind us that stories ought not be taken at face value. Further, they ought to be studied within social contexts and perhaps especially settings for the would-be exertion of dominance. Evaluations of what narratives do should be based on careful research. We think that these points are well taken. The authors of this book's chapters are keenly aware that stories can and do inspire and sustain the bad things of the world. It is not difficult to find current examples of destructive stories, from the most bizarre conspiracy theories to the largely taken-for-granted storied ideologies that sustain global inequality. We recognize as well that storytelling gets manipulated and even coerced (e.g., Fox 1999; Zhang and Dong 2019). These hazards are beyond question. Still, we press on.

Notwithstanding the aforementioned criticisms, we note that stories can do good for particular people in particular situations, and furthermore, that most people have a sense of that promise. Stories can comfort, inspire, and uplift. More lastingly, they can promote positive changes in the world. These are the topics we are committed to exploring.

Stories Doing Good

The idea that storytelling is "good" is actually widespread. Indeed, that idea informs the charge that some stories are co-opted, marginalized, or silenced altogether: these things are wrong because to tell one's stories reflects and promotes agency and dignity.

Some may question the notion of *intrinsically* good stories, though we consider as strong candidates the story of the Good Samaritan in the Bible, that of the prophet Muhammad helping a woman who threw garbage at him, or the story of Buddha rejecting a gift. Our emphasis in this book, however, is on stories *doing* good more than on their *being* good.

There is not space here to include all the ways in which stories may do good, but let us mention a few to give the reader a sense of what we mean by it. A long tradition holds that life stories can mend wounds of traumatized pasts, preparing people to face the future. Narratives are a way to "make sense" of crises, such as forced migration (Jackson 2002), illness (Frank 1995), or imprisonment (Maruna, Wilson, and Curran 2006). "Recovery tales" (Plummer 1995) and "reform narratives" (Presser 2008) facilitate the individual's capacity for "making good" (Maruna 2001). Gergen and Gergen (1983) broadly call these "progressive narratives," which project advancement toward a favorable goal. Within criminology and the sociology of crime, studies of desistance have been framed in these terms, though the upward trajectory of such narratives has broader application. The storyteller relegates misery or misconduct, and the suffering or transgressive self, to the past; the future (self) will be different.

The field of narrative psychology centers storytelling as a means, and a generally positive one, to knowing oneself. Indeed, Strawson (2004), cited earlier, problematizes that view. Sociologists have made a distinct but related observation, that we let *others* know where we stand by telling stories. Scott and Lyman (1968) attend to storytelling—the giving of "accounts"—as a form of social action for mending the junctures between expected and actual behavior. Also, within cultures stories present "positive models to emulate and negative models to avoid" (Polkinghorne 1988: 14). Shared stories do important work in creating the collective consciousness that integrates and makes societies possible (Durkheim 2015).

In powerful works by Arthur Frank (1995), Judith Herman (1992), and Susan Brison (2002), the authors describe the power of stories to give *meaning* to suffering and map a path beyond it. More broadly, stories give meaning to life itself. Hence the centering of stories within religion. From the earliest appearances of human collectives, people have put immense narrative work into making meaning of human existence. The Mayan Popol Vuh (tales of creation) and the Norse cosmogony starting with Ginnungagap (a gaping abyss) are among known feats of humans' astonishing storytelling imagination. Faced with uncertainty, people go to great lengths to create myths. Harari (2017) argues that "humans conquered the world thanks to their unique ability to believe in collective myths," not only about their origins but also about freedom, equality, and material sustenance. Consider that no reality inheres in "money": its reality stems from people's belief in it. Stories big and small do indispensable work for whatever gets called "society" and "social life." Accordingly, whereas Lyotard (1984) conjectured that the "grand narratives" of modern society would give way to a multitude of small local stories, the former seem now to coexist with the latter in providing direction for human life.

The power of stories means that specialized or professional storytellers hold a particularly important position within societies, from the storytellers in Machiguenga culture famously described in Vargas Llosa's *El Hablador* (2010), to the Celtic seanchaí, authors or ancient and modern prophets and priests, and further on to modern-day politicians, television hosts, and other "influencers." Even the degree to which any of these storytellers might be despised illustrates their power. If not for their power to influence society, why would they be derided? Conversely, the absence of storytellers is a frightening scenario, reflecting a society where we did not share some basic stories.

Stories do "good" work on a micro-sociological level as well. In everyday conversations, small stories (Bamberg and Georgakopoulou 2008) can, through "comic corrective" (Bauman 1986) or boundary drawing (Lamont and Molnár 2002), provide continuous minor feedback, permitting the amendment of undesirable behavior in a relatively tension-free way. Stories also do good, in the telling, by creating moments of immense pleasure in the telling or the hearing: they produce the temporary refuge of a distraction or laugh (Tutenges and Rod 2009). Arguably, the good that comes from "oral literature as verbal art" (Bauman 1986: 9) should be appreciated more than it has been in both sociology and criminology.

Personal narratives can do good by giving voice to suffering, marginalization, and oppression. Ricoeur famously wrote, "The whole story of suffering cries out for vengeance and calls for narrative" (1984: 75). In other words, storying one's misery is as important as anything else that one does. Storytelling is a kind of redress, a blow to regimes of silence, and a counter to discursive masters. Through narrative, tellers can assert subjectivity and a point of view and make claims to truth, including truths about victimization and trauma (McGarry and Walklate 2015; Serisier 2018). It is thus no wonder that they receive so much use in contexts of recovery and social protest. In contextualizing present circumstances and suggesting ways forward, stories issue calls for action (Plummer 1995; Polletta 2006). People rise up against oppression equipped with understandings gained through prognostic frames (stories of the problem), diagnostic frames (stories of the solution), and motivational frames (stories of why one should act now) (Snow and Benford 1992).

Of course, the aforementioned stories can also be, and are, used to promote harmful ideologies. However, protest narratives surely provide an opportunity for carving out opposition toward harmful master narratives and for envisioning another future. Without them, change for the better would be difficult, if not impossible.

Narratives, Resistance, and the Everyday

Beyond narratives in the sphere of organized movements, "personal" narratives can construct less recognized forms of resistance, such as in response to stigmatizing stereotypes (Lavin 2017). That fact brings us to the realm of the everyday. The "everyday" is that which is ordinary, habitual, and often overlooked (Highmore 2011). Lefebvre (1991: 87) likens everyday life to "fertile soil":

> A landscape without flowers or magnificent woods may be depressing for the passer-by; but flowers and trees should not make us forget the earth beneath, which has a secret life and a richness of its own.

The metaphor of the fertile soil draws attention to that which lies beneath, and sustains, manifest social phenomena. Harms with structural roots and ramifications are challenged daily, though accounts of such are often overlooked as "just" stories. Small resistances and stories of such have not received enough attention, in our view. Along these lines, both Lynn and McNeill, in their chapters, consider the narratives of the men and women about their involvement with the justice system. While their narratives testify to harm, they also find the "good" in surprising ways. "If the everyday remains a primary site of the enforcement of injustice, it remains a place for hope and resistance too" (Ferrell, Hayward, and Young 2015: 89). Everyday narrative resistance can be a rejoinder to multiple, even contradictory, discourses, hence Sandberg and Colvin's (2020) observation: counter-narratives can "talk back" *both* to harmful subcultural narratives *and* to cultural prejudices (17). Fleetwood and Ilan in this volume are similarly oriented toward the multiple audiences to whom a narrative may be directed. Narratives are good at negotiating multiple discursive demands inasmuch as they permit play and creativity.

Whereas the contributors to this volume come from multiple disciplines, the three authors of this chapter are positioned within criminology. We have pioneered the paradigm known as narrative criminology. And so we turn next to narrative criminology for thinking about stories doing good.

Narrative Criminology

Narrative criminology advances the idea that stories influence harmful deeds and arrangements (Fleetwood et al. 2019; Presser 2009; Presser and Sandberg 2015). Stories inspire people to act and also provide discursive frameworks for legitimizing action. Influential stories include life stories, event stories, stories of the group/community/nation, and mere hints of stories, or tropes, that reflect dominant, not-needing-to-be-enunciated logics (Sandberg 2016).

Narrative criminology has a critical dimension and critical potential (Presser and Sandberg 2019). Among other things, it theorizes harm and not necessarily lawbreaking. Presser (2018) has elaborated this dimension in her studies of meat eating and punishment of "criminals." Narrative criminologists have been, furthermore, unusually reflexive about starting assumptions and blind spots, perhaps especially about how researchers conceptualize and shape the phenomena they strive to understand. An important insight of narrative criminology is that stories are various and complex, and so too are their impacts.

Nothing intrinsic to the narrative criminology approach inclines the researcher toward harm as opposed to beneficence. A criminological model for the latter focus is control theory, a major perspective that promises to theorize *non*-offending (conceived as "conformity"). That promise has been largely unfulfilled, as assessments of the theory typically aim to predict the discipline's standard outcomes based on crime. Control theories do not seek "to account for variation in occupational behavior, meritorious achievement, or prosocial contributions to the welfare of society" (Akers and Sellers 2013: 113). It seems that criminology is more attracted to darkness than to lightness. Certainly, criminologists want to know what causes harm for the sake of intervening. However, we should also seek to understand what helps to lift humanity and support well-being. Such understanding could ultimately help to change the nature of what we face.

Whereas we three have studied the stories of various harm-doers and harm-resisters for two decades, we have also been fortunate to hear good stories through our research—stories that counter harm and direct ways toward justice and well-being. Fleetwood (2019) studied narratives posted on Hollaback London, a branch of a global organization dedicated to campaigning against street harassment. She finds that "reading narratives can generate dispositions for self-defence. Hollaback narratives do not just offer storylines or scripts for resisting street harassment but foster a style for doing so" (1711). Interviews with young

Muslims in Norway led Sandberg to a view of narrative resistance to both violent terrorism and mainstream non-Muslim hostility (Sandberg and Colvin 2020). Interviews that Presser and colleagues (2018) conducted with meat eaters and vegans yielded stories of achieving awareness and growth. Ideas from narratology and sociology have guided these research efforts.

Interdisciplinary Insights

Narratology offers theories and concepts for understanding good stories out of bad circumstances. First, formalizing the idea that stories and the stuff of stories are not the same, is the important narratological distinction between the narrative discourse and the events to be, potentially, narrated.

Troubles from which "good stories" may emerge are complicating actions (Labov and Waletzky 1967)—the unforeseen and perhaps difficult present events or experiences. Whereas complicating actions are elemental to stories, they are not the whole story. Among other things, audiences will want to know their "resolution." What "finally" happened and why? What was the experience of that happening like (Fludernik 1996; D. Herman 2009)? Good out of bad (circumstance) is a rather common storyline, the stuff of narrative genres including the heroic quest (Campbell 1949), the "rags to riches" story (Weiss 1969), the restitution story of illness (Frank 2010), and the underdog story (Presser 2018). Especially popular stories deliver something unexpected. The endings of the darkest and the most ordinary stories are not foretold: surprising and even good turns of events are always possible.

Smith (1981: 169) states that "no narrative version can be independent of a particular teller and occasion of telling and, therefore, . . . we may assume that every narrative version has been constructed in accord with some set of purposes or interests." Contemporary rhetorical narratologists agree that "texts are designed by authors to affect readers in particular ways" (Phelan 2017: 6). They show narrative to be "the product of co-enunciation and co-construction processes" (Chanfrault-Duchet 2000: 62). Stories are assembled within social interactions, and, as contemporary psychotherapy makes plain, "our" stories get revised through dialogue, and revised versions can be deployed for growth.

Narratologists are mainly interested in how narratives are constituted, whereas social scientists are interested in the public life of stories—how they play out in social contexts and what they owe to social experience. Sociology inspires us with ideas about the social embeddedness *and* flexibility of people's stories. Ken Plummer (2019) notes, "As people make their own narratives—but not usually in moments and structures of their own choosing—a politics of empowerment and enhancement of lives becomes possible, creating new opportunities for better worlds" (xii).

Concerning the deep socialization of discourse—shaping, regulating, and controlling what can be said or even imagined—Fleetwood (2016: 181) conceptualizes a narrative habitus that includes "vocabulary, narrative formats, tropes, discursive formats and subject positions." Creativity is possible only within the limits prescribed by the habitus, she argues. Habitus structures storytelling, not least by honing expectations, internalized and largely insensible, of what a "true" story is. Cultural and socially situated expectations influence choices about what stories to tell and how to tell them (see Presser 2004), which reminds us that we can "story" hard times in a range of ways, albeit limited.

Discourse generally is co-constructed. We use common language and linguistic forms. We draw on available metaphors, idioms, tropes, and story genres; we cannot make sense to ourselves and others otherwise. And yet, language-in-use tends to be hybridized (Fairclough 2013; Sandberg 2013). Discourse analysts refer to this tendency as intertextuality or interdiscursivity, and the phenomenon suggests resourcefulness, and thus opportunities for finding and creating good, alongside constraint.

The Chapters

The chapters that follow are organized as studies of stories that do good (part 1), and studies of telling stories effectively (part 2). Relatively speaking, part 1 is more inclined toward the positive themes discernible in stories and the positive effects of their telling. In (subtle) contrast, part 2 devotes more attention to the affordances of the story form within specific social contexts. As such, the contributions in part 2 are more concerned to engage the problematics of good storytelling. As Polletta and colleagues contend in chapter 7, "What makes for a good story depends on what the purposes of the story are."

Part 1. Stories That Do Good

1. Sveinung Sandberg and Sébastien Tutenges ponder the "good stories" shared, over years of ethnographic work, by marginalized people involved in street crime and substance abuse. They have heard stories about overcoming trauma, turning away from harm-doing, and making life better for oneself and others. The analysis yields a typology of storytelling as healing, uplifting, harm-limiting, and/or imaginative. Respectively, the four types of storytelling have the effect of reducing some suffering; creating a sense of well-being in the moment; redirecting some (more) harmful trajectories; and envisioning a better future. The chapter foregrounds a view of goodness bound to social context: some stories "may not be *intrinsically* good" but rather "may *do good* for particular people in particular situations." The interview emerges as one site for conjuring changed selves and better circumstances.

2. Vanessa Lynn illuminates the narratives of two former prisoners depicting past prison experiences as life-serving. Mass incarceration in the United States has wreaked untold harms on Black men and their communities. Yet, during in-depth interviews with Lynn, two formerly incarcerated men, Miles and Travis, told positive stories about their time in prison, recounting, for example, their having discovered community; grown intellectually, spiritually, and socially; and arrived at beneficial self-understandings. Lynn innovates with the concept of narrative portraiture. The interviewees are portraitists who, helped by Lynn as interlocutor, offer complex, holistic renderings of their lives.

3. Jennifer Fleetwood and Jonathan Ilan find good stories in "fresh home rap," a thematic genre of UK rap music from men and women who have recently been released from prison. Drawing on street cultural tropes typically associated with criminality, such as the pursuit of a lavish lifestyle, fresh home raps nonetheless make space for the possibility of pursuing legitimate rather than criminal careers. The raps center joy and flourishing as well as triumph over the tedium of prison and the injustice that brought them there; they emplot new beginnings.

4. Christina Ergas relates stories of cooperation and mutual aid that people in two urban ecovillages, in the United States and Cuba, told in the face of climate disaster. Ergas was audience to these stories during four years of field research. Whereas popular dystopian tales of climate crisis thematize doom, the ecovillagers' stories center on and furthermore motivate regeneration and solidarity. The stories cast community as a united protagonist and envision "outsiders" as potential insiders to the community.

Part 2. Good in the Telling

5. Paul Joosse maintains that philosophers might usefully deploy narrative forms for arguing their points, as "storying philosophical arguments helps us to actually accomplish what they aim to do—which is to do good." Joosse takes the case of Dr. Martin Luther King Jr's 1968 "I Have Been to the Mountaintop" speech to demonstrate the powerful capacities of narratives, among them the capacity to construct a sense of the uncanny, to invite ready connections to canonical tales that imply big and undeniable truths, and to position tellers among listeners rather than in an elite position "above." King used these capacities to conjure a social justice vision that, however long the odds, would seem inevitable.
6. Fergus McNeill analyzes the case of Mary, who had fifty years prior experienced recognition and support from probation officer Grace, in Scotland. Mary recalls Grace's interventions within the broader context of carceral and other systems that would narrow her life options along gender and class lines. Grace's contributions included inviting Mary to share, often in the space of a "beautiful tearoom," the specifics of her difficult home life and the future she wanted for herself, and advising Mary to leave criminal history out of "her story" as she pursued an opportunity to train as a nurse. Officer Grace's own sharing of details from her life undercut the hierarchized distance and one-way storytelling dynamic typically associated with state agents of supervision. Here, then, storytelling is a tool of present and future social mobility and fulfillment. Finally, McNeill observes that Mary's telling of the story to him

allowed her to reinstate some prior gaps and to give due credit to Grace, a feat that underscores her narrative agency.
7. Francesca Polletta, Tania DoCarmo, and Kelly Marie Ward evaluate the role secured for personal stories in political advocacy work. They note a tendency for advocates and their advisors to offer would-be supporters a sense of false intimacy with victims of injustice at the expense of the latter group's actual empowerment. However, the authors "resist a characterization of professionalized storytelling as by definition bad," instead drawing on interviews with professionals to develop ideas about storytelling for social reform that is more effective *and* more ethical—for example, positioning personal storytelling as just one step in the activist agenda.
8. Robin Kundis Craig examines the narratives told by young climate activists and the narratives that have been told about them. These narrators are best positioned to develop and share stories centering on harm to future generations. Their positionality permits them to tell highly compelling stories of human rights violation—that is, of harm to children and not simply the environment. Their conversancy with social media has allowed them to tell global stories and to have such stories heard near and far, with salutary effects on mobilization.
9. The narratives of those who have survived sexual violence helped to propel feminist activism beginning in the 1960s. Tanya Serisier conceptualizes such stories as gifts that survivors bestow. Serisier examines "the processes by which feminists themselves learned to receive the gift . . . and furthermore insisted on this process within wider public cultures." Storytellers bear the burden of telling in culturally recognizable and resonant ways. While some survivor stories are thus received, others seemingly "beyond the bounds of the tellable" go unheard. Storytellers and their supporters have turned bad stories into good in the sense of being crucial and consequential. A next step is to broaden the range of hearable and concerning survivor stories—for example, featuring those with flat plotlines and relatively agentive victims.
10. The book draws to a close with Charlotte Andrews-Briscoe and Molly Andrews telling a story of coteaching a class in Luzira Upper Prison for men, in Uganda. Class content itself was centered on a

story—that of Nelson Mandela as he tells it in his autobiography, *Long Walk to Freedom*. Mandela's narrative prompted animated discussions among men in prison about fighting for justice under constrained circumstances. It also occasioned a mother-daughter collaboration that gave deeper insights into the different justice efforts that each has chosen to undertake.

Conclusion

This project was born of our own search for hope and levity. Our spirits were brought down by illness, death, political strife, and corruption. In a series of online conversations at the start of the project, we wondered about the possibilities of re-storying the present. Soon enough, we took up questions, sometimes fantastical, of the social construction of lived reality and the nature of freedom from pain and oppression. The result of these explorations is a body of work that we hope reaches beyond its basis in self-help for discouraged criminologists and sociologists, to a critique of criticality itself and a modest offering of creative solutions for today and tomorrow, for all of us.

REFERENCES

Akers, Ronald L., and Christine S. Sellers. 2013. *Criminological Theories: Introduction, Evaluation, and Application*. 6th ed. New York: Oxford University Press.

Atkinson, Paul. 1997. "Narrative Turn or Blind Alley?" *Qualitative Health Research* 7 (3): 325–44.

Bamberg, Michael, and Molly Andrews, eds. 2004. *Considering Counter-Narratives: Narrating, Resisting, Making Sense*. Philadelphia: John Benjamins.

Bamberg, Michael, and Alexandra Georgakopoulou. 2008. "Small Stories as a New Perspective in Narrative and Identity Analysis." *Text & Talk* 28 (3): 377–96.

Bauman, Richard. 1986. *Story, Performance, and Event: Contextual Studies of Oral Narrative*. Cambridge: Cambridge University Press.

Björninen, Samuli, Mari Hatavara, and Maria Mäkelä. 2020. "Narrative as Social Action: A Narratological Approach to Story, Discourse and Positioning in Political Storytelling." *International Journal of Social Research Methodology* 23 (4): 437–49.

Brison, Susan J. 2002. *Aftermath: Violence and the Remaking of a Self*. Princeton: Princeton University Press.

Campbell, Joseph. 1949. *The Hero with a Thousand Faces*. New York: Pantheon.

Canham, Hugo, and Malose Langa. 2017. "Narratives of Everyday Resistance from the Margins." *Psychology in Society* 55: 3–13.

Chanfrault-Duchet, Marie-Françoise. 2000. "Textualisation of the Self and Gender Identity in the Life-Story." In *Feminism and Autobiography: Texts, Theories, Methods*, edited by Tess Cosslett, Celia Lury, and Penny Summerfield, 60–75. London: Routledge.

Durkheim, Emile. 1995. *The Elementary Forms of Religious Life*. Translated by Karen E. Fields. New York: Free Press.

Fairclough, Norman. 2013. *Critical Discourse Analysis: The Critical Study of Language*. 2nd ed. London: Routledge.

Fernandes, Sujatha. 2017. *Curated Stories: The Uses and Misuses of Storytelling*. New York: Oxford University Press.

Ferrell, Jeff, Keith Hayward, and Jock Young. 2015. *Cultural Criminology: An Invitation*. 2nd ed. London: Sage.

Fleetwood, Jennifer. 2016. "Narrative Habitus: Thinking Through Structure/Agency in the Narratives of Offenders." *Crime, Media, Culture* 12 (2): 173–92.

Fleetwood, Jennifer. 2019. "Everyday Self-Defence: Hollaback Narratives, Habitus, and Resisting Street Harassment." *British Journal of Sociology* 70 (5): 1709–29.

Fleetwood, Jennifer, Lois Presser, Sveinung Sandberg, and Thomas Ugelvik, eds. 2019. *The Emerald Handbook of Narrative Criminology*. Bingley, UK: Emerald.

Fludernik, Monika. 1996. *Towards a "Natural" Narratology*. New York: Routledge.

Fox, Kathryn J., 1999. "Changing Violent Minds: Discursive Correction and Resistance in the Cognitive Treatment of Violent Offenders in Prison." *Social Problems* 46 (1): 88–103.

Frank, Arthur W. 1995. *The Wounded Storyteller: Body, Illness, and Ethics*. Chicago: University of Chicago Press.

Frank, Arthur W. 2010. *Letting Stories Breathe: A Socio-Narratology*. Chicago: University of Chicago Press.

Gergen, Kenneth J., and Mary M. Gergen. 1983. "Narratives of the Self." In *Studies in Social Identity*, edited by Theodore R. Sarbin and Karl E. Scheibe, 254–73. New York: Praeger.

Halverson, Jeffry R., H. L. Goodall Jr., and Steven R. Corman. 2011. *Master Narratives of Islamist Extremism*. New York: Palgrave Macmillan.

Harari, Yuval Noah. 2017. *Homo Deus: A Brief History of Tomorrow*. London: Vintage.

Herman, David. 2009. *Basic Elements of Narrative*. West Sussex, UK: Wiley-Blackwell.

Herman, Judith. 1992. *Trauma and Recovery*. New York: Basic Books.

Highmore, Ben. 2011. *Ordinary Lives: Studies in the Everyday*. London: Routledge.

Jackson, Michael. 2002. *The Politics of Storytelling: Violence, Transgression, and Intersubjectivity*. Copenhagen: Museum Tusculanum Press.

Keen, Suzanne. 2007. *Empathy and the Novel*. New York: Oxford University Press.

Labov, William, and Joshua Waletzky. 1967. "Narrative Analysis: Oral Versions of Personal Experience." In *Essays on the Verbal and Visual Arts*, edited by J. Helms, 12–44. Seattle: University of Washington Press.

Laclau, Ernesto, and Chantal Mouffe. 1985. *Hegemony and Socialist Strategy: Towards a Radical Democratic Politics*. London: Verso.

Lamont, Michèle, and Virág Molnár. 2002. "The Study of Boundaries in the Social Sciences." *Annual Review of Sociology* 28 (1): 167–95.
Lavin, Melissa F. 2017. "She Got Herself There: Narrative Resistance in the Drug Discourse of Strippers." *Deviant Behavior* 38 (3): 294–305.
Lefebvre, Henri. 1991. *Critique of Everyday Life: Foundations for a Sociology of the Everyday*. London: Verso.
Lyotard, Jean-François. 1984. *The Postmodern Condition: A Report on Knowledge*. Minneapolis: University of Minnesota Press.
Mäkelä, Maria. 2018. "Lessons from the Dangers of Narrative Project: Toward a Story-Critical Narratology." *Tekstualia* 1 (4): 175–86.
Maruna, Shadd. 2001. *Making Good: How Ex-Convicts Reform and Rebuild Their Lives*. Washington, DC: American Psychological Association.
Maruna, Shadd, Louise Wilson, and Kathryn Curran. 2006. "Why God Is Often Found behind Bars: Prison Conversions and the Crisis of Self-Narrative." *Research in Human Development* 3 (2): 161–84.
McAdams, Dan P. 1993. *The Stories We Live By: Personal Myths and the Making of the Self*. New York: William Morrow.
McGarry, Ross, and Sandra Walklate. 2015. *Victims: Trauma, Testimony and Justice*. London: Routledge.
McKenzie-Mohr, Suzanne, and Michelle N. Lafrance. 2017. "Narrative Resistance in Social Work Research and Practice: Counter-Storying in the Pursuit of Social Justice." *Qualitative Social Work* 16 (2): 189–205.
Miller, Jody, Kristin Carbone-Lopez, and Mikh V. Gunderman. 2015. "Gendered Narratives of Self, Addiction, and Recovery among Women Methamphetamine Users." In *Narrative Criminology: Understanding Stories of Crime*, edited by Lois Presser and Sveinung Sandberg, 69–95. New York: New York University Press.
Phelan, James. 2017. *Somebody Telling Somebody Else: A Rhetorical Poetics of Narrative*. Columbus: Ohio State University Press.
Plummer, Ken. 1995. *Telling Sexual Stories: Power, Change and Social Worlds*. London: Routledge.
Plummer, Ken. 2019. *Narrative Power: The Struggle for Human Value*. Cambridge: Polity.
Polkinghorne, Donald E. 1988. *Narrative Knowing and the Human Sciences*. Albany: State University of New York Press.
Polletta, Francesca. 2006. *It Was Like a Fever: Storytelling in Protest and Politics*. Chicago: University of Chicago Press.
Presser, Lois. 2004. "Violent Offenders, Moral Selves: Constructing Identities and Accounts in the Research Interview." *Social Problems* 51 (1): 82–101.
Presser Lois. 2008. *Been a Heavy Life: Stories of Violent Men*. Urbana: University of Illinois Press.
Presser, Lois. 2009. "The Narratives of Offenders." *Theoretical Criminology* 13 (2): 177–200.

Presser, Lois. 2018. *Inside Story: How Narratives Drive Mass Harm*. Berkeley: University of California Press.

Presser, Lois, and Sveinung Sandberg, eds. 2015. *Narrative Criminology: Understanding Stories of Crime*. New York: New York University Press.

Presser, Lois, and Sveinung Sandberg. 2019. "Narrative Criminology as Critical Criminology." *Critical Criminology* 27 (1): 131–43.

Presser, Lois, Jennifer L. Schally, and Christine Vossler. 2018. "Life as a Reflexive Project: The Logics of Ethical Veganism and Meat-Eating." *Society & Animals* 28: 713–32.

Ricoeur, Paul. 1984. *Time and Narrative*. Vol. 1. Translated by Kathleen McLaughlin and David Pellauer. Chicago: University of Chicago Press.

Sandberg, Sveinung. 2010. "What Can 'Lies' Tell Us about Life? Notes towards a Framework of Narrative Criminology." *Journal of Criminal Justice Education* 21 (4): 447–65.

Sandberg, Sveinung. 2013. "Are Self-Narratives Strategic or Determined, Unified or Fragmented? Reading Breivik's Manifesto in Light of Narrative Criminology." *Acta Sociologica* 56 (1): 69–83.

Sandberg, Sveinung. 2016. "The Importance of Stories Untold: Life-Story, Event-Story and Trope." *Crime, Media, Culture* 12 (2): 153–71.

Sandberg, Sveinung, and Sarah Colvin. 2020. "'ISIS Is Not Islam': Epistemic Injustice, Everyday Religion and Young Muslims' Narrative Resistance." *British Journal of Criminology* 60 (6): 1585–1605.

Scott, Marvin B., and Stanford M. Lyman. 1968. "Accounts." *American Sociological Review* 33 (1): 46–62.

Serisier, Tanya. 2018. *Speaking Out: Feminism, Rape and Narrative Politics*. Cham, Switzerland: Springer.

Smith, Barbara Herrnstein. 1981. "Narrative Versions, Narrative Theories." In *American Criticism in the Post-Structuralist Age*, edited by Ira Konigsberg, 162–86. Ann Arbor: Michigan Studies in the Humanities.

Snow, David A., and Robert D. Benford. 1992. "Master Frames and Cycles of Protest." In *Frontiers in Social Movement Theory*, edited by Aldon D. Morris and Carol McClurg Mueller, 133–55. New Haven: Yale University Press.

Strawson, Galen. 2004. "Against Narrativity." *Ratio* 17: 428–52.

Tutenges, Sébastien, and Morten Hulvej Rod. 2009. "'We Got Incredibly Drunk . . . It Was Damned Fun': Drinking Stories among Danish Youth." *Journal of Youth Studies* 12 (4): 355–70.

Weiss, Richard. 1969. *The American Myth of Success: From Horatio Alger to Norman Vincent Peale*. Urbana: University of Illinois Press.

Vargas Llosa, Mario. 2010. *El Hablador*. Madrid: Punto de Lectura.

Zhang, Xiaoye, and Xianliang Dong. 2019. "The Archived Criminal: Mandatory Prisoner Autobiography in China." In *The Emerald Handbook of Narrative Criminology*, edited by Jennifer Fleetwood, Lois Presser, Sveinung Sandberg, and Thomas Ugelvik, 427–44. Bingley, UK: Emerald.

PART I

Stories That Do Good

1

What Good Can Stories Do?

SVEINUNG SANDBERG AND SÉBASTIEN TUTENGES

Abdi was a twenty-one-year-old former gang member who blended in perfectly among the people selling drugs on the streets of inner-city Oslo. He knew how to carry himself with the kind of intimidating coolness typical of street cultures worldwide. He was a gifted storyteller and often entertained people with movie-like narratives about his past: how he had worked as a drug dealer, handled weapons, carried out robberies, learned some hard lessons, and left the gang. He used his gifts not only to entertain and to present himself as streetwise, but also to educate street youths who, in his view, were naïve in their fascination with all things criminal. For although he often expressed himself in a tough and uncompromising way, replete with "gangster" slang and violent imagery, his moral evaluation of gangsters was anything but romantic. Rather, his narratives were generally presented in the genre of tragedy (Frye 1957) with an emphasis on the suffering associated with crime and deviance. Sharing such narratives was his way of trying to convince people on the street to stay out of trouble. As he put it, "I went from committing crimes to trying to prevent them."

Storytellers and their stories are key to all social groups. They have the capacity to bring people together, raise spirits, and make life meaningful. However, criminalized storytellers and stories are not usually appreciated in the mainstream, although they may be romanticized and find audiences in popular culture. Indeed, they are often considered unreliable and untrustworthy. People involved in crime, excessive drug use, and violent street culture may find it difficult to publicly voice their stories in their own words, in spite of the widespread preoccupation with their situation. They are often spoken about by various experts and decision makers but are rarely allowed to speak for themselves. The result is a skewed representation of these environments, with a narrow focus on problems, harm, and disintegration at the exclusion of resources, harm reduction, and solidarity. Stories concerning and emphasizing "the bad" occupy center stage—not least in social scientific research—whereas stories that concern and promote "the good" are relegated to the shadows.

This chapter turns the tables by exploring how storytellers and stories can alleviate pain, prevent harm, and otherwise do good for criminalized people. We try to avoid the romantic storytelling of the subaltern that has a long history in literature, film, and music as well as leftist politics and social movements, and instead emphasize a more nuanced and complex portrayal of these people and environments, highlighting agency and "good-doing" without leaving out the destruction, violence, harms, and antagonism that are also part of these milieus. We place particular emphasis on Abdi, whom Sébastien met during a recent ethnographic study in Oslo, but also revisit and present storytellers and stories from other research projects over the last two decades. In this sense, our chapter is myopic, but bear with us. Our primary aim is to create a typology of stories that do good to people living on the margins of society—and to accomplish this aim, we draw on our own research, since this is what we know best.

Our approach is inspired by the ethnographic branch of narrative criminology (Fleetwood and Sandberg 2021). Rather than considering stories mainly for their internal organization and meaning, narrative ethnographers explore the way stories are performed on specific social occasions and their effects (Gubrium and Holstein 2009). Hence, our emphasis is on storytelling as a dynamic, collaborative performance with meanings that shift depending on a variety of situational factors, such as where, when, among whom, and for what purposes the storytelling takes place (Presser 2010). The studies we draw from are based on narrative criminology's foundational concern with looking for narratives that motivate and sustain harm (e.g., Presser and Sandberg 2015; Sandberg and Ugelvik 2016). Most of our previous research sought to understand narratives as antecedents for harm, but those harmful narratives were certainly not the only ones present. Here we dig out those that could also do good in the context of harm. We identify four basic types of good storytelling: healing, uplifting, harm-limiting, and imaginative. This typology is by no means exhaustive, but includes important ways that storytelling can do good in environments usually associated with bad.

Healing Storytelling

What we describe as healing storytelling is a type of narration that serves to diminish suffering, either one's own or someone else's. Healing storytelling is seen when people talk about traumatic memories in order to alleviate the burden of those memories (Jackson 2013), or when past failures are recounted and redefined in a manner that makes it easier to live with them in the present (McAdams 2013). It is a broad category that includes several closely intertwined forms and functions of storytelling. What we discuss below, for example, includes stories that witness and validate surviving extreme situations, stories that make sense of bad experiences, and stories that produce meaningful identities. Healing stories often emphasize that something good ultimately came out of what was initially bad. Hence the quest narrative of illness that Frank (2010) famously describes, where hardship becomes a source of transformation. This new self can be an improved version of some former self.

The healing work of storytelling can quite straightforwardly be seen in "bad trip stories" told by people who use illegal drugs. As one participant in a study of psychedelic drug use put it, "The bad trips are what gives you the *most* insights," adding that these experiences provide insight into "who you really are." Another participant in the same study agreed, stating that "even if it was intense and really scary for me, I really see the value of it" (Gashi, Sandberg, and Pedersen 2021). These individuals ascribed meaning to what would otherwise have been meaningless suffering. In another study of individuals who had negative experiences with cannabis, we compared how these Western participants talked about the bad-trip episodes with a ritual practice among the Kuranko people of Sierra Leone during which young men go out into the bush to meet the "Djinn" (Sandberg and Tutenges 2015). The Djinn are capricious spirits who can both rob people of their lives and bestow upon them great treasures, and the Kuranko people consider it necessary to make regular contact with these spirits in order to secure vitality for themselves and their community (Jackson 2013). In secular Western societies, the underworld, with its illicit drugs and other capricious forces, plays a role akin to the bush and its Djinn: it is risky to go there, yet many people do, in part for the treasures they may get out of it, such as immediate thrills, social prestige, and hard-earned life lessons.

At other times the healing work of storytelling is more convoluted and complex. In two studies (Sandberg and Pedersen 2009; Tutenges 2019), we conducted ethnographic fieldwork in the same open drug market in Oslo. During these fieldwork excursions we witnessed many instances of healing storytelling being told by young marginalized ethnic minority men selling drugs on the street. Such healing discourse seemed to be a constant factor in an otherwise changing and tough world. In the social environment of the street, displaying signs of vulnerability is widely regarded as a show of weakness, and many try to hide emotional pain—for instance, by putting up a hard façade. However, emotions such as sadness and fear can be both difficult and damaging to conceal (Brackett 2019), and street youths—like anyone else—feel compelled to express them. While it may not be possible to do so overtly through open declarations or displays of vulnerable body language (e.g., crying) in public, storytelling can be another, more subtle way to express painful emotions.

Abdi often turned to storytelling to express his emotions. His stories and the way he performed them were often brimming with shame, sadness, despair, fear, and hate. Consider the following story told during an interview, in which Abdi describes the first job he did for his gang: "I got a call and was told to jump someone. . . . When we went to the guy's place, he comes out and my friend hits him with a baseball bat, so he falls to the floor. We start kicking him, we robbed him, and when he got up, I pulled out my knife, held it to his neck, and looked into his eyes, which changed me." Abdi told this story with a stern look on his face, but the memory clearly pained him. "I wish I could reverse the knife incident," he said. Abdi could not change the past, but through storytelling, he could express and perhaps alter his feelings about what had happened while sharing some of the lessons he had learned with his listeners. Storytelling became a way to transcend extreme experience, surpassing and overcoming difficulties, and perhaps more importantly, a way to present a new and different self. The otherwise meaningless or "bad" event is thus assigned meaning and provided with a sense of purpose by being a moment of change and by linking past harms he had committed with present insights. It is in this sense that we propose that storytelling can be healing.

In other research projects, we observed numerous similar examples of storytelling that seems to be beneficial in terms of assuaging and/

or making meaning out of past suffering. In studies of individuals incarcerated for large-scale drug dealing, we found that "hard life" stories were an important part of their narrative repertoires (Sandberg and Fleetwood 2017). These stories dwelled upon troubles such as domestic violence, substance misuse in families, and being brought up in marginalized neighborhoods, and were often told as part of larger life stories. "Hard life" stories are "sad tales" (Goffman 1961), forms of "oppression discourse" (Sandberg 2009), that reflect the marginalization, suffering, and abuse that many in the lowest strata of societies experience. What often happens in street stories, however, is that trauma and suffering are put into a context where they become something one can learn from, or something disconnected from the "real" self. The storytelling can thus be a way to rise above difficulties and move on.

Interviewed while in prison for drug dealing, Johannes talked about a traumatic childhood in which his father, "a heroin addict and a criminal," died when Johannes was a child; subsequently his mother married another drug user. Johannes framed the story as an exciting experience and connected it to his present street persona (Sandberg and Fleetwood 2017: 375). Another interviewee in the same study had experienced domestic abuse growing up and dealt with these experiences through complex storytelling, combining reflexive learning and moral tales with laughter as a means of coping with distressing experiences. The combination of justifying the violence and laughing about it made it a highly ambiguous story, but one that nevertheless made these early childhood experiences manageable (Sandberg and Tutenges 2019: 572–73). Others in the same study used more altogether humorous stories to reinvent traumatic events as funny ones. Arguably, such "hard life" stories, humorous or not, make sense of bad experiences and show how the narrator has survived extreme situations. Subsequently, and as a consequence of such narration, they produce new and meaningful identities.

Turning a tragic event into a humorous one can be a way of dealing with such events, making it possible to live with them and to move on with life (Lynn, this volume). This is clearly what goes on in drinking stories, a narrative genre that uses incongruity and transgressions to trigger interest, to entertain, and to challenge commonly held views. We have studied binge drinkers on numerous occasions, and turning potential trauma into funny drinking stories is a recurring theme in our data (e.g., Tutenges and Rod 2009). There are a multitude of ways to tell a story about previous suffering, and storytellers can twist them in all kinds of different directions. The use of humor is one way of making injuries, trauma, and pain bearable—and it can be an effective one, especially where suffering and victim positions must be combined with different forms of "rough" (Way 1993) or "street" (Mullins 2006) masculinities.

In a more recent study (Sandberg, Agoff, and Fondevila 2021), incarcerated Mexican mothers were interviewed about their prison conditions, their relationships with children and families, and their criminal careers.[1] Much of what took place in these interviews can be interpreted as healing storytelling. When these mothers talked about their children, it was against the background of years of guilt, shame, and neglect. For example, one incarcerated mother had been a sex worker and erotic dancer, and justified this work, as well as her absence from her daughter, by pointing out that her motivation had been to earn money so that her mother could raise her child: "It was to support my mother, who provided for my daughter," she explained. Many of the mothers justified previous neglect by pointing out that they had at least provided for their children both before and after going to prison. Such storytelling can be written off as standard accounts, "a linguistic device employed whenever an action is subjected to valuative inquiry" (Scott and Lyman 1968: 46), but we believe that they had immense and existential importance for the women. With tellers facing the stigma of being both poor women and mothers, these stories helped explain difficult decisions and destinies, both to themselves and to others.

What has typically been cast negatively as excuses, justifications (Scott and Lyman 1968), and neutralizations (Sykes and Matza 1957) in criminological theory can, in fact, do very important work for storytellers (Maruna 2001). Such "excuses" make it possible to avoid associating previous bad behavior too closely with the present self, facilitating processes of identity and behavioral transformation (Maruna and Copes 2005). Behavior that is considered bad (crime, substance use, violence, and so forth) may be constructed as the product of external factors, or carried out in the service of some greater good, instead of being an integral part of the self of those who have committed it, and this can serve to heal wounds and thus make life livable.

A recurrent theme throughout our studies is a tendency for people to use storytelling to deal with trauma, cope with tragic circumstances, and reinterpret the past to make the present better (Jackson 2005). This is what we describe as healing storytelling: the power of stories to "repair" by turning bad experiences into valuable ones, moving on from trauma, and producing new meaningful identities. Healing stories can be ones that individuals tell themselves or ones that they tell others in order to get a certain version of events and themselves confirmed. Generally, this is a type of storytelling that retrospectively looks back at events (McNeill, this volume) and provides them with new meaning, sometimes years after they happened.

Uplifting Storytelling

Whereas healing storytelling tends to be retrospective and aimed at reducing suffering, uplifting storytelling tends to be centered on the present and aimed at creating immediate well-being. For example, this type of storytelling can take the form of humorous performances aimed at eliciting a good laugh and the relief that comes from laughing together (Sandberg and Tutenges 2019), or it can center on "war stories" aimed at generating a sense of thrill, pride, and often masculinity (Kurtz and Upton 2018). The audience is key to this type of storytelling: the mood of the moment is based on interactional collaboration—hence the tendency for jokes to belly-flop when told to unwilling listeners. Arguably, being present in storytelling situations and doing narrative ethnography (Gubrium and Holstein 2008) are thus necessary to fully understand the role of uplifting storytelling.

Abdi often used his gifts for storytelling to captivate and uplift his listeners. For example, in one interview he recounted a story about an encounter with a gang leader that proved decisive for his criminal career. He was sixteen years old and wanted to be part of the gang, but first had to go through some unexpected trials. He went to a big house occupied by the gang and was led down to the basement, where he found more than he had bargained for:

> There's like twenty people around my age, around their early twenties, and everyone got guns, there is cocaine, drugs, kilos of drugs stacked up in the

basement, and there is a PlayStation 3 where everyone is playing FIFA. And then there's another door where the offices were. I remember walking in and I was getting excited and thinking it was so cool, they were playing rap music, this is real! They opened the door, and I was told to wait outside while everyone was looking at me. They called me a newbie and said that I had to be careful and not make eye contact when I go in, and not to look at the ladies. I was surprised when they said "ladies." I went in and the whole room was mirrored. There were prostitutes in this room, like six of them, a desk in the middle with money all around. A guy was sitting there and smoking a joint and goes, "You wanna join the gang?"

Abdi maintained eye contact as he told this story, skillfully building up the suspense, not once pausing to search for words. The whole performance was masterful, giving the impression that he had delivered it many times before—presumably via different versions tailored to the listeners before him. For, as Bauman points out, "narratives are keyed both to the events in which they are told and to the events that they recount, toward narrative events and narrated events" (1986: 2). The version Abdi told during the narrative event of the interview took the form of a "gangster story" similar to those featured in popular movies and music (Fleetwood and Ilan, this volume). The pace was fast, the tone hard, and the focus was on money, might, and misogyny.

Abdi told us that, as he stood there in front of the gang leader, he tried to act "cool" in order to be accepted: "It was like a job interview, and my résumé was my reputation for beating people up, selling drugs, and stuff like that." However, Abdi lost his cool when the man with the joint suddenly pulled out a gun and commanded him to shoot one of the women in the room. "Shoot this girl right now if you want to join the gang!" the man yelled.

> I started shaking and nodding my head. I was sixteen and scared. He takes the gun, loads it and puts it to my head and goes, "Shoot this bitch or I will shoot you cuz you're in my main place." I said, "No. I wanna go home. I want to join the gang, but I'm not gonna kill someone." He says, "All right." He grabs my hand, aims at the girl, and pulls the trigger. I closed my eyes, but there was nothing in there. The girl was laughing, knowing there was nothing in there.

The story exposes the innocence of the protagonist, the sixteen-year-old Abdi, as well as the probable assumptions of the listener, who is led to expect the worst from the gang leader. Abdi concluded that he "felt horrible that day" but conveyed that he had also experienced a mix of other feelings, including pride and excitement. His story was movie-like in character, something that may contribute to a sense of bonding between storyteller and audience (Polletta, DoCarmo, and Ward, this volume). Performed skillfully in the right context, this type of storytelling can indeed be uplifting and may give people a sense of tuning into one another and being part of a common body (Tutenges 2022). This feeling of bonding may be strengthened by Abdi's position in the story, as the newcomer and outsider, admitting that he was not fully in control or confident in the situation, a feeling to which audiences can easily relate. Such a storytelling technique is well known: the naïve protagonist getting caught up in a situation beyond their control. It makes it easy for the audience to identify with the storyteller, and the confusion inherent in the situation invites elements of humor, drama, and excitement. It is also worth noting that the role of the woman also changed abruptly in this still very sexist story, from that of the innocent victim to a central conspirator in the dark joke, adding additional layers to an already complex storytelling event.

In Durkheimian terms, the hallmark of successful storytelling performances is that they generate high levels of collective effervescence, meaning a state of heightened intersubjectivity marked by intense, transgressive, and yet mutually attuned actions and emotions among two or more individuals (Tutenges 2022). These effects are most pronounced when storyteller and listener are physically close to each other and focus fully on the ongoing performance (Collins 2004). By these standards, Abdi performed the story about his meeting with the gang leader with great success because it raised the level of effervescence in the storytelling situation. We felt completely engrossed in Abdi's performance and immersed in the narrative universe that he conjured up. One must assume that this was a story he had told similarly on other occasions with similar effects. It is possible that Abdi embellished his story, but what matters more than fidelity to past events in uplifting storytelling is that "the audience enters into the spirit of the performance by not questioning it but by taking it in a situational mood, whatever will build up the highest level of momentary collective effervescence" (Collins 2004: 85).

It is interesting to observe how, despite the fifteen-year gap between our two ethnographic fieldworks in an Oslo street drug market, the drug dealers in each often told many of the same stories, with similar content, a similar sense of humor, and similar theatrics. We have previously described this as gangster discourse (Sandberg 2009), pointing out how these stories tend to focus on pleasant or exciting drug experiences, successful crime, sexual encounters, and tricking the police. The emphasis in our analyses has tended to be on the pride and respect such storytelling engenders. We have *not* stressed the no less important role that these stories play in lightening the atmosphere among the youths, making it enjoyable and fun to hang out in these sometimes freezing cold Norwegian drug markets, and solidifying the social bonds within the group. Uplifting storytelling can be a way to make the life in a tough and hostile environment not only bearable, but pleasant, fun, and enjoyable. Studies of incarcerated populations have called attention to similar stories that play an analogous role among prison inmates, perhaps also incorporating additional elements such as mockery of prison guards and stories of the dark comedy of prison life. Such stories can serve important functions, including managing emotional pain and effectively challenging the hierarchies of prisons (Ugelvik 2014).

Uplifting storytelling has clear parallels with another major research area of ours, drinking stories, which perhaps resonate more strongly with mainstream society than stories of street youths. We mentioned earlier that drinking stories can be used as a way of dealing with trauma or problematic experiences. The main narrative work they do, however, is entertainment, lifting the spirits of those participating in these storytelling sessions. It is difficult to understand these stories without emphasizing the role of the audience and the narrative context of storytelling. Addressing taboos and focusing on themes such as sex, bodily harm, bodily fluids, lawbreaking, and pranks (Sandberg, Tutenges, and Pedersen 2019), these stories are often told during pre-drinking sessions where they serve as mood-altering techniques that help people to transition from ordinary states of consciousness to states of collective effervescence (Tutenges and Sandberg 2013: 541). It is in this sense that not only drinking, but also drinking stories may be said to be intoxicating.

What we call uplifting storytelling describes what takes place in the here-and-now of storytelling sessions. The role of audiences is key to this kind of narrative performance, perhaps more so than in the other types of storytelling outlined in this chapter. As demonstrated above, we find many of the same ingredients in uplifting stories told among marginalized ethnic minorities selling drugs on the street and in the drinking stories told by middle-class youths. However, there are also important differences—for instance, in the manner these stories are told. These differences go back to what Fleetwood (2016) calls the narrative habitus of storytellers: the embodied stories, the sense of storytelling contexts, and appropriate themes, which differ substantially from group to group. Gaining fluency in these matters can take years to achieve, and someone considered a gifted storyteller on the street will probably find less resonance in a middle-class pre-party. The stories and their performance become an embodied part of who people are.

Harm-Limiting Storytelling

Another form of narrative work does good in the present in a different and more direct way. Sometimes during different kinds of conflicts or situations that may escalate into trouble, storytelling can intervene and ease conflict, thereby reducing or helping to avoid harm. Our concept of harm-limiting storytelling is inspired by the drug research field and draws in particular on two insights from this literature: recognizing that the outcome is not necessarily ideal (that the intervention of storytelling may not *completely* prevent harm) and seeing harm reduction primarily as a bottom-up approach (Marlatt 1996), meaning that it emerges from the same environment as the harm itself. In our research we have encountered harm-limiting storytelling in studies of violence, destructive drug use, and recruitment to terrorist organizations—but such storytelling is also present in, for example, politics and social movements (Craig, this volume).

Abdi recalled a conversation with a police officer that illustrates the powerful effects storytelling can have in the context of street culture. This conversation happened at a time when Abdi was about to leave his gang. As he put it, he went up to a police officer and told him "everything":

> I was scared of losing my life. He said he wouldn't arrest me because he also was a father, and that he would just take the knife from me and give

me a caution, and told me I was doing the right thing. He explained the difference between being in the military and being a gangster. He said I was fighting against the government, while the military also fight, but they fight for the government and country. It's the same thing [being in the military and being in a gang], where you have a leader, and you have brothers, and they are closer to you than your family. But the truth about being a soldier, he explained to me, is that when he left the military, he had left with respect and honor, and people look up to him for it, while as a gangster people will be scared and disgusted by you. He opened my eyes by saying that.

Abdi told the police officer about wanting to leave the gang, got this story confirmed, and was also provided with several narrative resources for moving from gang life to more conventional life. The interaction and the stories the police officer told him changed his life. Especially drawing parallels with other hyper-masculine environments such as the military seemed to have a profound effect; it made it possible for Abdi to hold on to certain gendered ideals when changing milieus. Narrative may work as metaphors in this way (Lakoff and Johnson 2003), highlighting similarities between contexts that might be worlds apart. This ability to recognize similarities across story settings is part of the allure of stories.

Harm-limiting storytelling is not constrained to street culture. One participant in a study of violence and nightlife drinking (Pedersen, Copes, and Sandberg 2016) described how she often tried to reframe would-be violent conflicts with verbal interventions like "No, that's not what happened," or "That's not something to be upset about," or "He's just drunk." In her experience, she could often resolve conflict by explaining the context of the perceived offense or blaming alcohol for provocations and other problematic behavior. Such narrative interventions can ease tension by shifting the blame onto something other than the harm-doer. In a variant of a classic neutralization technique (Sykes and Matza 1957), the denial of responsibility—"It wasn't my fault"—is transformed into "It wasn't her/his fault" to avoid further conflict. There are many other stories and cultural representations that can similarly be appealed to during violent conflicts.

Harm-limiting storytelling does not just refer to narrative interventions in company with others but can also take the form of stories that people tell themselves, and only occasionally seek to have confirmed by others. A study of female methamphetamine users in Alabama showed that the participants possessed certain stories that reduced the harm of their drug use (Copes, Sandberg, and Ragland 2022). Importantly, the women staked out narrative boundaries separating themselves from other meth users who were "bad mothers" or "tweakers" (derogatory slang for users), did not pay attention to their health and appearance, and/or engaged in "immoral" practices such as selling sex. In their own stories, they emphasized being "good mothers," and these functioned to constrain their drug use. One woman stated, "I don't want [drugs] in the house, no I don't. I mean like, on the weekends when my daughter isn't here we do it in the house." Stories of parenting priorities might have placed limitations on their drug use, primarily as self-stories, or stories they told themselves. The women were also able to use these stories when talking to others—for example, when explaining why they could not use drugs at particular times or in particular places.

Harm-limiting storytelling can be directed at far-reaching harms, such as extremism and terrorism. It can, for example, take the form of "bogeyman" narratives, as found in research on Somali Canadians who reject the Somali jihadist group Al-Shabaab, "positioning the recruiters as odious agents, recruits as weak-minded dupes and [research] participants as knowledgeable storytellers who can forewarn others against recruitment" (Joosse, Bucerius, and Thompson 2015: 811). This form of harm-limiting storytelling was also important in the street environment of which Abdi, our research participant, was part. The young men in his milieu were heavily involved in crimes such as violence and drug dealing, but were deeply critical of political and religious extremism, describing jihadists as evil people who harmed innocents, as bad Muslims who defamed Islam, and as cowards who violated the code of the street (Tutenges and Sandberg 2021).

As mentioned above, harm-limiting storytelling is more directly influential when done *in situ* when harm is about to happen. One young man from another large project we have organized was on his way to Syria to fight for ISIS when his mother intervened.[2] "My mom said she needed me here," he told us, and outlined how she had convinced him to stay (Ellefsen and Sandberg 2022: 7). Such harm-limiting storytelling can also extend over a longer period of time. Another participant explained how, over a year, she was in constant conversation and narrative exchange with a friend who was drawn to violent jihadism: "Sometimes I felt I was about to lose her," she explained, but "I cannot see sisters go into that trap" (Mohamed and Sandberg 2019: 193–94). The stories she would tell as part of her efforts to make her friend less extreme included alternative and more moderate interpretations of the most arousing extremist narratives such as stories about jihad, Sharia, *shahid*, the Caliphate, *kuffar*, and al-Qiyāmah (Sandberg and Colvin 2020).[3]

Convincing someone engaged in a radicalization process that they are wrong and should take a different path is usually a hard task that requires a pre-established relationship of trust and continuous storytelling, combined with accompanying displays of love and commitment. As with other forms of prevention, harm-limiting storytelling seldom works in isolation. It is, nevertheless, a crucial part of deradicalization, since jihadism, like most other forms of religious and political extremism, has its foundation in a powerful repertoire of narratives (Halverson, Goodall, and Corman 2011).

With the concept of harm-limiting storytelling, we refer to episodes where present-time narration eases conflicts or otherwise changes the circumstances, motivations, or trajectories toward harm. Arguably, this could also be described as preventive storytelling, but we prefer the term "harm-limiting" because in many of the instances we describe, some harm has already taken place, and the storytelling does not necessarily *prevent*, but *limits* harm. For example, the aforementioned meth-addicted women did not quit their use but tried to keep it within certain bounds. Importantly, storytelling is just one among many factors that can limit harm, but we believe that it should be reckoned with as a powerful one.

Imaginative Storytelling

What we describe as imaginative storytelling is a type of narration based on fictional representations of reality. Much in the same way that narratives can motivate and sustain harmful behaviors, they can also enable people to imagine different kinds of futures. This storytelling can carry great significance because it allows for engrossment in creative narrative scenarios of what could be, ought to be, or might be. When reality is hard to face and hope is running dry, imaginative storytelling can provide moments of relief or create new hope. In imaginative storytelling, or "joint fantasizing" (Poppi 2024), narrators distance themselves from their present circumstances and find new pathways for change, often outside the sphere of "the real." Imaginative storytelling is closely linked to healing storytelling because it often draws on personal sufferings in the portrayal of imagined pasts, presents, or futures. The narrative atmosphere it creates is also related to uplifting storytelling. However, imaginative storytelling not only works to alleviate suffering or amplify pleasure in the here-and-now, but also points toward the future and may make the imagined one come true.

An example of imaginative storytelling can be found in a captivating desistance story told by Hetav, who was part of the same street milieu as Abdi. Hetav's story centered on a life-changing conversation he once had with an imam in a mosque, during which the imam had talked to him about a particular verse from the Quran (Tutenges 2019). What he took from this conversation was the idea that in life, "either you pray or you get preyed on." This inspired him to start praying and, eventually, to opt out of crime—or so he said. On the face of it, this story seems similar to Abdi's about his meeting with the police officer. The fact that Hetav was still deeply involved in drug dealing might lead one to dismiss his story, yet it can provide some important insights into his lifeworld. The story shows that he considered Islam a saving force that could give him a new beginning in life, full of religious devotion and virtue (Linge 2023). The storied transition from crime to religion was to a large extent an imaginary scenario, but perhaps some of it might someday come true. Rather than being an accurate description of harm-limiting storytelling, it laid out a potential future scenario for Hetav and other street youths.

In the fieldwork in the same drug market fifteen years earlier, another young man who sold drugs similarly explained that he wanted to get married, have children, and get away from crime (Sandberg 2010). After summarizing the opportunities a benevolent welfare state and a supportive family would give him, he stated more downheartedly that "I've been in those fucking starting blocks for ten years already." He had tried to get a job, move to his parents' home country, and engage with a "straight" woman, but nothing worked. He was always pulled back into drug use, drug selling, and violent crime, where he had accumulated skills over a decade in an environment where he felt at home. These hopes for the future still continuously motivated him to try to change his criminal lifestyle. Although his situation had not really changed, without imaginative storytelling, his life would have been even darker. To quote a cynical and much-debated line from the nineteenth-century playwright Ibsen, "If you take the life lie from an average man, you take away his happiness as well." Stories that include dreams, hopes, opportunities, and agency can potentially inspire future change, but they also do "good" in the present.

Arguably the best example of imaginative storytelling we have is from a recent study of incarcerated fathers in Mexico, conducted in parallel with the study of mothers discussed earlier. These fathers had often not seen their children in many years, but they creatively rewrote their previous history with them and described how things would change for the better as soon as they were released from prison (Sandberg, Agoff, and Fondevila 2020). One of the fathers confidently declared, "I'm not just saying it, I will prove it." Another had not seen his children in ten years but was certain that he could manage to achieve a better relationship with his children when he was released, "with psychological help." A third had not seen his daughter for twenty years, but still envisioned a happy future with her. Although in one way sad, given that the likelihood of these imagined outcomes becoming a reality seemed relatively low, the stories or dreams of fatherhood provided a constant source of motivation for the incarcerated fathers to get the best out of their time in prison and to change their lives when they came out. Imaginative storytelling can serve as means to "anticipate and constructively move towards an indeterminate future" and may thus pave the way for personal or social change (Wagoner, de Luna, and Awad 2017). As with the young men selling drugs on the streets of Oslo, the imaginative storytelling kept incarcerated Mexican fathers going under difficult circumstances and inspired and envisioned alternative and better futures.

Imaginative storytelling has been particularly important for desistance research in criminology. *Making Good* by Maruna (2001), for example, deals directly with the power of storytelling for prisoners who want to change their lives, as does Presser's (2008) discussion of the reform narratives of violent men. Fleetwood and Ilan (this volume) also describe the theme of imagination in the "fresh home" narratives of hip-hop lyrics. The imaginative storytelling of people living under difficult circumstances, especially if they have committed criminal offenses, is often viewed with skepticism and cynicism. Family members, social workers, prison guards, and many more have heard such stories numerous times before and ended up disappointed when the reality turned out to be different. Still, even though the future scenarios envisioned in this type of storytelling might not always come true, the storytelling itself can be a positive force in situations characterized by hopelessness. Without glimpses of hope or visions of a better future that such storytelling provides, people may despair and miss out on opportunities for making positive changes. So, although sometimes dreamlike and far from representing factual truth, imaginative stories may do a lot of good.

Conclusion

In this chapter, we have described how stories can do good in marginalized environments. In these efforts, we have deployed a qualifier of the "good," which is surely problematic. Our argument is that while most stories may not be *intrinsically* good, they may *do good* for particular people in particular situations. The way we have streamlined our own story makes us vulnerable to criticism. Distinguishing good from bad is not easy—an argument most famously laid out in Nietzsche's *Beyond Good and Evil* (1966). Our approach to these grand questions is pragmatic: Good is whatever eases the lives of—and the lives of those proximate to—the criminally involved, for example, helping them out of a life of crime, reducing the harm they inflict, or limiting their destructive drug use. This coincides in many respects with their own understanding of good, which makes our project more justifiable. Many works on the subject of good from the fields of ethics and moral philosophy arrive at a similarly straightforward understanding: "To do good means contributing to the furthering of happiness, well-being, or love of life. Or, to put it briefly, contributing to furthering happiness in the world and combatting unhappiness" (Thomassen 2003: 83).

Adding to the problem of defining good is another, equally thorny question: How can we be sure that that which appears to be promoting good does not actually end up doing harm? The history of humankind provides many examples—for example, the great political ideologies or world religions—and there are also endless smaller instances of storytelling that, although intended to do good, end up doing harm. We cannot know, for example, whether the examples of storytelling we discuss in this chapter really ended up doing good. The good they were doing may have been temporary, and participants' conceptions of good may have corrupting effects, as mainstream attitudes might have it. Even uplifting storytelling, while doing good in the situation of storytelling, may eventually have reinforced criminogenic and harmful stories and lives. The possible real-life outcomes of storytelling are uncertain, fluid, and in constant change. For the purpose of this chapter, however, which is to suggest a typology of forms of storytelling, we believe that it is sufficient to trust the storytellers and our own intuitions. While we cannot know the endings and all possible consequences of these particular instances of storytelling, we do believe that they illustrate healing, uplifting, harm-limiting, and imaginative storytelling as forms of narrative performances doing good.

The sociology of social problems and criminology has been our research field for the last two decades, and in this field there is a vast body of research on the ways in which narratives promote harm (e.g., Presser 2018; Presser and Sandberg 2015). Not surprisingly, only a few studies address the way stories and storytelling work to promote personal and common good (e.g., Maruna 2001). The main aim of our chapter has been to highlight, analyze, and attempt to understand such storytelling, especially in a context less strictly focused on desistance from crime and outside therapeutic or institutional settings. Our goal has been to understand such storytelling better, in terms of both narratology (Bauman 1986) and the narrative work (Frank 2010) it performs, but we also believe that understanding good storytelling generally adds to our understanding of marginalized milieus. In the study of social problems and harms, an emphasis on good has been warranted for a long time.

We have demonstrated how storytelling can be used to cope with past trauma, create positive experiences in the present, encourage harm-limiting behavior, and inspire better futures. A single instance of storytelling, or an individual story, can do all these things at once, but they are analytically separable as four different forms of narrative work. We believe that there are good reasons to emphasize the good that stories can do for everyone, everywhere, but that it is especially important in research on places and people that are usually associated with bad. Such an emphasis can counter stereotypes of marginalized people and environments, envisage "good-doers" often neglected by the public, media, and research—and even inspire more good.

NOTES

1 For a description of the project this study was part of, see the CRIMLA website, www.crimeinlatinamerica.com.
2 For a description of the project, see "Radicalization and Resistance" on the website of the Department of Criminology and Sociology of Law, University of Oslo, https://bit.ly/radicalization-resistance.
3 "Jihad" refers to holy war; Sharia is Islamic Law; *shahid* is an Islamic word for martyrdom; the Caliphate is the Islamic State that is promised Muslims in the Quran; *kuffar* refers to infidels; and al-Qiyāmah is the Day of Reckoning.

REFERENCES

Bauman, Richard. 1986. *Story, Performance, and Event: Contextual Studies of Oral Narrative.* Cambridge: Cambridge University Press.
Brackett, Marc. 2019. *Permission to Feel: Unlocking the Power of Emotions to Help Our Kids, Ourselves, and Our Society Thrive.* New York: Celadon.
Collins, Randall. 2004. *Interaction Ritual Chains.* Princeton: Princeton University Press.
Copes, Heith, Sveinung Sandberg, and Jared Ragland. 2022. "Protecting Boundaries: How Symbolic Boundaries Reduce Victimization and Harmful Drug Use." *Crime & Justice* 69 (3): 533–58.
Ellefsen, Rune, and Sveinung Sandberg. 2022. "Everyday Prevention of Radicalization: The Impacts of Family, Peer and Police Intervention." *Studies in Conflict and Terrorism.* https://doi.org/10.1080/1057610X.2022.2037185.
Fleetwood, Jennifer. 2014. *Drug Mules: Women in the International Cocaine Trade.* Basingstoke, UK: Palgrave Macmillan.
Fleetwood, Jennifer. 2016. "Narrative Habitus: Thinking Through Structure/Agency in the Narratives of Offenders." *Crime, Media, Culture* 12 (2): 173–92.
Fleetwood, Jennifer, and Sveinung Sandberg. 2021. "Narrative Criminology and Ethnography." In *The Oxford Handbook of Ethnographies of Crime and Criminal Justice,* edited by Sandra Bucerius, Kevin Haggerty, and Luca Berardi, 246–69. Oxford: Oxford University Press.
Frank, Arthur W. 2010. *Letting Stories Breathe: A Socio-Narratology.* Chicago: University of Chicago Press.
Frye, Northrop. 1957. *Anatomy of Criticism: Four Essays.* Princeton: Princeton University Press.
Gashi, Liridona, Sveinung Sandberg, and Willy Pedersen. 2021. "Making 'Bad Trips' Good: How Users of Psychedelics Narratively Transform Challenging Trips into Valuable Experiences." *International Journal of Drug Policy* 87: 1–7.

Goffman, Erving. 1961. *Asylums: Essays on the Social Situation of Mental Patients and Other Inmates*. London: Pelican.

Gubrium, Jaber F., and James A. Holstein. 2008. "Narrative Ethnography." In *Handbook of Emergent Methods*, edited by Sharlene Nagy Hesse-Biber and Patricia Leavy, 241–62. New York: Guilford.

Gubrium, Jaber F., and James A. Holstein. 2009. *Analyzing Narrative Reality*. London: Sage.

Halverson, Jeffry R., Harold L. Goodall Jr., and Steven R. Corman. 2011. *Master Narratives of Islamist Extremism*. New York: Palgrave Macmillan.

Jackson, Michael. 2005. *Existential Anthropology: Events, Exigencies, and Effects*. Oxford: Berghahn.

Jackson, Michael. 2013. *The Politics of Storytelling: Variations on a Theme by Hannah Arendt*. Copenhagen: Museum Tusculanum Press.

Joosse, Paul, Sandra M. Bucerius, and Sara K. Thompson. 2015. "Narratives and Counternarratives: Somali-Canadians on Recruitment as Foreign Fighters to Al-Shabaab." *British Journal of Criminology* 55 (4): 811–32.

Kurtz, Don L., and Lindsey L. Upton. 2018. "The Gender in Stories: How War Stories and Police Narratives Shape Masculine Police Culture." *Women & Criminal Justice* 28 (4): 282–300.

Lakoff, George, and Mark Johnson. 2003. *Metaphors We Live By*. Chicago: University of Chicago Press.

Linge, Marius. 2023. "Muslim Narratives of Desistance among Norwegian Street Criminals: Stories of Reconciliation, Purification and Exclusion." *European Journal of Criminology* 20 (2): 568–85.

Marlatt, Alan G. 1996. "Harm Reduction: Come as You Are." *Addictive Behaviors* 21 (6): 779–88.

Maruna, Shadd. 2001. *Making Good: How Ex-Convicts Reform and Rebuild Their Lives*. Washington, DC: American Psychological Association.

Maruna, Shadd, and Heith Copes. 2005. "What Have We Learned from Five Decades of Neutralization Research?" *Crime and Justice* 32: 221–320.

McAdams, Dan P. 2013. *The Redemptive Self: Stories Americans Live By*. Rev. ed. Oxford: Oxford University Press.

Mohamed, Idil A. A., and Sveinung Sandberg. 2019. "'Jeg kan ikke se søstre gå I den fella': Unge muslimer som forebyggere." In *Forebygging av Radikalisering og Voldelig Ekstremisme*, edited by Stian Lied and Geir Heierstad. Oslo: Gyldendal Akademisk.

Mullins, Christopher W. 2006. *Holding Your Square: Masculinities, Streetlife and Violence*. Cullompton, Devon: Willan.

Nietzsche, Friedrich. 1966. *Beyond Good and Evil*. New York: Vintage.

Pedersen, Willy, Heith Copes, and Sveinung Sandberg. 2016. "Alcohol and Violence in Nightlife Settings: A Qualitative Study." *Drug and Alcohol Review* 35 (5): 557–63.

Polletta, Francesca. 2006. *It Was Like a Fever: Storytelling in Protest and Politics*. Chicago: University of Chicago Press.

Poppi, Fabio I. M. 2024. "Per imaginem ad Veritatem: Joint Fantasizing of Crime." *Criminal Justice Studies* 37 (2): 99–123. https://doi.org/10.1080/14786 01X.2024.2337438.
Presser, Lois. 2008. *Been a Heavy Life: Stories of Violent Men*. Urbana: University of Illinois Press.
Presser, Lois. 2010. "Collecting and Analyzing the Stories of Offenders." *Journal of Criminal Justice Education* 21 (4): 431–46.
Presser, Lois. 2018. *Inside Story: How Narratives Drive Mass Harm*. Oakland: University of California Press.
Presser, Lois, and Sveinung Sandberg, eds. 2015. *Narrative Criminology: Understanding Stories of Crime*. New York: New York University Press.
Sandberg, Sveinung. 2009. "Gangster, Victim, or Both? Street Drug Dealers' Interdiscursive Construction of Sameness and Difference in Self-Presentations." *British Journal of Sociology* 60 (3): 523–42.
Sandberg, Sveinung. 2010. "'The Sweet Taste of Sin'—A Muslim Drug Dealer in a Nordic Welfare State." *Journal of Scandinavian Studies in Criminology and Crime Prevention* 11 (2): 103–18.
Sandberg, Sveinung, Carolina Agoff, and Gustavo Fondevila. 2020. "Stories of the 'Good Father': The Role of Fatherhood among Incarcerated Men in Mexico." *Punishment & Society* 24 (2): 241–61.
Sandberg, Sveinung, Carolina Agoff, and Gustavo Fondevila. 2021. "Doing Marginalized Motherhood: Identities and Practices among Incarcerated Women in Mexico." *International Journal for Crime, Justice and Social Democracy* 10 (1): 15–29.
Sandberg, Sveinung, and Sarah Colvin. 2020. "'ISIS Is Not Islam': Epistemic Injustice, Everyday Religion, and Young Muslims' Narrative Resistance." *British Journal of Criminology* 60 (6): 1585–605.
Sandberg, Sveinung, and Jennifer Fleetwood. 2017. "Street Talk and Bourdieusian Criminology: Bringing Narrative to Field Theory." *Criminology and Criminal Justice* 17 (4): 365–81.
Sandberg, Sveinung, and Willy Pedersen. 2009. *Street Capital: Black Cannabis Dealers in a White Welfare State*. Bristol, UK: Policy Press.
Sandberg, Sveinung, and Sébastien Tutenges. 2015. "Meeting the Djinn: Stories of Drug Use, Bad Trips and Addiction." In *Narrative Criminology: Understanding Stories of Crime*, edited by Lois Presser and Sveinung Sandberg, 150–73. New York: New York University Press.
Sandberg, Sveinung, and Sébastien Tutenges. 2019. "Laughter in Stories of Crime and Tragedy: The Importance of Humor for Marginalized Populations." *Social Problems* 66 (November): 564–79.
Sandberg, Sveinung, Sébastien Tutenges, and Willy Pedersen. 2019. "Drinking Stories as a Narrative Genre: The Five Classic Themes." *Acta Sociologica* 62 (4): 406–19.
Sandberg, Sveinung, and Thomas Ugelvik. 2016. "The Past, Present, and Future of Narrative Criminology: A Review and an Invitation." *Crime, Media, Culture* 12 (2): 129–36.

Scott, Marvin B., and Stanford M. Lyman. 1968. "Accounts." *American Sociological Review* 33 (1): 46–62.

Sykes, Gresham M., and David Matza. 1957. "Techniques of Neutralization: A Theory of Delinquency." *American Sociological Review* 22 (6): 664–70.

Thomassen, Niels. 2003. "The Ethics of Understanding." *Danish Yearbook of Philosophy* 38 (1): 83–98.

Tutenges, Sébastien. 2019. "Narrative Ethnography under Pressure: Researching Storytelling on the Street." In *The Emerald Handbook of Narrative Criminology*, edited by Jennifer Fleetwood, Lois Presser, Sveinung Sandberg, and Thomas Ugelvik, 27–43. Bingley: Emerald.

Tutenges, Sébastien. 2022. *Intoxication: An Ethnography of Effervescent Revelry*. New Brunswick: Rutgers University Press.

Tutenges, Sébastien, and Morten Hulvej Rod. 2009. "'We Got Incredibly Drunk . . . It Was Damned Fun': Drinking Stories among Danish Youth." *Journal of Youth Studies* 12 (4): 355–70.

Tutenges, Sébastien, and Sveinung Sandberg. 2013. "Intoxicating Stories: The Characteristics, Contexts and Implications of Drinking Stories among Danish Youth." *International Journal of Drug Policy* 24 (6): 538–44.

Tutenges, Sébastien, and Sveinung Sandberg. 2021. "Street Culture Meets Extremism: How Muslims Involved in Street Life and Crime Oppose Jihadism." *British Journal of Criminology* 62 (1): 1502–17.

Ugelvik, Thomas. 2014. *Power and Resistance in Prison: Doing Time, Doing Freedom*. London: Palgrave Macmillan UK.

Wagoner, Brady, Ignacio Brescó de Luna, and Sarah H. Awad. 2017. "Introduction: Imagination as a Psychological and Sociocultural Process." In *The Psychology of Imagination: History, Theory and New Research Horizons*, edited by Brady Wagoner, Ignacio Brescó de Luna, and Sarah H. Awad, ix-xii. Charlotte, NC: Information Age Publishing.

Way, Peter. 1993. "Evil Humors and Ardent Spirits: The Rough Culture of Canal Construction Laborers." *Journal of American History* 79 (4): 1397–42.

2

"I Actually Came Out on Top!"

Narratives of Formerly Incarcerated People Who Made Prison Work

VANESSA LYNN

In the hectic pace of the world today, there is no time for meditation, or for deep thought. A prisoner has time that he can put to good use. I'd put prison second to college as the best place for a man to go if he needs to do some thinking. If he's motivated, in prison he can change his life.
—Malcolm X, *The Autobiography of Malcolm X*

Malcolm X's autobiography resonates through time, touching generations worldwide. He describes his time in prison as marking a turning point—the place where he undergoes a profound political, religious, and racial awakening (DeGloma 2010). In a recent op-ed for the Marshall Project, "I Hate to Admit It, but Prison Is a Blessing in Disguise," Jy'Aire Smith-Pennick (2021) likewise shares his story of achieving positive change in prison:

> I would have to be a fool to not take advantage of these life-changing opportunities. And that's what it all boils down to—opportunity. To truly change, I had to alter my way of thinking. But without opportunities, I would be a person with a good head on his shoulders in the same position.

Some highly influential criminologists have emphasized prison as a site of deprivation, suffering, and pain (Sykes 1958; Warr 2016). Others have shed light on the deleterious consequences of racialized mass imprisonment on individuals, families, and communities (Clear 2007).

However, I join those scholars who argue that people who are incarcerated find opportunities in prison to improve their personal and social conditions (Bullock, Bunce, and McCarthy 2019; Comfort 2008; Crewe and Ievins 2019; Kazemian 2019; Schinkel 2014; Ugelvik 2014; Wright 2020). Stories mediate the discovery of opportunities in prison—indeed, the good created there.

To understand a person's story about prison, we must listen to their whole life story. Thus, I draw on the method of narrative portraiture to depict the lives of two formerly incarcerated Black men in the United States (Lawrence-Lightfoot and Davis 1997). Narrative portraiture is a qualitative method that allows the researcher to apply an aesthetic approach to the representation of the complexity of the lives of the people being studied. In this chapter, I explore the narrative portraits of Miles and Travis, two formerly incarcerated men.[1] The narrative portraits teach us that these men reflect on stories they told themselves to make sense of their past and anticipate the future, which sparked personal change while incarcerated. These portraits also reveal that these men *value* sharing stories of rehabilitation and growth while they were incarcerated. Overall, these portraits could be considered a form of narrative resistance: the good was realized despite the harms of prison.

Prison Paradox

Criminologists and sociologists have long documented and theorized the inner workings of prison: its culture, the pains of imprisonment, strategies for adaptation, and the development of hierarchies and other social relationships (Crewe 2012; Foucault 1977; Jacobs 1977; Sykes 1958). Many view prison as a criminogenic environment. For example, Sykes (1958) proposed the deprivation model of inmate culture, arguing that the pains of imprisonment and the deprivation of material and symbolic needs lead to a prison culture of violence. Goffman (1968) viewed the prison as a total institution that erases identity and thus forces prisoners to develop new identities. Contemporary conversations about decarceration and abolition take for granted that prison is altogether bad.

Research on reentry also highlights the barriers and collateral consequences of reentering society after prison with the stigma of a criminal conviction. Studies of post-incarceration life focus on successful reintegration into society: finding housing, getting a job, getting married, raising children, and so forth (Petersilia 2004; Travis 2005). Securing these means of living is undoubtedly important but does not guarantee a successful return to society. Trimbur (2009) argues that interactions with racial and class hierarchies shape reentry experiences. Williams, Wilson, and Bergeson (2019) similarly found that sanctions post-incarceration, encountered by Black men, are a form of racialized oppression that deeply impacts one's sense of masculinity, especially when looking for employment. Some, of course, persevere despite the odds.

We know that some people take advantage of their time incarcerated. Sykes (1958) describes informal arrangements in prison that maintain order, create a system of solidarity, and develop prisoners' leadership skills. Kreager and Kruttschnitt (2018) claim that deprivation may lead prisoners to find ways to cope "with dignity, resist exploiting peers, and provide community goods that encourage inmate solidarity and passive resistance to formal authority" (263). While prisons are seen as incapacitating places, researchers argue that "prisons can and should aim to be capacity-building" (McNeil and Schinkel 2016: 618). Crewe and Ievins (2019) theorize that prison can also be viewed as a reinventive institution; for incarcerated men and women, therapeutic programs provide modes of reinvention to rebuild a sense of self-worth and the capacity for trust and intimacy. Kazemian (2019) explores the positive growth that people incarcerated experience in the French prison system, demonstrating that desistance can be achieved in prison. Given these dynamics, we can say that prisons are characterized by contradictions. Toch (1992) describes the hostility and stressors of life in prison; however, he also examines the positive processes that incarcerated people engage in to ameliorate their stress. He explains that they create "their own responsive worlds. . . . The prison setting accommodates a large number of those worlds" (236).

Viewing the prison solely through the lens of the pains of imprisonment prevents us from learning about effective programs and the work done by incarcerated persons to find healing and build community. However, it is not my intent to condone the existence of prison as a site of violence and deprivation. Prisons deeply and adversely impact individuals, families, communities, and societies. The portraiture methodological approach gives the researcher the opportunity to provide a holistic picture of how people experience incarceration.

Portraiture

Developed by Lawrence-Lightfoot and Davis (1997), portraiture is a methodological approach that seeks to marry science and art; it is a method within the phenomenology tradition, with goals, techniques, and standards of ethnography. Portraiture follows a tradition in critical race scholarship that encourages shifting how we look and represent the "other." Tuck and Yang (2014) argue that social sciences have a legacy of documenting "pain stories from communities that are not White, not wealthy, and not straight . . . both for its voyeurism and for its consumptive implacability" (227). Because so much of the research on the "other" focuses on pain and suffering, there is a need to also look at the strength within these communities (Tuck and Yang 2014). Critical race theorists have shared the same concerns about deficit theorizing, that is, research that depicts only the deprivations experienced by communities of color (Yosso 2005: 75). Yosso (2005: 77) offers the "community cultural wealth" framework for conducting education research, which centers "the knowledge, skills, abilities, and contacts possessed and utilized by communities of color to survive and resist macro and micro-forms of oppression." Portraiture is an approach that invites the researcher to look for and embrace the representation of the strength in study participants with nuance, balancing the reality of the deficits.

This chapter marries both narrative and portraiture perspectives to show how formerly incarcerated persons make sense of their lives over time and the complex nature of prison life. A portraiture approach allows researchers to embrace complexities while also centering on "goodness" (Lawrence-Lightfoot 2005). Narrative portraiture can be used to develop multidimensional narratives, inquiring into the issues of personal and institutional life. The narrative portraits in this chapter reflect both the strengths *and* pains of prison life. They explore how lives before incarceration inform prison life and conditions. This method entails an attitude of respect in seeking understanding and in representing people's lives and experiences.

Implementing a portraiture methodology means determining the context and choosing a unified representation to frame the aesthetic whole (Lawrence-Lightfoot and Davis 1997). The research takes place in personal, cultural, and historical contexts. Narratives contain multiple events and perspectives told in contexts and about contexts within which the researcher and the researched live. As such, the researcher constructs a narrative—paints a portrait—that represents the complexities of human life, capturing the interaction of values, personality, structure, and history in a holistic fashion (Lawrence-Lightfoot and Davis 1997).

Stories are created between people. As a portraitist, I listened to the perspectives and realities that the participants chose to share and the stories that they wanted to tell, and in turn, that I wanted to relay to future audiences. The people's lives included in this research took shape within a specific historical context. The background of these portraits is the understanding that mass incarceration is the result of multiple haunting regimes of injustice. I use the word "haunting" as Gordon (2008: 183) does to emphasize that the regime produces "something-to-be-done." Indeed, in every regime of injustice, those affected develop strategies for social resilience that help them both cope and resist.

Narratives are a key vehicle of meaning-making and an impetus to action (Presser and Sandberg 2015). Narrative criminologists explore how stories affect the storyteller among others; narratives are told to counter the "pains of imprisonment," such as in Warr's (2020) study of the "narrative labor" of men incarcerated with life and indeterminate sentences. More recently, Warr has explored the narrative labor of Black incarcerated men in particular: they must mitigate their Blackness to construct a more acceptable self, a rehabilitative self, that is associated with whiteness (Warr 2022). Kazemian (2019) describes the "desistance narratives" of incarcerated people who use past adversity and trauma as catalysts to enact positive change. In this chapter, I offer narrative portraits based on what two men shared at my prompting, about realizing potential and achieving personal change despite life histories of trauma and the struggle of imprisonment.

Eliciting the Narratives of Formerly Incarcerated Men

The two narrative portraits are drawn from a project involving interviews with twenty-three formerly incarcerated Black and Brown men in New York state (Lynn 2022). The research explored retrospective experiences of three types of prison programs: art-based, cognitive behavioral therapy (CBT), and higher education. The twenty-three men were open about their experiences and had "good" and "bad" stories to share. In focusing on three types of prison programs, the study attempted to capture opportunities for personal change. Almost all participants turned a telling moment with me as an opportunity to remember something good about their past experiences in prison or upon release. However, it was the interaction between Travis and Miles as storytellers and me as an audience that distinguished these two interviews. I was struck by Travis's sensitivity and eagerness to tell his stories, which turned it into a cathartic experience. Miles had longed to tell his story and reconnect with his brother, which I was keen to hear. Both men provided opportunities for me to paint multiple snapshots of good stories, but also of past stories that led to good experiences.

I relied on networks of nonprofit organizations providing volunteer services to incarcerated people. Miles received my flyer from someone whom I interviewed before; both lived in the same homeless shelter. Travis received my flyer from the nonprofit organization that taught art in prisons. Travis's and Miles's two narrative portraits were created from a four-hour interview each. I encouraged "walking probes" by inviting the men to bring me to a location that had meaning to them. Miles asked me to drive in the neighborhood where he grew up. Travis was not interested in such a visit, so we met in a coffee shop. An interview guide was designed to provide both structured and unstructured narratives. For example, to invite narratives about their lives before incarceration, I initiated the interviews with "Tell me about how it was growing up in [location] for you." To understand their incarceration and participation in prison programs, I asked questions about whether they participated in rehabilitation programs, whether they liked them, and why or why not.

In fact, the interview did not generally follow the guide, as participants tended to organically raise preferred topics before I even asked a question. For instance, Travis spent valuable time describing his numerous accomplishments while incarcerated that did not involve prison rehabilitation programs. When I inquired further, it was as if it would never end; he kept adding instances of being productive. It was as if the interview became cathartic.

The stories the men told followed a set of narrative formulas, including the "code of the street" as a discourse to discuss lives in poor urban communities during the tough-on-crime and crack era (Anderson 2000; see also Brookman, Hopes, and Hochstetler 2011; Copes, Hochstetler, and Williams 2008; Sandberg 2009). The stories also followed the narrative construction of prison as redemptive, which can serve the purpose of shame management (Kazemian 2019; Maruna and Ramsden 2004). These formulas also provide the contexts to portray the beauty and the ugliness of the participants' experiences. I would stress that the participants turned bad experiences into good stories at the time of the interview, but we cannot infer that they view their lives in general as good.

Travis

Travis and I arranged to meet at a coffee shop in a gentrified section of Harlem in New York City. On a cold February day, the shop was noisy and quite busy. Travis was born in the Bahamas and, when I met him, was forty-two years old. His father was a welder working throughout the Caribbean islands, and his mother was a nurse. Travis was a good student, had skipped a grade, and enjoyed his comfortable life in the Bahamas where he grew up.

VANESSA: And from birth to age twelve in the Bahamas, how was that?
TRAVIS: Excellent. It was fun.
VANESSA: School?
TRAVIS: School was good. I was doing excellent in school until I came up here; they didn't understand how I was in the eleventh grade.
VANESSA: They did not transfer you to the proper grade?
TRAVIS: They ended up putting me in the tenth grade until my paperwork came in from home that I was in the eleventh. They didn't know that I skipped a grade.
VANESSA: Oh, you skipped a grade?
TRAVIS: Yeah. Fifth grade, and I skipped sixth.
VANESSA: And what did you like the most about school?
TRAVIS: I liked math. I liked reading a lot. Just learning in general.
VANESSA: Learning in general?
TRAVIS: I just liked learning more things and a fun-filled challenge.

When he was twelve years old, Travis moved to the South Bronx. This was 1987, considered the peak of the crack epidemic (Johnson, Golub, and Dunlap 2000). He was doing well in school, with his older sister teaching him what she learned about in school. But a second turning point for Travis occurred at age thirteen, when an eighteen- or nineteen-year-old boy living in his building was playing with a gun and shot him in the head. Travis was left with a bullet near his eye, which was too risky to operate on, forever altering his life. Despite this tragedy, Travis laughed a lot over the course of the interview, which I asked him about:

VANESSA: You laugh a lot . . .
TRAVIS: I was always a person that laughs.
VANESSA: Okay.
TRAVIS: It's a part of my personality. Sometimes I look at certain things and if I take it seriously, it's going to turn me into something different. So I try to always put a sense of humor.
VANESSA: That is a totally legit reaction, absolutely.
TRAVIS: I used to just react—that's what got me into trouble—because after being shot, I told myself when I came out the hospital, I started getting into fights. I can't get into fights because the bullet is still there.

Travis's laughter might be a coping mechanism to alleviate the trauma of that painful experience and give it meaning (Sandberg and Tutenges 2019). In turn, humor enables him to make his trauma tellable. He pragmatically attributes his incipient antisocial behavior to his being shot in his head, resulting in trauma not addressed through any counseling. Travis had dreams and aspirations, but they all fell through as a result of being shot.

I seen a lot of my friends in the Bahamas, they fly the planes, so their brothers taught them how to fly a plane and they got their permits and I'm gonna be a pilot. I was always inspired by it, by that. But when that happened, I'm like, well, that's out the window. My father said he was going to sign me up for the military and everything and I said okay. Well, I'm looking forward to that, and then that didn't happen. And when I went to school, I tried to go and finish school and people started to tease me about my eye so that, you know, I just stopped talking, you know.

Travis dropped out of high school. He started hanging out on the streets of the South Bronx. A study revealed that in 1990, 85 percent of people incarcerated come from seven neighborhoods in New York City, the South Bronx being one of them (Center for NuLeadership 2013). He became involved in street culture and violence, including selling drugs. His parents sent him to South Carolina to escape trouble, but he also found trouble there. Shortly after, he was sent to live with his strict, "no-nonsense" aunt in Brooklyn. Eventually his father brought him to the "hot seat" in his family living room, where family members were sent to have a serious talk when they were in trouble. The problem this time was that his father had found Travis's nine guns:

TRAVIS: About nine guns—a couple handguns—submachine guns.
VANESSA: What?
TRAVIS: Submachine guns.
VANESSA: What?
TRAVIS: 45 MP machines, 9 mm. and 45s.

Talking to Travis, I was in disbelief. I didn't inquire further about how a teenager could purchase so many guns, but the reason why he felt he needed the guns was clear to me. He had explained that he had been shot and didn't feel safe; with that many guns, there was no way he would get hit again. At the same time, youth violence increased in urban areas in the late 1980s and early 1990s. This increase was framed in sensational news coverage as "crack violence" and a crisis in cities like New York. While the expansion of the crack market was associated in the public eye with an increase in violence, recent research finds that the period also increased young Black men's access to guns as a result of a "positive supply shock in gun markets in the 1985–1993 period," which put more guns on the market at a cheaper price (Bartley and Williams 2022: 340). Travis came of age during the peak of the crack epidemic and all that it entailed; here, we see how expanded access to guns shaped his life.

Within his story of oppression and the typical narrative of hustle in inner-city America, Travis also interspersed stories of family support. His family intervened and attempted to keep him out of trouble on multiple occasions. Travis reconstructs his story with family intervening as a collective, whether putting him in the hot seat or sending him away. After he was arrested a few times, his mother wanted to send him to North Carolina, but a few days later, still in New York, he was arrested again.

Travis spent nine years in prison. He felt at the time that this was an injustice and that his life was over. During his early years in prison, he ran into trouble and spent much of his time in solitary confinement. During that time, he ran into his brother, who was also incarcerated in solitary confinement. His brother tried to talk sense into him:

> TRAVIS: So came out my cell to take a shower, and I was like, "Oh no, look at this. What a wonderful thing." So we went to the yard and we was in the cages and, looking at me, said, "Bro, I love you, man." I said, "I love you too, bro." He said, "Man, I need you home. Whatever you are doing, stop it. Go home." . . . He said, "If you want to spend the rest of your life here's prison, then don't call me your brother. I don't want to have anything to do with you." I said, "What?" He said, "You heard me. How we going to help each other? You can't do nothing for me here, because all you can do is but so much." I said, "You know what? You are right, bro. This is it, man." He said, "Okay, that's what I want to hear. . . . Man, you're a smart kid and you've been a smart kid. I don't know what's wrong with you or what got into you. I don't know if that gunshot wound that got to you?"
>
> VANESSA: He said that?
>
> TRAVIS: Yeah. Tear drop fall out of my eye. He was like, "Why you crying?" I was like, "Nobody ever hit me with that punchline right there. I never really talked about it."

Travis's brother was able to put the finger on the unaddressed trauma Travis had been carrying since he was thirteen years old. His brother's story appears as a narrative intervention that positively impacted him as it sparked his will to change. The good story his brother told him in prison, reminding him of the good in him, led to his awakening and seeking (or making) good experiences through the institutional structures available.

Having earned his GED in prison, Travis attended college when he returned home. It was a logical continuation of his interest in learning, the narrative identity he carried from his childhood in the Bahamas. However, sustained fear for his life led him to carry a gun for safety. The bullet still stuck in his head defined his life-course trajectory from incipience to persistence, with a felt, urgent need to carry a firearm a constant. Even though he had done nothing wrong, Travis had to go to court to address a false robbery allegation and face the risks of going to trial for a "twenty-five-to-life" sentence. He blamed his lawyer for pushing him into taking a plea deal, resulting in a new, fourteen-year sentence.

These choices were, of course, made within a very particular context. Travis had tremendous potential, but that potential was reshaped by his interaction with the prison system, the trauma of being shot as a thirteen-year-old, and his coming of age during the violence in the 1990s in New York City. At the same time, those social forces and feelings of guilt for putting his family through this ordeal also inspired Travis to be more involved in a positive prison life during his second sentence. His narrative of this prison sentence exemplifies Flaherty's temporal agency as "the modification of one's own experience" (Flaherty 2011: 19). Accepting a shorter sentence gave Travis the "temporal tolerance" (Flaherty 2011) to engage with himself and others during his incarceration. His work during this time involved taking advantage of the institutional context of prison to reclaim his potential.

Without the good story that he remembered his brother telling him and without the institutional support he sought out, Travis would not have been able to tell his own good story in that moment with me. Travis listed for me all that he contributed to. He joined the Caribbean African Unity organization (CAU), explaining that it "is basically an organization that represents the interests of Caribbean nationals who enter the system." The organization also hosted cultural and political classes taught by incarcerated men with master's degrees. He taught classes after a member of the Black Panthers, who led a class on leadership, reached out to him: he saw his ability to defuse tensions between gangs. He participated in the Alternative to Violence Program (AVP) following his involvement with the CAU. Travis was telling a story of someone who availed himself of every possible opportunity, and he spoke excitedly and at length about his program experiences:

TRAVIS: I forgot to share with you—when I was in Otisville, I did a program. I started [a] gun buyback program.
VANESSA: You started that?
TRAVIS: Yeah, I did it there. It was on the news and everything.
VANESSA: Yeah, yeah, I've heard about that.
TRAVIS: In Otisville.
VANESSA: You did that?
TRAVIS: I did [the organizing]. I got the whole organization together, and I said, "I want each one of you on this committee. This is gonna be a committee for us. We're going to call it the 'Community Restoration Project.'" So a lot of us—we could make plans in our community—and we haven't done anything to slow it down. So this is our way of helping, in that sense.

The seemingly oppressive prison environment was at odds with Travis's story of prison humanizing its population. His story of prison rehabilitation experiences constructs an image of incarcerated people working to improve themselves and their community, identifying problems and solutions. At one point, to explain the impact of the crack epidemic, Travis explained how it had destroyed the community and how the "whole thing just went crazy—there was no loyalty, no trust, no nothing." In prison, he created a way to make up for that missing community. Travis became a Muslim, joined the Caribbean African Unity organization, started a gun buyback program, and took college courses from an accredited, prestigious school. Travis believed in social change and wanted to be a part of it. He used his time in prison to create opportunities he had not had before. He maximized his sense of agency in accord with Emirbayer and Mische's (1998) definition of agency as "a temporally embedded process," oriented toward the future, and occurring in the present but with a sense of reflectiveness and evaluation of himself in the past.

The interview with Travis lasted more than four hours, and if I hadn't needed to interrupt our time together, it could have lasted longer. The study's focus on prison programs, by virtue of the questions I asked participants, allowed Travis to tell a story of turning a seemingly negative experience—prison—into a positive one involving service to a tight community. He shared a story of incarcerated folks working together to create safe communities inside and outside the walls. In line with Schinkel's (2014) conclusion that incarcerated people seek rehabilitation tailored to them as individuals, his story further depicts the ways people in prison can thrive and achieve personal growth outside institutionally mandated programs (Kazemian 2019).

Travis's narrative portrait includes multiple stories, and the experience of telling them enacts something good. He used laughter while sharing a story to cope with trauma. He shared a story of building community and working together, a story that made an impression on me as a listener who so frequently thinks about the bad that prison does. The good story led to another story that he subsequently returned home, his large family still supporting each other as he was living with and caring for his mother. His narrative, as he told me during the four-hour interview, depicts his struggles and eventual successes before and during incarceration. Travis's narrative portrait starts with his potential and ends there; it is an overall story of realization—of lost and found promise.

Miles

It was a hot, sunny, humid day in August 2016. I drove to pick up Miles from the homeless shelter where he lived and waited for him in my car with the air conditioning on the highest setting. I hadn't met Miles before, but I had described my car so he would know how to find me. After a few minutes, a dark-skinned, short Black man approached my vehicle. I stepped out to introduce myself. Miles was wearing black shorts, a black tank top, and a black shirt. He was also sporting a huge smile. He had contacted me after getting my flyer from another man, Ilan, whom I had interviewed the week before. The two men lived in the same shelter; they had met while taking the same prison-based college classes. Miles heard that Ilan and I drove to where he grew up, and Miles was excited to share the same experience. Excited might be an understatement: Miles was adamantly ready. As soon as we started talking, Miles was eager to tell his life story:

> VANESSA: We are going to Jamaica. Thank you again for taking the time.... Tell me a little bit about growing up in Queens, and tell me about your family and how it was where you grew up.

MILES: First, I'm glad you asked, 'cause I finally can get it off my chest instead of holding it in for so long.

VANESSA: Wait, you've never told your story to nobody?

MILES: Never.

VANESSA: In no programs? While you've been incarcerated?

MILES: I gave them pieces. I didn't give them everything.

VANESSA: And who's "them"?

MILES: When I gave them my autobiography, I gave them pieces.

VANESSA: What autobiography?

MILES: The autobiography I had to do for Writing 1, that was the first assignment.

VANESSA: And before, through the courts?

MILES: Nope.

VANESSA: Intake?

MILES: Nope.

VANESSA: In prison, nobody ever asked you about your story?

MILES: They asked me, but it wasn't . . . no, I didn't. It wasn't the time.

VANESSA: Why?

MILES: Because I didn't feel comfortable.

VANESSA: So now you're comfortable.

MILES: Yep, because you asked—different way—different approach. The way they asked me is demanding.

VANESSA: How?

MILES: And then once they get the story, they throw it in your face and they judge you with it, and they put different things in your file, and they classify you, and they put you in a certain category to how you was raised, and, it's like they diss you.

My time with Miles also extended to four hours. Miles, I would later find out, needed help. Going back to where he grew up was his chance to find his younger brother, whom he hadn't seen in fifteen years. He took the opportunity to share his story on his own terms with me, and not with his lawyer, the prosecutor, or the judge, which led us to drive for hours, looking for—and eventually finding—his brother. In fact, there is little incentive or opportunity to share one's story through the criminal justice system. Most defendants resolve their case with a plea deal (Subramanian et al. 2020). Miles never had to share his story, whether through the court system or while incarcerated, or when he was asked to tell about his life, he was not comfortable doing so. Miles's current story includes the present moment of telling his story freely; it was a good moment because he wanted to tell it.

Miles, thirty-four, was born in 1981 to a mother who had been addicted to crack and later abandoned him, his older sister, and his younger brother. Miles had never told his story because it was so traumatic. His story also identifies the crack era as a social context that forever shaped his life story. Although he was born and grew up at the height of the crack epidemic, he came of age during a decline in crime and violence (Johnson et al. 2000). His account of his childhood echoes the metaphorical characterization of crack as a weapon of destruction, impacting every family member in its path:

> VANESSA: And how did it impact your life—the crack era and the war on drugs?
> MILES: It messed my childhood up because it took my mom from me, it took my mother from me, it totally destroyed my family . . . 'cause my mother wasn't the only crackhead in my family either.

Miles initially attributes his childhood trauma to crack and his mother, but he later adds more detail that reflects a short moment of stability in his life:

> MILES: I don't have many memories of Queens with the lady 'cause I was a kid. The only memories I have with the lady was me going to school.
> VANESSA: Okay, how was school?
> MILES: School was good, I was an excellent student. I was good! I was an excellent student. I had the highest reading percent average.
> VANESSA: So you remember enjoying school and being good at it?
> MILES: Yeah, and I absolutely remember, and after I was taken from the lady that raised us, my life has never been the same. She wiped us, me and my little brother, we were like Batman and Robin. If something broke, Miles and Chris did it, something stolen, we did it, we were boys, and things like that.

Miles navigated the foster care system and group homes as a child. Miles shared how his situation went "downhill" shortly after he was taken away from the stable, caring foster home and instead placed into a group home:

> MILES: Uh, no, no, we don't go to school in group home. Once I was taken away from Ms. Ida, the first home. It was a wrap, everything went downhill. Everything went downhill.
> VANESSA: So how was school? You came back to school?
> MILES: I used to go to that elementary school, right down the block, right there.
> VANESSA: So after group homes, you went back to school?
> MILES: Hum hum, I was never the same. School was wack. I wasn't interested in anything. Everything is boring. The only thing I was interested in is what I was doing in the group home, the wild stuff—beating up people, getting beat up, stealing, cutting school—that became a habit. Lying, stealing, not listening, becoming hardheaded—that became my habit. I have an estimate it started at nine, but I know I was real young, real young.

Instability and disruption made Miles feel isolated. Still, that sense of isolation was mitigated when he found a social network of other boys his age whose experiences were similar to his. After leaving the group home, Miles began living with his grandmother, but he also joined a gang. He started to neglect school due to his involvement in gang activities.

Eventually, Miles was incarcerated for robbery in the first degree, along with the members of the gang he was affiliated with. Miles completed a five-year prison sentence before being re-incarcerated six months later for a ten-year sentence. One would think that five years might be significant enough for someone to want to get the desistance process started; however, Miles told me that the first sentence did not motivate him in that way; his sense of collective belonging was still tied to his gang:

> VANESSA: When you came home, the prison experience didn't turn you off from doing the things to make you go back?

MILES: It didn't do anything because I didn't learn a lesson. I carried too much hate. So when I came home—you didn't write me a letter, I don't care no more, I don't care about you, nobody else, so what. And I took that. I carried it with me to the point where I went back to the gang, where I felt the love was at, until doing the time for my ten years. I started to mature. I started to realize, hold on, you're growing up now, man. When you come home, you're gonna be this age, so you got this much time.

VANESSA: When did you say that to yourself?

MILES: I said that in 2010.

VANESSA: What made you say that to yourself?

MILES: I started to look at the old-timers that was not doing anything with themselves. They were not doing anything! No one was doing anything with themselves, all they was doing was talk about another person. They would criticize, and I said, "You know what, I don't want to be like that." And I started spending a lot of times with myself, and the time I started spending to myself, I started to value myself more. I started to grow out of certain habits, like being in groups.

VANESSA: Which one?

MILES: Like gang group, just being around a lot of people. It started to fade away, I started to feel uncomfortable.

Both times Miles was incarcerated, he was in a gang. The gang represented love and belonging, a constant that he was looking for from his mother. However, during his second sentence, he decided to leave the gang life because he "started to mature" and told himself, "Hold on, . . . I don't want to be like that," which led him to spend more time by himself. Miles had a narrative reflection, a story he told himself to make sense of his present conditions among older prisoners and what his future would be like if he didn't make a personal change. Narrative was evidently a vehicle for agentively thinking things through to himself (Emirbayer and Mische 1998). His narrative reflection was then a catalyst for personal change. A program did not aid Miles's self-reform. He changed despite what prison had to offer. Miles developed a temporal agentic orientation to overcome his past feelings of anger and hate that made him realize that gang life was not compatible with his present experience, seeing "old-timers not doing anything." He evaluated that current situation with a vision of himself going home in the future, "at this age."

His gang let him go, and, like Travis, he started pursuing things that he never had time to explore previously, including vocational programs, his GED, and eventually higher education opportunities. However, while Miles did not have access to the social capital of prison activists and prison organizers as Travis had, his options were no less exceptional:

> VANESSA: How did you get out of [the gang]?
> MILES: I just left, I just left it alone.
> VANESSA: They didn't say anything?
> MILES: They wanted to, but because of who I was, and everybody had love for me, they see that I was doing the right thing after where I came from. "Leave him alone! If you do something to him, I'll do something to you," and people just left me alone, they just left, like, "Nah, he going to school. He wants to go to school." I actually have a computer repair certification, I got my food handler [certification], I have college credits.
> VANESSA: So how did you get to the college program? Why did you apply?
> MILES: The reason why I applied is because I wanted to go to college. I wanted to do something different. I wanted to see if I could do it. I really wanted to see if I could do it; I wanted to challenge myself. At first, I wasn't gonna do it. I said, "Nah, man, nah," but then I said, "If you want to do something for yourself, man, you gotta get off your ass and do it, give it a shot. You don't got nothing to lose. Give it a shot."

Miles, like Travis, found a supportive and helpful community within the prison. The community aided in the desistance process and his overall transformation, but a narrative reflection ultimately sparked his motivation. He observed those who were unproductive in the prison community, and felt angst at the prospect of becoming like them (Paternoster and Bushway 2009). It enabled his narrative reflection and led him to be his own agent of change (Emirbayer and Mische 1998).

Miles's stories emphasize episodes of actualizing agency. In prison, he was overcoming the "not caring" thought processes of his youth, engaging a process that centers on a self-reflexive and agentic decision to mature. The college program Miles enrolled in was also transformative. He exposed himself to writings that helped him put his biography and sense of personal responsibility into perspective:

VANESSA: Who have you ever blamed for that childhood?
MILES: Hum.
VANESSA: If you ever blamed somebody?
MILES: The government. If I can blame anybody for it, I blame Ronald Reagan for it.
VANESSA: You thought about that?
MILES: Yeah, now that I'm conscious. Back then, nuh, I would operate, "Mommy, it's your fault." But it's not my mother's fault—you know what I'm saying? I know what drug do, and I know why they put it in the neighborhoods, and I know what it was for.
VANESSA: When did you come to that conclusion?
MILES: I came to that conclusion in 2012–13, something like that.
VANESSA: Based on what?
MILES: Based on reading. Since I started reading, I started to become more conscious, and these types of people we used to be [unintelligible] around, and talking around, they used to hit some of my thoughts right on the nail.
VANESSA: Who was the people?
MILES: They were regular prisoners, conscious prisoners in the yard, talking, some of the prisoners were college students, some of them were people running programs, some were just good with writing.

Miles's narrative started with a downhill trajectory due to the crack epidemic and effects on his family, which led to not caring, getting into trouble, and ultimately, expecting death. These circumstances led to his incarceration. Miles then shared a story he used to tell himself, that it was his mother's fault, but he changed that story to blaming Reagan. This shift in assigning responsibility can be seen as a device that allowed him to make peace with his experiences and his mother. The story itself provided something good for him, such as peace and love for his mother. A few years after the interview, when we spoke again, Miles had left the shelter and moved in with his mother; they were trying to rebuild their relationship. His transformational experiences in prison allowed him to reconstruct the disruption of his past through education and through reflective and imaginative distancing, another agentic tool to shape one's response to problematic situations (Emirbayer and Mische 1998).

> MILES: But I actually—but, you know, even though I did the time that I did, hey, look who I am, look what I gain, look what I became?
> VANESSA: What do you mean?
> MILES: I came out on top! I didn't come home at the bottom! I actually came out on top! I got school.
> VANESSA: You couldn't have been on top without having gone to prison?
> MILES: I could have, but I also—other things could have happened. I was going in a different route, a total different route. I was still gang member, I was hanging out, I was on parole, getting high, I was running all up and down Jamaica Avenue, and everything like that. I stayed in this precinct over here, it was like, that became my second home.

Miles pursued higher education as a challenge to himself and gave himself opportunities to explore his interests in reading and writing. College for him, then, became not only a space centered around the goal of earning a degree, but an opportunity to challenge himself, do something good for himself, and explore the relationship between himself and society. In contrast to typical depictions of prisoners as ruthless and violent, he describes how people surrounding him uplifted him by providing the necessary tools or leaving him alone. His story positions him as finding the strength to achieve something good, of coming out on top and overcoming both his hard start in life and oppressive government regimes. The struggles of his first prison sentence can help explain the strength he found during his second sentence. Miles was elated to recall these moments, focusing on specific experiences of his time in prison. As we drove home after he had reunited with his brother, Miles could not stop smiling. It is possible that this positive turn of events allowed him to focus on the positive that happened despite and even because of prison.

Conclusion

Narrative portraiture aims to "depict social phenomena through people's stories of everyday life experience [and is thus] able to bridge the gap between individual and society" (Rodríguez-Dorans and Jacobs 2020: 613). Then, as theorized by narrative criminology, stories inspire actions. Stories can promote harm but can also do the opposite; they can alleviate pain and trauma (Presser and Sandberg 2015; Sandberg and Tutenges 2019). This chapter presents two narrative portraits of formerly incarcerated Black men and their stories of personal change and prison life. The narrative portraiture perspective allowed me to capture the good and bad as they featured in their storytelling.

Prison research has a history of emphasizing hypermasculinization and prisons' cultures of violence. Prison is seen to potentially stifle the abilities of long-term prisoners to develop a prosocial narrative identity (Warr 2020). However, scholars have also explored how prisons provide structure and discipline and, for some, rehabilitation. Often, prison is a site of possible transformation, given the access it may provide to specific programs or social services (Kazemian 2019; Schinkel 2014). This chapter shows that in listening to the whole story of a person's life, we can better understand how people might construct good experiences in prison and their own good selves who take advantage of these. I presented Travis's and Miles's narrative portraits, recounting how specific stories allowed them to better themselves while incarcerated. Travis and Miles positioned prison as a positive influence; they shared multiple stories that show the good that happened—that they made happen—despite being incarcerated.

Their choice to focus on the good they did while incarcerated was a move to regain agency, and sharing their stories gave them agency too. For both Miles and Travis, their prison sentences did not annihilate their agency; on the contrary, in prison they sought out educational opportunities and created new opportunities to help others by giving back to their communities. Telling stories that promote specific temporal experiences over others is an example of time-work: theoretically, it integrates agency with temporality; practically, people are agents in choosing to tell stories that favor or suppress specific experiences they had over time (Flaherty 2011). Personal narratives are thus a vehicle for agency in contrast to the loss of liberty that characterizes imprisonment. As such, recounting these experiences about themselves and other incarcerated people allowed them to change the hegemonic narrative that bad people are in prison and the criminological understanding that people learn to commit crimes while incarcerated.

In the story of being an overachiever in prison, Travis is proud of his accomplishments, and when sharing this story with me, he can shine his pride. Similarly, Miles shared plenty of stories that did him good. While incarcerated, he told himself a story that motivated him to change, led him to summon the courage to enroll in college, and allowed him to make peace with his mother. Ultimately, deciding to do the interview to tell his story led him to reunite with his brother. In sum, storytelling in the present allowed the narrators to turn traumatic and painful experiences into stories of success and positive experiences, allowing them to feel pride and delight at that moment.

Americans and their leaders are attempting to reckon with the problem of mass incarceration. The voices of people directly impacted by incarceration are increasingly being heard; people do not have to be defined by their worst mistakes. Smith-Pennick's (2021) is one of the many stories the Marshall Project highlights in its online publication. Travis's and Miles's narrative portraits show two men for whom stories created avenues for responding to trauma and systems of oppression; their stories are the source of self-resilience. Using laughter while sharing a story of trauma helps to turn it into a story of resilience. The stories they told me also do something good for us readers: they change perceptions of the work incarcerated people do to rebuild themselves and their communities; they make prison a restorative place. As Presser notes, "Given the logics of prison—harm seeking, exclusionary, individualistic, state-dominant, irrelevant to victims, passivizing and coercive" (2014: 21), until we can reduce or eliminate prisons, prison administration should make prisons more restorative—emphasizing encounter, amends, reintegration, and inclusion. Future research should consider creating narrative environments where people under correctional control can create, shape, and tell good stories.

NOTE

1 Pseudonyms are used.

REFERENCES

Anderson, Elijah. 2000. *Code of the Street: Decency, Violence, and the Moral Life of the Inner City*. New York: Norton.

Bartley, Wm. Alan, and Geoffrey Fain Williams. 2022. "The Role of Gun Supply in 1980s and 1990s Youth Violence." *Contemporary Economic Policy* 40 (2): 323–48. https://doi.org/10.1111/coep.12556.

Brookman, Fiona, Heith Copes, and Andy Hochstetler. 2011. "Street Codes as Formula Stories: How Inmates Recount Violence." *Journal of Contemporary Ethnography* 40 (4): 397–424.

Brosens, Dorien. 2019. "Prisoners' Participation and Involvement in Prison Life: Examining the Possibilities and Boundaries." *European Journal of Criminology* 16 (4): 466–85.

Bullock, Karen, Annie Bunce, and Daniel McCarthy. 2019. "Making Good in Unpromising Places: The Development and Cultivation of Redemption Scripts among Long-Term Prisoners." *International Journal of Offender Therapy and Comparative Criminology* 63 (3): 406–24.

Center for NuLeadership on Human Justice and Healing. 2013. "The Seven Neighborhood Study Revisited." https://nuleadership.org.

Clear, Todd R. 2007. *Imprisoning Communities: How Mass Incarceration Makes Disadvantaged Neighborhoods Worse*. Oxford: Oxford University Press.

Comfort, Megan. 2008. "'The Best Seven Years I Could'a Done': The Reconstruction of Imprisonment as Rehabilitation." In *Imaginary Penalities*, edited by Pat Carlen, 252–74. New York: Routledge.

Copes, Heith, Andy Hochstetler, and Patrick J. Williams. 2008. "'We Weren't Like No Regular Dope Fiends': Negotiating Hustler and Crackhead Identities." *Social Problems* 55 (2): 254–70.

Crewe, Ben. 2012. *The Prisoner Society: Power, Adaptation and Social Life in an English Prison*. Oxford: Oxford University Press.

Crewe, Ben, and Alice Ievins. 2019. "The Prison as a Reinventive Institution." *Theoretical Criminology* 24 (4): 568–89.

DeGloma, Thomas. 2010. "Awakenings: Autobiography, Memory, and the Social Logic of Personal Discovery." *Sociological Forum* 25: 519–40.

Emirbayer, Mustafa, and Ann Mische. 1998. "What Is Agency?" *American Journal of Sociology* 103 (4): 962–1023.

Evans, William N., Craig Garthwaite, and Timothy J. Moore. 2022. "Guns and Violence: The Enduring Impact of Crack Cocaine Markets on Young Black Males." *Journal of Public Economics* 206. https://doi.org/10.1016/j.jpubeco.2021.104581.

Flaherty, Michael G. 2011. *The Textures of Time: Agency and Temporal Experience*. Philadelphia: Temple University Press.

Foucault, Michel. 1977. *Discipline and Punish*. New York: Random House.

Garland, David. 2001. *The Culture of Control*. Oxford: Oxford University Press.

Goffman, Erving. 1968. *Asylums: Essays on the Social Situation of Mental Patients and Other Inmates*. New York: Anchor.

Gordon, Avery F. 2008. *Ghostly Matters: Haunting and the Sociological Imagination.* Minneapolis: University of Minnesota Press.

Haslam, Alexander S., and Stephen D. Reicher. 2012. "When Prisoners Take Over the Prison: A Social Psychology of Resistance." *Personality and Social Psychology Review* 16 (2): 154–79.

Jacobs, James B. 1977. *Stateville: The Penitentiary in Mass Society.* Chicago: University of Chicago Press.

Johnson, Bruce, Andrew Golub, and Eloise Dunlap. 2000. "The Rise and Decline of Hard Drugs, Drug Markets, and Violence in Inner-City New York." In *The Crime Drop in America*, edited by Alfred Blumstein and Joel Wallman, 164–206. Cambridge: Cambridge University Press.

Kazemian, Lila. 2019. *Positive Growth and Redemption in Prison: Finding Light behind Bars and Beyond.* New York: Routledge.

Kreager, Derek A., and Candace Kruttschnitt. 2018. "Inmate Society in the Era of Mass Incarceration." *Annual Review of Criminology* 1: 261–83.

Lawrence-Lightfoot, Sara. 2005. "Reflections on Portraiture: A Dialogue between Art and Science." *Qualitative Inquiry* 11 (1): 3–15.

Lawrence-Lightfoot, Sara, and Jessica Hoffman Davis. 1997. *The Art and Science of Portraiture.* San Francisco: Jossey-Bass.

Lynn, Vanessa. 2022. "Eliciting Selves: Narrating Collective Redemption through Historical Representation." *Critical Criminology* 49 (3): 250–51. https://doi.org/10.1177/0094306120915912k.

Maruna, Shadd. 2001. *Making Good: How Ex-Convicts Reform and Rebuild Their Lives.* Washington, DC: American Psychological Association.

Maruna, Shadd, and Derek Ramsden. 2004. "Living to Tell the Tale: Redemption Narratives, Shame Management, and Offender Rehabilitation." In *Healing Plots: The Narrative Basis of Psychotherapy*, edited by Amia Lieblich, Dan P. McAdams, and Ruthellen Josselson, 129–49. Washington, DC: American Psychological Association.

McNeill, Fergus, and Marguerite Schinkel. 2016. "Prisons and Desistance." In *Handbook on Prisons*, edited by Yvonne Jewkes, Jamie Bennett, and Ben Crewe, 607–21. London: Routledge.

Paternoster, Ray, and Shawn Bushway. 2009. "Desistance and the Feared Self: Toward an Identity Theory of Criminal Desistance." *Journal of Criminal Law and Criminology* 99 (4): 1103–56.

Petersilia, Joan. 2004. "What Works in Prisoner Reentry? Reviewing and Questioning the Evidence." *Federal Probation* 68 (2): 4–8.

Presser, Lois. 2014. "The Restorative Prison." In *The American Prison: Imagining a Different Future*, edited by Francis T. Cullen, Cheryl Lero Jonson, and Mary K. Stohr, 19–32. Thousand Oaks, CA: Sage.

Presser, Lois, and Sveinung Sandberg, eds. 2015. *Narrative Criminology: Understanding Stories of Crime.* New York: New York University Press.

Rios, Victor M. 2011. *Punished: Policing the Lives of Black and Latino Boys.* New York: New York University Press.

Rodríguez-Dorans, Edgar, and Paula Jacobs. 2020. "Making Narrative Portraits: A Methodological Approach to Analysing Qualitative Data." *International Journal of Social Research Methodology* 23 (6): 611–23.

Sandberg, Sveinung. 2009. "Gangster, Victim, or Both? Street Drug Dealers' Interdiscursive Construction of Sameness and Difference in Self-Presentations." *British Journal of Sociology* 60 (3): 523–42.

Sandberg, Sveinung, and Sébastien Tutenges. 2019. "Laughter in Stories of Crime and Tragedy: The Importance of Humor for Marginalized Populations." *Social Problems* 66 (4): 564–79.

Schinkel, Marguerite. 2014. *Being Imprisoned: Punishment, Adaptation and Desistance.* New York: Springer.

Shelby, Tommie. 2016. *Dark Ghettos.* Cambridge, MA: Harvard University Press.

Smith-Pennick, Jy'Aire. 2021. "I Hate to Admit It, but Prison Is a Blessing in Disguise." Marshall Project, June 10. www.themarshallproject.org.

Subramanian, Ram, Léon Digard, Melvin Washington II, and Stephanie Sorage. 2020. *In the Shadows: A Review of the Research on Plea Bargaining.* Vera Institute of Justice, September. www.vera.org.

Sykes, Gresham M. 1958. *The Society of Captives: A Study of a Maximum Security Prison.* Princeton: Princeton University Press.

Toch, Hans. 1992. *Living in Prison: The Ecology of Survival.* Washington, DC: American Psychological Association.

Travis, Jacob. 2005. *But They All Come Back: Facing the Challenges of Prisoner Reentry.* Washington, DC: Urban Institute Press.

Trimbur, Lucia. 2009. "Me and the Law Is Not Friends: How Former Prisoners Make Sense of Reentry." *Qualitative Sociology* 32 (3): 259–77. https://doi.org/10.1007/s11133-009-9134-4.

Tuck, Eve, and K. Wayne Yang. 2014. "R-words: Refusing Research." In *Humanizing Research: Decolonizing Qualitative Inquiry with Youth and Communities*, edited by Django Paris and Maisha T. Wynn, 223–48. Thousand Oaks, CA: Sage.

Ugelvik, Thomas. 2014. *Power and Resistance in Prison: Doing Time, Doing Freedom.* New York: Springer.

Visher, Christy A., and Jeremy Travis. 2003. "Transitions from Prison to Community: Understanding Individual Pathways." *Annual Review of Sociology* 29: 89–113.

Wacquant, Loïc. 2010. "Crafting the Neoliberal State: Workfare, Prisonfare, and Social Insecurity." *Sociological Forum* 25: 197–220. https://doi.org/10.1111/j.1573-7861.2010.01173.x.

Warr, Jason. 2016. "The Prisoner: Inside and Out." In *Handbook on Prisons*, 2nd ed., edited by Yvonne Jewkes, Ben Crewe, and Jamie Bennett, 586–604. New York: Routledge.

Warr, Jason. 2020. "'Always Gotta Be Two Mans': Lifers, Risk, Rehabilitation, and Narrative Labour." *Punishment & Society* 22 (1): 28–47.

Warr, Jason, 2022. "Whitening Black Men: Narrative Labour and the Scriptural Economics of Risk and Rehabilitation." *British Journal of Criminology* 63 (5): 1091–1107. https://doi.org/10.1093/bjc/azac066.

Williams, Jason M., Shaun K. Wilson, and Carrie Bergeson. 2019. "'It's Hard Out Here if You're a Black Felon': A Critical Examination of Black Male Reentry." *Prison Journal* 99 (4): 437–58. https://doi.org/10.1177/0032885519852088.

Wright, Kevin A. 2020. "Time Well Spent: Misery, Meaning, and the Opportunity of Incarceration." *Howard Journal of Crime and Justice* 59 (1): 44–64.

Yosso, Tara J. 2005. "Whose Culture Has Capital? A Critical Race Theory Discussion of Community Cultural Wealth." *Race Ethnicity and Education* 8 (1): 69–91.

X, Malcolm. 1990. *The Autobiography of Malcolm X: As Told to Alex Haley*. New York: Ballantine.

3

Fresh Home

Narratives Celebrating Freedom from Prison and the Durability of the Street Self in UK Rap Music

JENNIFER FLEETWOOD AND JONATHAN ILAN

UK rap music might seem like an unlikely place to find "good" stories. Rap music, replete with descriptions of criminal acts and the sexual subjugation of women, is more usually consigned to the category of "bad story" to the extent that it is regularly the subject of censure, censorship, and blame for social ills, to the point of being used as evidence in criminal trials (see, e.g., Fatsis 2019a, 2019b; Ilan 2012, 2020; White 2017). Although rap is now firmly a part of pop/youth culture, police forces, prosecutors, and other relevant authorities seem to find little positive value in rap music, reflecting wider structures of class and race in evaluations of musical expression (see further Crockett Thomas et al. 2021; Peters 2019). In this chapter we implicitly challenge this "bad" categorization, reflecting on the "fresh home" theme in UK rap music, which celebrates a rapper's recent return from prison. We show that fresh home raps are charged with joyous sentiment and celebrate the durability of the rappers' street selves—how these individuals are able to endure the deep privations of prison—to emerge to become even more successful musicians. At its heart, fresh home invokes a classic "rags to riches" narrative but ultimately says something about contemporary marginality. For the most disadvantaged, the story of transcending marginalization and thriving uncompromised merits celebration in music.

Our analysis sits at the intersection between narrative and cultural criminologies, both of which explore how ideas about crime are embedded in culture and media, including personal narratives (Aspden and Hayward 2015). Cultural criminologists recognize culture as a site of politics and contested meaning, emphasizing the significance of music, emotions, and affect (Ilan 2019), areas that narrative criminology has arguably neglected. Culture may be diffuse and hard to pin down; narrative analysis offers a way to study personal narratives as an identifiable aspect of culture. Such analysis leads us to reflect on how meaning is constructed—here, the meaning of the prison experience in particular—and what narratives—in the present case, raps—can accomplish for their speakers (Presser and Sandberg 2015; Sandberg 2010). Further, a Bourdieusian approach to narrative (Fleetwood 2016) prompts us to consider how forms of creativity and resistance are nonetheless embedded in social structures and power relations.

Here we attend to UK rap music as a site of personal storytelling about the struggles of life at the margins and experiences of imprisonment, freedom, and resilience. Concretely, we analyze key fresh home raps and accompanying music videos released in 2019 and 2020 by high-profile artists Digga D, Potter Payper, Unknown T, and Headie One, and one lesser-known female rapper, Lavida Loca. These better-known male rappers have all had singles and/or albums that have featured high in the charts, even at the top. They have featured in mainstream broadcasting and can legitimately be viewed as producing part of contemporary British pop culture. We also included works by Lavida Loca as a female rapper who raps about criminal justice experience. All are widely held to have lived "road life" (life at the stronger end of UK street culture, where respect-based violence and crimino-entrepreneurialism are common), and their raps are seen to *authentically* represent that. Our choices reflect the time of our writing, but this period also marked a moment of unprecedented success for UK rap. Fresh home themes can be found across the micro-genres that constitute the wider UK rap/grime ecosystem (e.g., afrowave, trap, drill, real rap, and others). Here we focus on key songs released soon after an artist's imprisonment (respectively, "Daily Duppy," "2020 Vision Freestyle," "Fresh Home," "Ain't It Different," and "King's Back"). We contextualized our interpretation within each artist's repertoire and the wider canon of "fresh home" by artists including Tion Wayne, C Biz, Lil Sykes, SmuggzyAce, and others.

Our reading is informed by an ethnographically inflected, immersive media analysis outlined in detail elsewhere (Ilan 2020). Immersion in the culture surrounding these raps enables in-depth understanding of discourses, styles, and language in play (Gubrium and Holstein 2009).

Here, this involves reading specific media (such as music videos) within a fulsome and appreciative understanding of the culture that produces them. In practical terms, this requires attending to large amounts of complementary contextual material—from other examples of UK rap, to scene gossip roundups, radio shows, and interviews. Insight gained from this process can inform analysis as well as sampling with the aim of achieving an understanding of media that would make sense to those who produced them.

Lyrics are prominent in rap and foremost in our analysis. But, acknowledging the problem of logocentrism (Crockett Thomas et al. 2020), we also considered how musical backing tracks, videos, clothing, style, and other factors communicated themes visually and affectively. Factors as diverse as attire, gestures and movement, flow, musical cadence, and tone were all part of the stories being told. Reaction videos (in which rap fans watch and respond to music videos) and below-the-line comments provided further context and helped us to check our interpretations. Documentaries and video footage furthermore capture the experiences of Potter Payper and Digga D as they move out of prison into the supervision of the probation service and into rap careers whose possibilities seemed to have expanded while they were away. Seeing rappers joyfully rap and gesture along to tracks in smoky studio rooms is a reminder of the ways that music—like stories—has the power to literally move us.

What Is Fresh Home?

What we refer to in this chapter as "fresh home rap" can be understood as rap music and/or accompanying visuals that address a rapper's recent return from incarceration. Rap music is often autobiographical, reflecting the prominence of personal stories in popular culture (Plummer 2019). Fresh home is more of a lyrical theme than a genre; it might dominate a whole song or feature as a more minor, fleeting reference. Some contain complete narratives, while others feature narrative tropes (Sandberg 2016). Fresh home raps often find ways of combining a solemn tone with celebratory and joyful sentiments. While fresh home has become a recognizable theme in UK rap music,[1] it documents lived experiences from Britain's urban socioeconomic margins and thus might say something about the shared experiences, hopes, feelings, suffering, and struggles of those communities in particular. These themes echo back to the origins of hip-hop and rap in African American and Latino neighborhoods in the Bronx, New York, in the 1970s. However, UK rap has its own distinct history and trajectory, including a sonic palette and lyrical themes that more closely trace the Black British experience (Ilan 2012; Bramwell 2015).

Fresh home rap has a number of lyrical and compositional characteristics. It frequently references the lived experience of imprisonment, its privations, and the strategies that rappers have adopted to get through their sentence. It also celebrates its author's return home. Indeed, as will become clear, lyrics of fresh home raps are often written inside and can themselves constitute a strategy for surviving prison. A clear distinction is usually drawn then to life on the outside and the kinds of pleasurable experiences and consumer goods the rapper can enjoy there. There are some common visual motifs in music videos as well, especially footage of the rapper being met at the prison gates by their friends. The friendships temporarily disrupted by prison tend to be celebrated alongside the freedom of the released rapper, as those in the videos consume alcohol, smoke, dance, shout lyrics, and sport their designer clothing in a joyful scene.

Tion Wayne, a chart-topping rapper from Edmonton, North London, captures the spirit of fresh home in the refrain on "Home" (2018, GRM Daily), as he raps, "fresh out the can man I'm up, and the feds try get your boy down" over a poppy, danceable beat. As in a call-and-response, listeners can join in the celebratory, melodic chorus: "yeah, yeah, yeah." Here the unbridled joy of freedom and release is contrasted with the work of the "feds" (police), who, in a typically street cultural manner, are represented as antagonistic villains, a source of vexation, interference, and oppression. An affective charge is thus produced through a sense of triumph against the forces of injustice.

Fresh home rap represents an opportunity to narratively bridge recent experiences of deprivation and perceived oppression with aspirations for future success and flourishing. As is characteristic of personal narratives, fresh home raps tell us where the narrator has come from and projects into the future, connecting between prison and home (Crockett Thomas et al. 2020, 2021). They are interesting for narrative theorists as first-person accounts of imprisonment and involvement in crime, not necessarily as precise records of fact, but as carriers of meaning. While fresh home raps cannot be legitimate without an actual experience of prison, they are also a truth-fiction hybrid (Sandberg 2010). They are stylized performances, drawing on rap's generic conventions and vocabulary, and may project a larger-than-life persona. At the same time, they are an artistic baring of the soul, giving voice to intimate and real experiences. They are radically different from the kinds of stories told in interviews, in that they are carefully crafted, albeit aesthetically and musically, and intended to be heard (and perhaps danced to) by music fans in both live and recorded formats.

Marginality and Survival

UK rap and the "fresh home" themes cannot be understood separately from the socioeconomic and political conditions that have given rise to them. UK rap principally stems from the most disadvantaged parts of England's large metropolitan centers, such as London, Birmingham, and Manchester. Its artists are primarily Black. In common with those poorer, ethnic minority populations across economically developed nations, they might be said to experience "advanced marginality" (Wacquant 2009), a combination of relative material deprivation and sociocultural exclusion. In English urban centers, this looks like poorly paid, insecure work with few prospects for advancement, overcrowded housing—the outcome of a policy doctrine of austerity that has dramatically reduced youth provision—advancing gentrification, and disproportionate attention from institutionally racist police and criminal justice systems (see White 2020). In other words, the communities from which UK rap emerges do not merely tend to "have less" than is average in their society, but are acutely aware that they are discursively positioned as being "worth less" (see Ilan 2015). Yusef Bakkali (2019), in his work with men from these backgrounds, develops the portmanteau concept of "the munpain" to capture the jarring dissonance such individuals can feel when their struggles are simultaneously everyday, chronic, and monotonous and also traumatic and dramatic. Ebony Reid (2023) has developed the street concept of "the trap," which is how many disadvantaged men participating in the drug economy and urban violence understand their own criminal motivations. They feel that they have few other opportunities for economic advancement and cannot seem to extricate themselves from the mind-states and social positions that they feel call for these behaviors.

Historically, marginalization has prompted forms of music and sociability that can connect with audiences and themes that are shunned by mainstream forms of leisure culture. In diasporic and/or Black Atlantic terms (Gilroy 2016), this has been evident in genres such as dancehall and rap (Rose 1994; Henry 2006). British genres such as UK rap and grime take on this kind of significance; they have the power to generate feelings of belonging, conviviality, fun, and status (Bramwell 2015). They provide economic opportunities in the creative industries, broaden cultural horizons, and can be personally transformative (Ilan 2012; White 2016). These genres have nevertheless faced opprobrium and even (calls for) criminalization from authorities certain that they glorify crime and violence and even incite or evidence it—even though there is little to suggest that this is the case (White 2017; Fatsis 2019b; Ilan 2020). The rappers whose work we consider in this chapter paint a vivid picture of "road" or street life in England (Gunter 2008) and the painful experiences that underpin it. Potter Payper (of Irish and Algerian descent, raised in East London, widely considered an underground hero of UK rap) is lyrically candid about what he has experienced beyond drug dealing and prison, describing in mournful detail the rootless life of drifting between sofas, witnessing his father beat his mother, and the claustrophobia of grief that comes when someone close to him dies. Meanwhile, even rappers who cultivate a cold-blooded persona, such as Lavida Loca, a young female rapper, speak in interviews about the pain of being in the care system as children. In such a context, it is not difficult to understand why rappers might be keen to identify events worth celebrating and possess a determination to wring as much joy from them as possible.

Fresh Home as a Good Story

Here we describe some of the narrative features of fresh home raps and the good they can do for the narrator. Recognizing that "good" is contestable, we nonetheless trace diverse facets of the good story in fresh home raps. Below we organize this analysis into four themes. First, we show that fresh home raps reaffirm street culture and selves embedded in it. Second, we show that writing raps in prison offers a means for reflection and reconfiguration of self-narratives distinct from the prison as an institution. Third, street narratives also offer a way to negotiate the meanings of imprisonment—especially evident in lyrics around food. Lastly, we show that raps written in prison can sometimes be a resource for overcoming marginalization through music. In particular, fresh home raps offer a way to move beyond dealing drugs, even as rappers hold on to a personal narrative rooted in street culture.

Reaffirming Street Narratives and the Street Self

Prison forces a narrative rupture for street-oriented individuals, significantly limiting their capacity to claim success in crimino-entrepreneurialism (and indeed rap music careers, as imprisonment limits recording, touring, and so forth). More profoundly, prison may prompt a crisis in self-narrative (Maruna, Wilson, and Curran 2006: 168). Imprisonment disrupts a person's "taken for granted ways of acting and living . . . lead(ing) to reflection on issues of existence, life, and death, which are usually bracketed from everyday consideration" (Maruna et al. 2006: 168–69). In response to this rupture, Maruna et al.'s respondents (2006) told religious conversion narratives, effectively managing shame, giving purpose to imprisonment and claiming interpretive control over their present and future. Whether secular or religious, "desisters" could tell "redemption" narratives, telling of negative past experiences in positive terms and enabling them to form a coherent self-story with their offending past behind them (Maruna 2001). Such narratives, furthermore, can draw on a person's own sense of their capacity to desist from crime when returned to the circumstances that initially prompted their offending (see Schinkel 2015).

Fresh home raps resolve narrative crisis in a different way, by reaffirming personal narratives embedded in street culture. Like Maruna's desisters (2001), rap artists narrate themselves as essentially good, struggling against bad external forces. Their lyrics emphasize their experienced poverty, marginalization, and mistreatment at the hands of the police, while boasting about their capacity to rise above their circumstances through canny illegal business and virtuosic rapping. The bad is located in this injustice and in particular in the forces of criminal justice that are viewed as keen on precipitating the failure of the rapper. Imprisonment can be interpreted as a normal aspect of street life and thus personal narratives, whether as a result of criminality or the operation of an unjust system. Potter Payper (who served several prison sentences in his teens and twenties) raps, in "Filthy Free" (2020, Faceless Sounds),

> Welcome to London City it's a treacherous place,
> Real gangsters don't snitch lookin' death in the face...
> Everybody lost someone they can never replace,
> And a coffin or a cell is only seconds away.

Potter celebrates freedom against a backdrop of hardship, emphasized by the pain in his gravelly voice. Here he positions imprisonment or death as the likely result of participating in the more extreme aspects of street culture. The accompanying music video emphasizes the message: Potter is shown laying a wreath in a cemetery accompanied by young men wearing T-shirts saying "Free Ice" and "Free Eyes" (entreaties to release incarcerated friends). This imagery incorporates prison into his self-narrative, heading off a potential narrative rupture of the kind described above. The way in which the rapper might respond to incarceration, however, remains open. As this chapter goes to press, we're pleased to note that Potter Payper seems to have remained out of trouble with the law.

Fresh home sits alongside a host of street themes common to rap music: the speakers' violent potential, their skill at dealing drugs, the neighborhood they identify with (Ilan 2020). Like "street talk", these stories—when told convincingly—have considerable value (Sandberg and Fleetwood 2017). Rapping about dealing and/or violence demonstrates the speaker's fluency in the "code of the street" (Anderson 2000) and establishes their authenticity and narrative authority, despite their recent time away. While masculinity is ubiquitous in fresh home raps (as in UK rap more generally), women can also demonstrate their street cultural fluency. Several notable women have made careers rapping about typical themes of drug dealing and violence. Fresh home likewise enables women to tell personal narratives about crime and prison, without undertaking the usual "repair" work necessary for accomplishing traditional femininity (Fleetwood 2015). Lavida Loca raps about her five years in prison in a matter-of-fact way, offering no explanation or repentance that might reclaim "respectability" ("King's Back," "Voice of the Streets Freestyle"). Ongoing commitment to street culture reflects the ways that our personal narratives are deeply held and do not readily change (Fleetwood 2016; Sandberg and Fleetwood 2017). Fresh home raps become a means of demonstrating that the prison stay has been taken in the rapper's stride and will not change them—that their street authenticity is transcendent.

Of course, entanglements with criminal justice authorities can demand the presentation of personal change. UK rap artists may be subject to restrictions after imprisonment. Digga D had extremely stringent post-release conditions, initially requiring him to check in to an approved premise every three hours (BBC 3 2020). In "King's Back" (2019), Lavida Loca raps vividly about travelling out of town selling heroin and crack cocaine, and boasts about her violent potential. She raps aggressively over a stripped-down backing track in a minor key typical of drill, emphasizing her street authenticity. The accompanying music video depicts her in the kinds of places where she would sell drugs (on the street and in a filthy bedsit), dressed in a hoodie, sometimes wearing a balaclava. But, in an interview on YouTube, she recounts remaining under probationary supervision for more than a year after her release at the start of her career, attending fortnightly appointments as a "serious offender." She says, "If I acted how people expected, I'd be back in jail" (AmarudonTv 2020). We can read her video as a display of an authentic inner self-story that has significance beyond the experiences that formed it.

The lyrical content of raps can leave rappers vulnerable to official sanction. Notable rappers such as Digga D have been given Criminal Behaviour Orders (CBOs), effectively banning them from rapping about criminal themes or referencing particular people and incidents (GRM Daily 2021). As elite storytellers, they wrap such restrictions into their lyricism using wordplay, obscure slang, and knowing puns to safely imply their intended meaning: "crafting ways to get around the censorship of the police by coding his language, littering his verses with intricate *double entendres*, metaphors and similes so only those in the know would be able to decipher it" (GRM Daily 2021). Digga D's fresh home rapping may serve thus to triumphantly evade the efforts of hated law enforcement, generating an affective reward for both musician and audience. He narrates himself as the master of both streets and lyricism, affirming that prison has not changed his essence. This continues a trend popularized in part by Headie One and RV's drill anthem "Know Better," which is built around a series of "shhh" sounds replacing specifics, indicating that the rappers do not wish to implicate themselves.

Fresh home raps reject "going straight'" desistance narratives. Indeed, some rappers would seem to be tempting fate by lyrically claiming a return to drug dealing:

> Fresh home, I bought coke and whipped it.
> (Headie One, "Ain't It Different"; 2020, Relentless)

It would be a mistake to read this lyric, claiming criminal conduct, literally, however (see Ilan 2020). Rather, it indicates an ongoing validation of drug dealing as a means to material success and thus a reaffirmation of street culture. Fresh home raps indeed more usually tend to imply that music will be the earning strategy for the released rapper, so affirming the street self becomes an important resource to compete in the "economy of authenticity" and street cultural potency that tends to inform the contemporary rap market (Ilan 2020).

Imprisonment can disrupt how individuals narrate themselves, but as Warr (2020, 2022) notes, prison offers inmates very little that would enable them, especially racially minoritized men, to tell a different kind of story about themselves. While for some, prison may be an opportunity to tell different kinds of self-stories, fresh home raps reaffirm personal narratives connected to street culture. That street narratives can endure prison reflects the depth at which personal narratives are held—in Bourdieusian terms, they are part of the habitus (Fleetwood 2016; Sandberg and Fleetwood 2017). Raps include elements of boasting and exaggeration (see Crockett Thomas et al. 2021), but they nonetheless reveal authentic elements of the authors' realities. They also reflect that "growing up marginalized often comes with an absence of other stories, and a well-developed repertoire of street stories that . . . further bind people to the street field" (Sandberg and Fleetwood 2017: 377). Fresh home raps reject institutional demands to show contrition. Instead, they celebrate the triumph of the pleasurable aspects of street life and the resilience of the street self in the face of perceived and experienced oppression.

Reflection through Street Self-Narratives

Imprisonment prompted rappers to reflect deeply about their lives, as Maruna et al. (2006) would predict. However, reflection was not on the terms of the penal institutions—that is, demonstrating willingness to abandon one's previous identity and show amenability to change oneself (Warr 2020). Unknown T spent a year in HMP Belmarsh on remand charged with murder (and was later found not guilty). He explains to the interviewer in an online documentary (No Jumper 2020), "Some people need a wakeup call in life and that was my one." Prison was a pivotal experience for many other rappers in our sample. Unknown T appears to validate carceral notions of reform and personal change for the better; however, as he and others who have spoken about their time in prison publicly are keen to emphasize, their reflection tends to be *in spite of* rather than because of what was available in prison. Rappers often refer to being in "seg" or "basic" in their lyrics and in documentary interviews, implying a capacity to reject prison regimes. Prisoners in segregation have limited access to participation in educational or behavioral programs, which in any case may be of limited use in enabling them to tell new kinds of stories about themselves (Warr 2020).

Music is generally a means by which prisoners can pass time and even achieve personal development while incarcerated (Herrity 2018). In contrast to prison programs aimed at correcting "cognitive distortions" (Fox 1999) and/or imposing new identities on prisoners (Warr 2020, 2022), freestyling and writing raps in prison can be a resource for personal development and advancement that remains true to a self-narrative bound up with street culture. Beyond passing time and generating entertainment through writing, rappers are able to claim authorship of their own lives—they decide what prison will mean for them. Potter Payper recalls how his most recent stay in prison prompted him to reflect, deciding to use his prison time to work on his career and take himself seriously, saying, "In three years do you *put yourself back together* but do you put yourself the same as you remember, or bigger and better?" (Groundworks 2020, our emphasis). This was not his first time in prison, but he describes his personal epiphany: *this time* he has to make a change for himself. In telling his story, Potter positions himself as emerging from prison as a powerful writer who can use the experience of prison for good—to work on himself to change the story of who he is. He follows a well-trodden path, of course; many rappers, and indeed writers of many stripes, have used prison as a space for creativity. The rapper narrates his post-prison self as being able to behave differently, but this is not because he has essentially changed; it is simply that music has reduced his need to rely on criminal enterprise to generate income.

Reflecting the spirit of independent entrepreneurship that underpins both UK urban music and drug dealing (see Ilan 2012; White 2016), rappers are able to make something of their prison time: practicing, honing their skills, and perhaps developing a repertoire of lyrics and tracks that can be drawn on in their future career. In interviews, rappers emphasize the skill and dedication required to be able to maintain one's creativity, devoid of backing tracks, studio, support, and so on. As Unknown T describes,

> When I was writing "Fresh Home" there was no instrumental, no rhythm, literally just me and my cell mate, pen and paper. Literally. You understand that. Shit's not easy. Every single lyric, every single flow, every single flow and thought was through me. (No Jumper, 2020)

Rappers can furthermore use prison for networking, often striking up friendships and artistic collaborations with other rappers they encounter. Unknown T shared a cell with Digga D in HMP Belmarsh. In a BBC 3 documentary (2020), Digga D is shown leaving prison in a car jiving jubilantly to Unknown T's "Fresh Home," which was recorded and released to critical acclaim while Digga D was still in prison. In contrast to clichés about prisons as "universities of crime," they can be spaces for honing music.

In sum, fresh home raps evidence the speaker's ability to maintain an authentic self in prison, to survive its privations, and to make something of prison by tapping into their innate creativity and talent for performance. Their raps narratively bridge the inside with the outside by drawing on street cultural tropes and stories and a wide array of vernacular and styles of expression pertaining to that field. The rappers mark themselves as unchanged, or certainly not changed in the way that the authorities may have hoped, and ready to recommence their artistic (and perhaps criminal) careers after release.

Narrative Resistance: Lyrics about Food

Fresh home raps reflect on the relationship between life on the inside and outside prison. In particular, lyrics about food are a key narrative device through which distinctions can be conjured. Food is an everyday, essential, and body-linked item that can powerfully evoke changing realities (Ugelvik 2011). It also has rich potential for double entendres and wordplay: "food" is slang for drugs and "cheffing" for stabbing. Digga D's (post-prison) album is titled *Made in the Pyrex*, a reference to the heatproof cookware favored for making crack cocaine. Through simile, the title captures the sense that he was "made" in his experiences in the drug trade. Unknown T in "Fresh Home" (2020, Island-Universal) raps,

> Prison governors try give me category A . . .
> I'm eatin' noodles from a plastic plate.

Both the humble food of noodles and the plastic plate accurately capture sensory aspects of punishment (Herrity, Schmidt, and Warr 2021). Food features as a metonym for privations and (arbitrary) punishment. The rappers are thus burnishing their authenticity as street subjects who have consequential conflicts with the law. Lyrics about food are also deployed to narrate the rappers' attitude to prison, illustrating their agency in resisting prison discipline as well as their status while incarcerated (see also Ugelvik 2011). Fresh home raps contain numerous detailed references to prison cookery, where kettles become improvised devices to cook high-protein dishes from purchasable items like canned tuna or mackerel. This not only constitutes a supplement to power muscle building (insofar as prison can be an opportunity to get physically fit), it also lifts the narrator out of a position of dependency, so that he is no longer reliant on mandated mealtimes for his entire sustenance. The rappers invoke a spirit of autonomy and defiance in the face of an uncaring prison system. Echoing themes from road life on the outside, they emphasize personal self-reliance and innovation. Food can also be a status symbol in prison, where stacks of snacks display the prisoner's purchasing power, capacity to ward off would-be thieves, and networks on the outside who are willing to pay money into his account. Food references can poignantly speak to life squandered behind bars—for example, when Headie One in "Ain't It Different" (2020, Relentless Records) raps about birthday cake made from digestive biscuits, he vividly evokes the attenuated celebration of birthdays inside. This lyric says something about conviviality in prison, showing that meaningful occasions can still be marked. This level of vivid depiction of bittersweet celebration serves to reinforce the authenticity of the rapper whose intimate familiarity with imprisonment is revealed through descriptions of food.

Finally, food can also become a narrative device for celebrating freedom on the outside. The themes of conspicuous consumption and visceral pleasure are abundant in fresh home videos (and street culture more generally). Designer clothing, foreign cars, premium liquor, and scantily clad models form the visual backdrop to the rapper, who will often refer to luxury food and restaurants in direct and stark contrast to mean prison fare. Potter Payper's video for "Filthy Free" (2020, Virgin) has typical elements of this motif, but also alights on something as banal as milk (in this case branded oat milk), as he raps the refrain,

> Early mornin' with a milky tea,
> Cah I ain't filthy rich but I'm filthy free.

While rappers might be able to cook eggs in a kettle, fresh milk is much harder to come by. In rapping about tea, Potter celebrates his newfound freedom and pleasure in the simple things.

Beyond food, fresh home raps reference an array of privations of prison: uncomfortable beds, guards' keys, missing family, grieving for people killed, and (in breach of masculine taboos) even the effects of the prison on mental health. Fresh home raps—like rap and drill more generally—can endow stories of deprivation and suffering with value, making bad experiences into stories worth telling (Sandberg and Fleetwood 2017). Digga D raps about being stabbed in prison in retaliation for a prior incident ("Daily Duppy," 2020, Universal Music), and others rap about their readiness to be violent in prison, as on the streets. Nonetheless, a lot about prison goes "unsaid" (Presser 2019, 2022). In a scene-media interview, Potter Payper describes being assaulted by three guards (Tim Westwood TV 2020). This kind of victimization can be spoken of in interviews, but not in his music, where it would be incongruent with the narrative stance expected of a rapper. The genre imposes its own restrictions on the kinds of stories that can be told by attaching expectations to the rapper persona. Prison is furthermore often characterized by considerable boredom, especially in segregation or basic conditions. Such banal experiences do not readily make for a story worth telling within the confines of fresh home raps that are meant to be celebratory in tone. The privations of prison can thus be contained within formula narratives—such as discussions of food—that serve to elevate the narrator above the tough material and psychic conditions they have recently endured. The fresh home narrative serves to bracket off the prison experience as something that can be left behind: noodles on a plastic plate need not feature in a life of comfort and luxury.

From Street Hustles to Music Industry Hustles

Fresh home raps are personal narratives with a happy ending: they celebrate surviving prison and transcending institutional oppression. This sentiment animates lyrics but can be found beyond them, in the exuberant sprays of champagne that friends douse the rappers in as they emerge from the prison gates, and in the particular spring that seems to animate the throw of an arm gesture or the swing of a shoulder in music videos. There is an affective dimension to ways in which the fruits of freedom are presented: sparkling jewelry, crisp designer clothes, high-end liquor, and models dancing in swimwear. Conspicuously consumerist, these images and references serve as stark contrasts to the austere regimes of prison.

Fresh home raps are mostly written in prison and express optimism for moving out of drug dealing and crime. As well as affirming the street self and surviving prison, they map out the kind of lifestyle their authors intend to enjoy on the outside. Enacting the classic "rags to riches" narrative, rappers affirm their commitment to earning well to enjoy a lavish, luxurious lifestyle (to which prison is an unfortunate but temporary impediment). There is a central paradox, however. Their illicit search for participation in lavish lifestyles may have led to their incarceration.

Fresh home raps successfully manage this apparent paradox. They maintain a commitment to street culture (and illicit business) while also projecting a personal narrative about becoming rich through their music career—a legal endeavor. This trope is captured in the title of London rapper Fredo's 2017 mixtape "Get Rich or Get Recalled," released after he served two stints in prison.[2] The implication is that if one can't get rich through music, criminal entrepreneurialism beckons. As Lavida Loca explains, music is one of the few professions where former incarceration may not be a particular barrier:

> Through my sentence I started to think about what I wanted to do beyond prison, beyond road. . . .[3] Music is the only thing you're free to do. You could just put a video on YouTube and release your music. There are no restrictions and no one doing a DBS [criminal background] check on me. I could just do it. (AmarudonTv 2020)

Indeed, having a criminal past may offer a point of distinction in a crowded field. Both Fredo and Lavida Loca emphasize their real experiences in their music, often dissing "fake" rappers.

Instead of repudiating criminal entrepreneurialism, the rappers grapple with whether it will be required to supplement their musical income—one of the central themes in Headie One's "Both," in which he raps about counting up cash from dealing drugs *and* from live shows. Both strategies reflect his self-story as someone who works hard, despite humble beginnings. Likewise, on his "2020 Vision Freestyle," Potter Payper raps, "I'm rapping and I'm trapping, don't know which I prefer."

Fresh home ultimately offers the rapper the last word, allowing them to remain authentic to their self-narratives, embedded in street culture without being constrained by it. In rapping they can convert their street skills (hustle, entrepreneurialism, ability to tell authentic stories) into the field of music. They can—perhaps—leave crime (and prison) behind, not because prison has changed them, but because entrepreneurialism in the music industry can be storied as a natural progression from their prior, illegal careers. Reflecting this, rappers can thumb their noses at the judgments and perceived oppression of the state. As Potter Payper raps on the track "PMW" (2020), "I told probation I'm a rapper, now just leave me alone."

UK rappers may be under pressure to represent themselves as ideal street subjects, authentic voices of the street and potentially criminal and violent, to generate success in the music business (Ilan 2020). Interestingly, grime artists in the late 2000s and early 2010s tended to represent themselves as educated, aspirational, legitimate entrepreneurs (Ilan 2012).[4] Indeed, Chip, whose rap persona is explicitly non-criminal, continues to represent this narrative when he raps,

> And I ain't got no rap songs 'bout who my knife went in
> So sorry darg, you might not relate when I'm pennin', but
> Follow my trail, I'll teach you how to not go to jail.
> ("Daily Duppy," 2020)

In the early 2020s more ambivalent attitudes toward criminality seemed to be adopted by rappers, drawing on both discourses of street authenticity and a quest for mainstream, legal careers in the music business. These dual, apparently contradictory discourses are accommodated, ambivalently, within fresh home raps. For the elites that we describe here, telling their personal narratives through rap can be literally life changing. Success in the music industry changes lives, expands imaginations, and allows the crossing of all sorts of boundaries (White 2016). Caution should thus be exercised before too much stock is placed in the literal truth of claims that the rapper will continue to operate in the criminal sphere. For freedom to be truly sweet, it should not be so short-lived.

Continuity: Personal Narratives, Enduring Hardships, and New Beginnings

Fresh home raps deftly illustrate a number of narrative theoretical concepts. They reflect the heartfelt, practical nature of personal narrative in that they are embodied and part of our sense of who we are and how we navigate the world. When Digga D says he is "made in the Pyrex," he tells us that his raps—like himself—are born of the lived experience of cooking and selling crack cocaine. In theoretical terms, personal narratives are the product of the sedimentation of experience that shapes our "feel for the game," which Bourdieu calls "habitus" (Sandberg and

Fleetwood 2017; Fleetwood 2016). The relationship between narrative and experience, sedimented in the habitus, is part of what allows rappers to tell fresh home stories credibly and effectively. Their personal narrative—made in the streets—offers a way to endure the privations of prison. And so, prison experience is often part of the rappers' narrative self-presentation, but they cannot capitalize on their incarceration while it endures.

Secondly, rappers' narratives evidence purposeful reflection—the "creativity within limits" that Bourdieu describes (Fleetwood 2016)—of socioeconomic and cultural positioning. But, while fresh home themes share commonalities, they reflect rappers' individual points of view, tastes, experiences, and fantasies. Further, words and discourse are "elastic" and polysemous. We find agency and creativity in fresh home narratives; their speakers are shaped by social circumstances but not defined by them. Fresh home raps are born of and describe the rapper's lived reality, but they also project imaginatively *into* future success. For the elite rappers we discuss here, these stories of success in the music business became a self-fulfilling prophecy.

Resistance and Social Change

Fresh home raps are a highly crafted, sophisticated form of storytelling. The artists we describe here command language in immensely skillful ways; they perform their stories with incredible swagger and style, literally moving their audiences to join them. In short, rap music is a hugely popular, artful form of creative expression that says much about experiences of prison. While we focus on stories told by a group of cultural elites, their narratives have a wider resonance: their lyrics and videos might be understood as communicating something essential not only about prison, but about the street culture of Britain's socioeconomic margins (see similarly Kubrin 2005). Fresh home raps resonate in part because they answer back to the ministrations of an uncaring state and mainstream indifference to the suffering of the marginalized.

Fresh home rap themes are not straightforwardly progressive; their content is not self-evidently "good." They include an array of discursive justifications for doing hurt and harm to others, and women are objectified, although perhaps no more than in more "mainstream" music and popular culture. While they evidence hardships in prison, their framing of imprisonment as an inevitable consequence of serious criminality means that they cannot connect with progressive arguments regarding prison reform or abolition. Success is largely understood as an individual rather than collective endeavor, reflecting the neoliberal ideal of the all-conquering individual who can transcend their impoverished beginnings to achieve material success and legitimate success. Like the forms of UK "urban" music that host fresh home, it reproduces rather than challenges mainstream neoliberal consumerism (Ilan 2014), albeit while also expressing the discontent and anguish of those marginalized within this socioeconomic arrangement.

As we demonstrate, fresh home raps can nonetheless do good in the context of harms. Like rap more generally, they can make stories of personal hardship, oppression, and prison tellable. As Lavida Loca demonstrates, fresh home offers a rare opportunity to talk about crime and imprisonment in the first person without shame or apology—to claim authorship over experiences, good and bad. They carve out space to speak back to oppressive systems. Fresh home makes prison meaningful in a very particular way. Rappers profess allegiance to street cultural values, while also—from prison—professing a will to move away from crime through their music career. For some, the act of storytelling itself becomes part of this process, facilitating financial success in the music industry. This outcome itself is not necessarily progressive without question, in particular where contemporary rap careers have been characterized as the commodification of marginalization, crime, and criminalization (Stuart 2020).

Fresh home raps might offer some individuals ways out, but could this music prompt social change more broadly? Rap music might appear to be an authentic form of subculture, a platform for marginalized voices to "speak out" and tell of their experiences (Sandberg and Colvin 2020). As Fatsis argues, grime music—and in particular its gritty descriptions of life in austerity Britain—"alerts audiences to iniquities in our socio-political arrangements" (Fatsis 2019a: 454). Indeed, fresh home raps carve out space to speak publicly about the realities of imprisonment. Fatsis argues that grime music can be understood as a subaltern counter-public and its artists as public characters who can "resist political marginalization and reclaim their dignity and self-respect through their art" (Fatsis 2019a: 454). As we have shown above, UK rap music also documents prison as one facet of a larger, oppressive system.

But from a narrative perspective, we might also attend to how such music is heard and acted upon: which publics can fresh home engage? While "speaking out" about personal struggles can sometimes prompt political action (Polletta 2006), as Serisier notes in her study of women's "speaking out" against sexual violence, there is no shortage of personal testimony; rather, such stories may reach a limited audience (2018). The same question might be applied to fresh home raps: they might speak of marginalization, but are they *heard*? As we noted above, grime and drill may be heard but not understood, and so become subject to censure/censorship.

Rather than a spectacular form of resistance, we understand fresh home rap music as an everyday form that effectively communicates rage, defiance, and frustration, and celebrates momentary triumphs over oppressive systems (see also Crockett Thomas et al. 2021: 2). These themes are communicated not only in lyrics, but also by rappers' intonation and movement, the affective quality of musical backing-tracks, and the visual motifs in video. In particular, fresh home raps voice defiance against the penal system, which appears as arbitrarily punitive, especially in relation to the illicit drug business. Fresh home raps do not offer an explicitly articulated politics or speak to established social movements. Rather, they are an exemplar of an affective politics of defiance that "burns bright, with a body felt sense of power, but ultimately fizzes out" (Dimou and Ilan 2018: 14). They are a form of cathartic celebration, where in these few elite cases the enduring street self and its capacity to flourish despite the efforts of hated law enforcement animate the artist and audience. Although "affects and musical resonances are not universal" (Crockett Thomas et al. 2020: 139), fresh home raps nonetheless resonate widely. Overall, however, the operation of the criminal justice system as an edifice experienced as oppressive and unjust by marginalized communities remains unchallenged.

Narrative criminologists explore how narratives can offer a resource for political change. Personal narratives are an "everyday" form of culture with the potential to inspire a reconfiguration of perspectives (Fleetwood 2019). Ellefsen and Sandberg (2021) examine young Muslims' "repertoire for resistance" in their counter-narratives. Fleetwood (2019) argues that reading stories about others responding to street harassment can cultivate "dispositions for self-defence" that enable women to talk back to harassers (2019: 1711). Rather than offering epistemic justice (in having their stories heard) or narrative resources for resistance, fresh home raps are perhaps best understood as an act of defiance (see also Ilan 2014). In narrative terms, personal narratives collectively construct an attitude or disposition of defiance that has cultural resonance. In sharing rappers' narratives of their "rags to riches" journey, we can momentarily believe that, for anyone, a better life is possible. The narrative resolution of the happy ending remains seductive, even as we know of its implausibility in the real world.

Fresh home raps have wide appeal despite being about the niche theme of prison. They attract millions of views on YouTube and, in the case of Potter Payper's album, even achieve top music chart positions. Of course, "crime" music has consistently demonstrated commercial value in different contexts (Quinn 2005; Ilan 2012, 2020). The central theme of fresh home raps, however—overcoming antagonistic and oppressive institutions and regimes—has much wider cultural resonance. In the United Kingdom, young people have grown up under austerity, defunding of education grants and youth services, the rise of the gig economy, and the relentless squeeze of a housing crisis (White 2020). Even more privileged young listeners know what it is to live in an oppressive system that offers them no meaningful place or future. For these listeners, fresh home does not just tell the story of overcoming oppression, but affectively conveys this as a feeling.

NOTES

1. While US rap and hip-hop culture do speak about most of the themes covered in this chapter—and seem to contain a certain number of return rituals—for whatever reason the tight cultural concept that is "fresh home" does not seem to have emerged on that side of the Atlantic.
2. This title is a riff on 50 Cent's 2003 album *Get Rich or Die Tryin'*.
3. In the United Kingdom, "road" is a metonym referring to street-based criminal cultures. Gunter's (2008) research on road culture is exemplary.
4. Grime is a British genre of "urban music" often confused with rap music. The two are related (in terms of consisting of chanted lyrics over a backing track), but they are distinct (Ilan 2012).

REFERENCES

Anderson, Elijah. 2000. *Code of the Street: Decency, Violence, and the Moral Life of the Inner City*. New York: Norton.

Aspden, Kester, and Keith J. Hayward. 2015. "Narrative Criminology and Cultural Criminology: Shared Biographies, Different Lives?" In *Narrative Criminology: Understanding Stories of Crime*, edited by Lois Presser and Sveinung Sandberg, 235–59. New York: New York University Press.

Bakkali, Yusef. 2019. "Dying to Live: Youth Violence and the Munpain." *Sociological Review* 67 (6): 1317–32.

Bramwell, Richard. 2015. *UK Hip-Hop, Grime and the City: The Aesthetics and Ethics of London's Rap Scenes*. London: Routledge.

Crockett Thomas, Phil, Fergus McNeill, Lucy Cathcart Frödén, Jo Collinson Scott, Oliver Escobar, and Alison Urie. 2021. "Re-writing Punishment? Songs and Narrative Problem-Solving." *Incarceration* 2 (1): 1–19.

Crockett Thomas, Phil, Jo Collinson Scott, Fergus McNeill, Oliver Escobar, Lucy Cathcart Frödén, and Alison Urie. 2020. "Mediating Punishment? Prisoners' Songs as Relational 'Problem-Solving' Devices." *Law Text Culture* 24: 138–62.

Dimou, Eleni, and Jonathan Ilan. 2018. "Taking Pleasure Seriously: The Political Significance of Subcultural Practice." *Journal of Youth Studies* 21 (1): 1–18.

Ellefsen, Rune, and Sveinung Sandberg. 2021. "A Repertoire of Everyday Resistance: Young Muslims' Responses to Anti-Muslim Hostility." *Journal of Ethnic and Migration Studies* 48 (11): 2601–19.

Fatsis, Lambros. 2019a. "Grime: Criminal Subculture or Public Counterculture? A Critical Investigation into the Criminalization of Black Musical Subcultures in the UK." *Crime, Media, Culture* 15 (3): 447–61.

Fatsis, Lambros. 2019b. "Policing the Beats: The Criminalisation of UK Drill and Grime Music by the London Metropolitan Police." *Sociological Review* 67 (6): 1300–316.

Fleetwood, Jennifer. 2015. "In Search of Respectability: Narrative Practice in a Women's Prison in Quito, Ecuador." In *Narrative Criminology: Understanding Stories of Crime*, edited by Lois Presser and Sveinung Sandberg, 42–68. New York: New York University Press.

Fleetwood, Jennifer. 2016. "Narrative Habitus: Thinking Through Structure/Agency in the Narratives of Offenders." *Crime, Media, Culture* 12 (2): 173–92.

Fleetwood, Jennifer. 2019. "Everyday Self-Defence: Hollaback Narratives, Habitus and Resisting Street Harassment." *British Journal of Sociology* 70 (5): 1709–29.

Fox, Kathryn J. 1999. "Changing Violent Minds: Discursive Correction and Resistance in the Cognitive Treatment of Violent Offenders in Prison." *Social Problems* 46 (1): 88–103.

Gilroy, Paul. 2016. "Between the Blues and the Blues Dance." In *The Auditory Culture Reader*, edited by Michael Bull, Les Back, and David Howes, 323–34. London: Bloomsbury.

GRM Daily. 2021. "Digga D: The Resilient Shining Light of the Drill Scene." *GRM Daily*, February 25. https://grmdaily.com.

Gubrium, Jaber F., and James A. Holstein. 2009. *Analyzing Narrative Reality*. London: Sage.

Gunter, Anthony, 2008. "Growing Up Bad: Black Youth, Road Culture and Badness in an East London Neighbourhood." *Crime, Media, Culture* 4 (3): 349–66.

Henry, William Lez. 2006. *What the Deejay Said: A Critique from the Street!* London: Nu-Beyond Limited.

Herrity, Kate. 2018. "Music and Identity in Prison: Music as a Technology of the Self." *Prison Service Journal* 239: 40–47.

Herrity, Kate, Bethany E. Schmidt, and Jason Warr, eds. 2021. *Sensory Penalities: Exploring the Senses in Spaces of Punishment and Social Control*. Bingley, UK: Emerald Group.

Ilan, Jonathan. 2012. "'The Industry's the New Road': Crime, Commodification and Street Cultural Tropes in UK Urban Music." *Crime, Media, Culture* 8 (1): 39–55.

Ilan, Jonathan. 2014. "Commodifying Compliance? UK Urban Music and the New Mediascape." *Tijdschrift over Cultuur & Criminaliteit* 4 (1): 67–79.

Ilan, Jonathan. 2015. *Understanding Street Culture: Poverty, Crime, Youth and Cool*. London: Macmillan.

Ilan, Jonathan. 2019. "Cultural Criminology: The Time Is Now." *Critical Criminology* 27 (1): 5–20.

Ilan, Jonathan. 2020. "Digital Street Culture Decoded: Why Criminalizing Drill Music Is Street Illiterate and Counterproductive." *British Journal of Criminology* 60 (4): 994–1013.

Kubrin, Charis E. 2005. "Gangstas, Thugs, and Hustlas: Identity and the Code of the Street in Rap Music." *Social Problems* 52 (3): 360–78.

Maruna, Shadd. 2001. *Making Good: How Ex-Convicts Reform and Rebuild Their Lives*. Washington, DC: American Psychological Association.

Maruna, Shadd, Louise Wilson, and Kathryn Curran. 2006. "Why God Is Often Found behind Bars: Prison Conversions and the Crisis of Self-Narrative." *Research in Human Development* 3 (2–3): 161–84.

Peters, Eleanor. 2019. *The Use and Abuse of Music*. Bingley, UK: Emerald.

Plummer, Ken. 2019. *Narrative Power: The Struggle for Human Value*. Cambridge: Polity.

Polletta, Francesca. 2006. *It Was Like a Fever: Storytelling in Protest and Politics*. Chicago: University of Chicago Press.

Presser, Lois. 2019. "The Story of Antisociality: Determining What Goes Unsaid in Dominant Narratives." In *The Emerald Handbook of Narrative Criminology*, edited by Jennifer Fleetwood, Lois Presser, Sveinung Sandberg, and Thomas Ugelvik, 409–24. Bingley, UK: Emerald.

Presser, Lois. 2022. *Unsaid: Analyzing Harmful Silences*. Oakland: University of California Press.

Presser, Lois, and Sveinung Sandberg. 2015. "Introduction: What Is the Story?" In *Narrative Criminology: Understanding Stories of Crime*, edited by Lois Presser and Sveinung Sandberg, 1–20. New York: New York University Press.

Quinn, Eithne. 2005. *Nuthin' but a "G" Thang: The Culture and Commerce of Gangsta Rap*. New York: Columbia University Press.
Reid, Ebony. 2023. "'Trap Life': The Psychosocial Underpinnings of Street Crime in Inner-City London." *British Journal of Criminology* 63 (1): 168–83.
Rose, Tricia. 1994. *Black Noise: Rap Music and Black Culture in Contemporary America*. Hanover, NH: University Press of New England.
Sandberg, Sveinung. 2010. "What Can 'Lies' Tell Us about Life? Notes towards a Framework of Narrative Criminology." *Journal of Criminal Justice Education* 21 (4): 447–65.
Sandberg Sveinung. 2016. "The Importance of Stories Untold: Life-Story, Event-Story and Trope." *Crime, Media, Culture* 12 (2): 153–71.
Sandberg, Sveinung, and Sarah Colvin. 2020. "'ISIS Is Not Islam': Epistemic Injustice, Everyday Religion, and Young Muslims' Narrative Resistance." *British Journal of Criminology* 60 (6): 1585–605.
Sandberg, Sveinung, and Jennifer Fleetwood. 2017. "Street Talk and Bourdieusian Criminology: Bringing Narrative to Field Theory." *Criminology and Criminal Justice* 17 (4): 365–81.
Schinkel, Margerite. 2015. "Hook for Change or Shaky Peg? Imprisonment, Narratives and Desistance." *European Journal of Probation* 7 (1): 5–20.
Serisier, Tanya. 2018. *Speaking Out: Feminism, Rape and Narrative Politics*. London: Palgrave Macmillan.
Stuart, Forrest. 2020. *Ballad of the Bullet*. Princeton: Princeton University Press.
Ugelvik, Thomas. 2011. "The Hidden Food: Mealtime Resistance and Identity Work in a Norwegian Prison." *Punishment & Society* 13 (1): 47–63.
Wacquant, Loïc. 2009. *Punishing the Poor*. Durham: Duke University Press.
Warr, Jason. 2020. "'Always Gotta Be Two Mans': Lifers, Risk, Rehabilitation, and Narrative Labour." *Punishment & Society* 22 (1): 28–47.
Warr, Jason. 2022. "Whitening Black Men: Narrative Labour and the Scriptural Economics of Risk and Rehabilitation." *British Journal of Criminology* 65 (5): 1091–1107. https://doi.org/10.1093/bjc/azac066.
White, Joy. 2016. *Urban Music and Entrepreneurship: Beats, Rhymes and Young People's Enterprise*. New York: Routledge.
White, Joy. 2017. "Controlling the Flow: How Urban Music Videos Allow Creative Scope and Permit Social Restriction." *Young* 25 (4): 407–25.
White, Joy. 2020. *Terraformed: Young Black Lives in the Inner City*. London: Repeater.

MEDIA SOURCES

AmarudonTv. 2020. "Lavida Loca Interview: Beneath the Surface (The Perspective)." August 16.
BBC 3. 2020. "Defending Digga D." November 24.
Groundworks. 2020. "Potter Payper—Training Day 3: The Documentary."
No Jumper. 2020. "Unknown T Takes Us to His Hood after Beating His Murder Case." October 12.
Tim Westwood TV. 2020. "Potter Payper on Training Day 3, Mover, Time Away, 2020 Vision, Being Real in the Game—Westwood." September 20.

4

Real Utopian Stories to Counter the Climate Apocalypse

CHRISTINA ERGAS

Climate change is arguably the greatest environmental threat that humanity has ever confronted. Global in scale, it affects all planetary systems. It is largely driven by rising atmospheric concentrations of greenhouse gases (GHGs), such as carbon dioxide, methane, and nitrous oxide. While the burning of fossil fuels is the main cause of the rapid rise of CO_2, other anthropogenic activities such as deforestation primarily for agriculture also have climate impacts. Food-system emissions—including agriculture, retail, transport, and waste—account for 34 percent of GHG emissions (Crippa et al. 2021). Changes in food production, consumption, and waste practices are necessary to combat climate change. If global emissions continue to rise, scientists predict a likely four-degree (or more) Celsius rise in average global temperatures by the end of the century, a temperature that few living things could adapt to in such a short time (IPCC 2018). Climate change poses an existential threat.

Popular media stories about climate change-related catastrophe, such as cli-fi (climate change science fiction) or other sci-fi, often depict individuals escaping roaming bands of thieves/cannibals or resource wars in austere desert-scapes, such as *The Road* and *Mad Max: Fury Road*. These stories cast all persons as out for themselves (save perhaps small clusters of the selfless), disconnected from other hostile individuals and environments. Further, they impart lessons about the *need* for self-sufficiency and depict conflict that necessitates bunkers, hoarding, and fighting skills. In the world beyond popular culture, these theories manifest as individualistic "prepper" networks and luxury bunkers (Campbell 2018; Rushkoff 2018). However, these individualistic stories about surviving climate apocalypse run counter to disaster research that suggests that communities actually come together after major disasters to support each other, even if elites panic and double down on property protections (Clarke and Chess 2008; Solnit 2009).¹

People in the individualist West are disproportionately responsible for GHG emissions. They are also relatively unfamiliar with cooperative stories about collective action. Social psychological research suggests that these positive stories are necessary for climate adaptation and mitigation; they combat negative feelings, promote self/community-efficacy, and offer doable solutions (Norgaard 2009, 2011). Thus, stories of community-oriented cooperation, regeneration, and solidarity counter a possible self-fulfilling prophesy of dystopian apocalypse. This chapter aims to convey insights from such stories in hopes that if we can envision something better, we can create it (Eckstein 2003; Wright 2010).

An important note: apocalypse has already occurred for many. Climate disasters disproportionately affect Indigenous communities and communities of color—in many cases the same communities torn apart by Western colonialism. US-based Indigenous scholar Kyle Whyte (2018) argues that the current climate crisis and its effects on Indigenous communities are a continuation of ongoing colonial violence. This argument corroborates the research on the impacts of social inequity on emissions, which suggests that more equitable social organization is needed to combat the climate crisis (Ergas and York 2012). I choose to use the term "apocalypse" because its etymology is useful in thinking about the stories from my cases. Specifically, in Latin, *apocalypsis* means a revelation, and in Greek, *apokálypsis* is an uncovering or disclosure (*Merriam-Webster* 2023). From the perspective of the community members living within (the legacies of) violent settler-colonial societies, I propose viewing apocalypse as a threshold. On one side lies the detrimental practices that cause the catastrophic destruction of social and ecological complexity and reveal the untenable relations and contradictions in the sociopolitical system. On the other side of the threshold lie possibilities for different and more adaptive systems of social and ecological organization and the hope for utopia based in the radical, liberatory imaginaries of the most marginalized peoples—those who have long suffered apocalypse prior to large-scale collapse (Haiven and Khasnabish 2014). The stories herein are about the everyday actions of community members who practice their versions of liberatory imaginaries in order to survive collapse.

This chapter offers a glimpse into equitable and collectivist stories for survival. These stories draw on four years of field research at two case sites: an urban ecovillage in the Pacific Northwest (PNW) of the United States and an urban farm in Havana, Cuba. Since stories inform actions, and vice versa, I chose my case sites because they both engage in regenerative forms of agriculture—types of agriculture that aim to generate healthy, nutrient-rich soils, retain GHGs, minimize waste, conserve water, and protect wildlife habitat—and practice relatively democratic and equitable forms of social organization. Research suggests that both regenerative agriculture and equitable social relations can mitigate climate change (Ergas and York 2012; Ergas et al. 2021; Ergas, McKinney, and Bell 2021; McGee, Ergas, and Clement 2018). I explore the relationship between each community's stories and these more regenerative and equitable practices.

The PNW ecovillage and Cuban urban farm stories both have apocalypse as an (un)stated context. Ecovillagers' stories are contextualized by the imaginary of future apocalypse—of ecological collapse and subsequent civilization collapse. The Cuban urban farmers' stories organize around their past experiences of apocalypse that precipitated agricultural success and their communist victory, the economic and ecological collapse of the 1990s and the revolution of the late 1950s.

The first case, Asaṅga (a pseudonym), is a specific form of intentional community of those "who have chosen to live together with a common purpose, working cooperatively to create a lifestyle that reflects their shared core values" (Kozeny 1995: 18). Members of intentional communities may inhabit a single residence or a "cluster of dwellings" in a suburb, city, or rural space (Kozeny 1995: 18). Intentional communities include religious communes, urban housing cooperatives, or ecovillages, as in Asaṅga. Gilman (1991: 10) formally coined the term "ecovillage" to describe a community that combines sustainable ecology and community building. As described in their written materials, Asaṅga's ecovillagers share a narrative of being the change they wish to see in the world and see themselves as a model for sustainable living, both socially and ecologically.

The second case is an organic urban farm and workers' cooperative I call el Organopónico. It was formed soon after the collapse of the Soviet Union, Cuba's primary trading partner, which caused an economic crisis in Cuba in the 1990s precipitating food shortages and widescale hunger. In response, the Cuban government began to incentivize cooperative farming and organic food production. El Organopónico is named after a Spanish word for a type of raised bed used for growing plants in areas with poor soil quality. Cooperative workers at el Organopónico share stories about being *compañeros* (comrades), who work together to feed the Cuban people through hard times.

For both cases, I conducted semi-structured/in-depth interviews and participant observation and analyzed written community materials. I use pseudonyms for all respondents and sites to maintain confidentiality. At Asanga, I interviewed twenty-three of the twenty-seven adults who lived at the ecovillage at the time. At el Organopónico, I conducted many informal interviews with the men I worked with, and fifteen semi-structured interviews with thirteen women and two men.[2] I conducted all interviews in Spanish and after transcription, translated them into English (for more on methods in Cuba, see Ergas 2014, 2021; for more on the PNW, see Ergas 2010; Ergas and Clement 2016; Ergas 2021). From interviewees' statements, I draw out stories "organized around consequential events" that made a point (Riessman 1993: 3).

My central argument is that the good stories of climate change survival are psychologically necessary to empower people to enact change in ways known to be politically effective—that is, collectively, democratically, and equitably. To demonstrate the importance of such good stories, in the following sections, I describe the social psychology of climate change inaction; offer real utopian stories—where ideals meet practical actions to create emancipatory futures—as antidotes to such inaction; and share the stories from these cases. I end by discussing what these real-world examples and everyday good stories can tell us about climate adaptation, particularly about the importance of cooperation and the relationship between humans and the environment.

The Social Psychology of Inaction

Climate change is an overwhelming problem. It is global and various in its impacts and its inputs; it implicates very powerful actors and has no singular solution. Denial and other negative emotions can lead to inaction, allowing the anthropogenic causes of climate change to persist unabated. Climate inaction is sustained for a variety of reasons and at multiple scales. At the individual level, negative emotions, such as burnout, hopelessness, and helplessness, trigger denialism and inaction. Norgaard (2015) examines the cultural and political-economic contexts of climate change denial, or what she terms the "social organization of denial," which include norms of conversation, attention, and emotion to create an "insidious form of social control" (253). To dismiss disturbing information and avoid negative emotions like fear, guilt, and helplessness, people use avoidance strategies in conversation, such as changing the topic, telling jokes, trying not to think about it, or just refusing to bring it up, even in political contexts.

Norgaard (2011) observes that denial strategies in the United States include structurally supported denial, American exceptionalism, anti-intellectualism, and individualism. Specifically, under the George W. Bush administration, officials suppressed reports, falsified documents, and argued that the climate science needed further investigation. American exceptionalism generally places "the American way of life" as beyond examination, and so anything that challenges it, such as asking Americans to decrease their energy consumption, is undemocratic. Finally, a strong American ethos of individualism combined with a profound distrust of the political system serves to disempower people, especially when collective action is necessary, maintaining inaction in the face of large-scale social problems such as climate change (Norgaard 2011).

Individualism is an ideology that emphasizes autonomy, self-reliance, resourcefulness, and independence over the goals of a society, social group, or government (Callero 2018). Individualism has been promoted by Western politicians and institutions—such as Margaret Thatcher, Ronald Reagan, and the World Bank—and underlies many current political and economic programs, such as advancing austerity, market-based competition, and free trade as "efficient" governing mechanisms. Hyper-individualism, advanced in the United States, conjures images of white settlers conquering the "wild" West, surviving off the land alone with their families, and protecting themselves against the elements as well as brutish "others." Hyper-individualist values similarly underpin modern popular cli-fi stories.

Individualism is a politically misleading ideology in that it depicts individuals as politically inferior actors who are powerless in the face of a global crisis, such as climate change. Collective strategies are the only available means that most people have to create large-scale change, particularly if they lack wealth or status. Thus, stories that feature collective solutions to climate mitigation and adaptation are important to inspire such action, especially within individualist cultures.

Social psychological research suggests that individuals need stories about solutions to avoid falling into a state of denial about pressing problems (Norgaard 2009). Giving people facts about environmental crises does little to empower them; it may even overwhelm them with negative emotions like fear and guilt that render them debilitated. To combat socially organized denial, Norgaard (2009) argues, we must have honest conversations about what needs to change, how to make that change, and the benefits to such change. Norgaard further emphasizes bolstering positive feelings, such as hope, and adds that we must

> build on positive stories of success; create a sense of community by building on the knowledge that individuals are part of a larger committed and motivated citizenry; highlight the caring which IS present in order to build a sense of pride and community; provide specific opportunities to engage in realistic actions; and suggestions should be realistic in order to be deemed credible. (47; emphasis in original)

Norgaard maintains that "to elicit a response, people must be given not only information, but something to do" (2009: 47), and suggests that actions should be doable. Informing people about existing projects like urban farming and ecovillages may empower them to act. When people know that there are things that they can do, they may develop a sense of self-efficacy that in turn allows them to feel more concerned about, rather than deny, these problems (Krosnick et al. 2006; Kellstedt, Zahran, and Vedlitz 2008; Norgaard 2009, 2011). That concern may more readily translate into action and make alternative futures easier to imagine and realize.

Real Utopian Stories as Countermeasures

Stories, even utopian ones, have the power to move people beyond climate change denialism and empower them to act. Stories help construct collectives in that they bring people together around a shared narrative.

Presser (2013: 25) notes that "stories make things happen because they guide human action." Eckstein (2003: 13) further contends that stories have the power to effect transformative change: "Carefully told and carefully heard, stories do have the potential to act as a bridge between engrained habits and new futures, but their ability to act as transformative agents depends upon disciplined scrutiny of their forms and uses." Stories have consequences as they inform individual actions, institutions, and laws, as well as social movements and countermovement. Stories also shape what individuals can even imagine as possible—inhibiting creativity or conceiving of visionary imaginaries—and therefore doable.

The word "utopian" is often used dismissively, referring to an "impractical scheme for social improvement," and its schemers are seen as naïve dreamers (*Merriam-Webster* 2022). It is defined as an ideal or imagined place in which everything is perfect. Fittingly, the word comes from the Greek roots *ou* and *topos*, meaning "no/not" and "place," respectively. Perhaps to temper the appearance of naivete and to thwart criticism, sociologist Erik Olin Wright (2010) suggests that utopian ideals must meet with practical actions to create emancipatory futures. In his book *Envisioning Real Utopias*, Wright argues for examining alternatives to rising income and power disparities brought on by an unbridled capitalism. With these concerns in mind, he defines real utopias:

> The idea of Real Utopias embraces this tension between dreams and practice. It is grounded in the belief that what is pragmatically possible is not fixed independently of our imaginations, but is itself shaped by our visions. . . . Nurturing clear-sighted understandings of what it would take to create social institutions free of oppression is part of creating a political will for radical social changes to reduce oppression. A vital belief in a utopian ideal may be necessary to motivate people to leave on the journey from the status quo in the first place, even though the likely actual destination may fall short of the utopian ideal. Yet, vague utopian fantasies may lead us astray, encouraging us to embark on trips that have no real destinations at all, or worse still, which lead us toward some unforeseen abyss. (2010: 6)

Wright (2010) suggests that we investigate the feasibility of radically different kinds of institutions and social relations that could potentially advance the democratic egalitarian goals historically associated with the idea of socialism. To this I would add, the envisioning process should consider different institutions and social relations that also benefit the natural environment. Wright (2010) cautions against attempting to implement utopian fantasies with no prior assessment, warning of catastrophic unintended consequences. Instead, he advocates for "utopian ideals that are grounded in the real potentials of humanity, utopian destinations that have accessible waystations" (2010: 6). Model sites, like those described below, are best understood as such waystations: not a destination, but part of the journey.

The foci for this chapter are the ways in which stories influence actions and how telling stories may affect the actions of others. I offer the ecovillagers' and cooperative farmers' stories as two examples, among many, that counter prevalent individualist, climate apocalypse narratives to prevent self-fulfilling prophesies. Instead, the stories that were told impart values of cooperation, interdependence, regeneration, and care.

Real Utopian Stories

Asaṅga

I first encountered Asaṅga in the summer of 2004 and regularly visited for several months that year. I returned to conduct research in 2007, lived there for three months, and then continued to visit monthly through the winter of 2008. The 2004 visit was my first experience with an environmentally conscious community. I walked away inspired to imagine life beyond the conspicuous consumption I was familiar with in the United States. When I returned to the ecovillage to research sustainable living, I turned compost, cleaned rabbit cages, and swept the kitchen in exchange for my sleeping arrangement (for more details, see Ergas 2010; Ergas and Clement 2016; Ergas 2021). In what follows, I retell ecovillagers' collective stories about why they believe that sustainability is necessary; how they practice it; and how they share this vision with their community.

Sustainability as Necessary

The term "sustainability" has many definitions. Similarly, ecovillagers have various understandings of the word. Everything, from protecting the environment, to internal mental processing, to dealing with conflict in personal relationships, is covered under ecovillagers' definitions of sustainability. Discussion of the term came up in most interviews, articulated in conjunction with a pronounced need for immediate attention given potential collapse. For example, in a discussion about the future of the earth, Ralph, a property owner, identified the repercussions if sustainable practices are not aggressively pursued. Ralph's sardonic sense of humor emerged as we deliberated over somber topics, such as climate change and the grim possibility of civilization collapse. He was preparing for future food shortages, and that was in part the motivation for an outdoor kitchen under construction at the time. He noted the dual fossil fuel crises: climate change and peak oil. Like many of his fellow community members, for whom civilization collapse as a result of extravagant consumerism was taken for granted, Ralph acknowledged the trouble already at hand. Peak oil—the point at which global petroleum supplies max out—has already occurred, and eventually, fossil fuel shortages will cause global food shipments to come to a halt. Ralph conceded that food canned and preserved in the ecovillage will not last long, given that many neighbors are not prepared. But he did not dwell on the dark scenario. Rather, he spoke of both the necessity *and the inevitability* of sustainability: We will achieve sustainability. There is no question about it. The real question is, Will it be with technology or with dust blowing in the wind? Permaculture and consensus are two practices that he and other ecovillagers engage in to sustain environmental survival and social relationships.

Sustainability as Practice

Ecovillagers share collective stories in biweekly meetings and workshops about sustainable human relationships, called consensus, and sustainable relationships with the land, called permaculture. They promote permaculture as a sustainable form of agriculture needed to stave off potential environmental crises and consensus decision making to sustain community, especially when conflict arises.

Permaculture

Permaculture is more than a regenerative form of agriculture. Permaculture guides ecovillagers' stories as well as actions because it prescribes how to construct buildings, communities, and social relationships, and it is an important framework for how they communicate about sustainability. Permaculture involves the development of "consciously designed landscapes which mimic the patterns and relationships found in nature, while yielding an abundance of food, fiber and energy for provision of local needs" (Holmgren 2004). Borrowing from Indigenous and traditional peoples' knowledge and practices, Holmgren (2004) emphasizes that "people, their buildings and the ways they organize themselves are central to permaculture. Thus, the permaculture vision of permanent agriculture has evolved to one of permanent culture" (xix). The key principles of permaculture are "care for the earth, . . . care for the people, . . . set limits to consumption and reproduction and redistribute surplus" (Holmgren 2004: 1). Permaculture classes are spaces where ecovillagers share stories about how to live more sustainably in community. Of the twenty-four interviewees I spoke with, eleven mentioned taking a permaculture class at some point. Emily, an ecovillage resident, taught permaculture at a rural ecovillage not too far from the city. When I asked about her political beliefs, Emily closely paraphrased Holmgren's principles:

> Permaculture. I'd call that somewhat of a political view, which is that we all need to become more sustainable where we are in order to protect the outlying areas. And the foundation for permaculture is care for the earth, care for the people, and share the abundance. It's very simple.

Like Ralph, who said that a sustainable future was not in doubt, Emily projects a highly accessible and positive future, here through permaculture. Carol, a young mother, expresses the interrelated nature of each of the three principles written by Holmgren in her narrative of sustainability, as encompassing the earth, personal relationships, and community:

> Sustainability is living in a way that enhances the quality of life for not just humans but for other species as well. So a given area or land base can maintain health or increase in health over time. Biodiversity would increase, for instance, or at least stay stable and not decrease. Sustainability in interpersonal relationships means that a relationship can continue, that when there's conflict there's a way to resolve the conflict. That goes for

whole communities, that [when] there's conflict in the community, there's a way for the community to resolve that and continue on with each other, and people don't have to leave.

To ecovillagers, permaculture is more than a community organizing framework. Many of them, in effect, wish to share their story of permaculture with the world by modeling it, teaching it, and sharing resources they garnered from it. Community meetings are another space where community members cultivate collective stories by practicing consensus and permaculture by sharing the abundance in the form of cooked meals, much of it from their gardens.

Consensus

Community meetings provide a space where collective, rather than individual, stories can emerge and be (re)defined through consensus. Consensus is a nonhierarchical form of decision making that ideally involves everyone in the process, allowing each member's voice to be heard and considering the needs of all group members. Ecovillagers engage democratically by convening regular village meetings, every two weeks or once a month, and practicing consensus. Consensus requires groups to arrive at solutions that everyone in the group can agree on. In some cases, groups decide to come to modified consensus because not everyone can agree on a solution. In these situations, some individuals may choose to set aside their personal feelings to allow the group to come to a decision. However, if someone strongly disagrees with a proposal, they may choose to block the proposal entirely, forcing the group to think through other options.

A story that multiple interviewees shared about consensus was over an issue that caused a bit of tension in the community. A disagreement about a gaggle of geese was discussed at a few meetings. Carol had brought the geese onto the property for her to eat. Many residents did not like the geese because they aggressively hissed and nipped; at the meetings, residents discussed moving them to a local farm. However, a vegan resident began to care for the geese and bonded with them. He told Carol that she could not eat them. He claimed that she had not been caring for them properly, so he had stepped in and had become attached. Carol insisted that the geese were hers to consume. Community members reached consensus during a meeting, when another resident asked whether Carol would take a few chickens to eat instead and allow the geese to move to a farm. She agreed, and in the end, the geese were relocated.

This story about the consensus process corroborates other good stories that community members share about the need for collective decision making for sustaining community, and it characterizes collective actors who have the potential to solve problems. A long-term resident commends the process:

> The way that works is we just get a notice out about the topic, when and where the meeting is, and anyone who cares just shows up, expresses their opinion, or hopefully, runs by consensus. Which, I'm really surprised at how well it has worked. As soon as we started using consensus, I thought we would get bogged down by all the details like what color the paint should be, but it hasn't worked out that way. People are really mature here, I'd say, and they understand. Although they haven't been formally trained in the process. . . . Some of us have, some haven't. . . . The general trend is that people understand that you only block for highly principled reasons and . . . you are flexible, and you always look for the third way. All those things that make consensus work. People seem to have a handle on that here. . . . I'm pretty impressed with [our] collective ability to come to solutions.

The account is mellow in its characterization—low mimetic, or "an attempt to describe life exactly as it is" with ordinary people (49), to use Frye's (1957) literary term—with medium (linguistic) modality (e.g., "really surprised" and "pretty impressed"). A counterfactual story of how it could have gone ("we would get bogged down") is likewise not so awful.

Ecovillagers meet to discuss community issues, grievances, and collective solutions. All meetings are potlucks and provide a space for nurturing relationships and collective stories about how to live sustainably. Consensus is characterized as a way of attempting equitable and sustainable community practices, such that everyone has an opportunity to make decisions and air grievances. It is a means to alleviate conflict, solve communal issues, and nurture communal bonds, stories, and identities, such as how they model sustainability for the rest of the world.

Modeling Sustainability

In addition to personal and interpersonal everyday work toward achieving sustainability, villagers relay their story of averting climate apocalypse to others. One way they do this is by giving tours to visitors in the community. The community's welcome materials state, "Our home serves not only as a place for us to live, but also as a model of sustainable living." Home, in this way, is a narrating object, or a place that tells stories (Ugelvik 2019). Their home tells stories about the residents, that they prioritize community and sustainability; the sociocultural context it is situated in, that of the larger consumer society the village space counters; its intended purpose, to model sustainability; and its past, as a space designed to build community around environmental concerns.

Huck, an elder resident who had lived at the ecovillage for six years, explained that the founders of the ecovillage had a vision that included tours where key members would "just waltz them through what's going on":

> Taking that even deeper, is when you come here, you are in some state in an educational halfway house situation. . . . So there's kind of a social, a strong social suggestion here that you can implement alternatives.

For Huck, the tours offer an immersive experience that makes real a story that others can enact as well.

Asaṅga residents are inspired by permaculture, which grounds those stories of humans living with the earth and each other more sustainably and counters dominant logics of individualism and consumerism. Community meetings offer space for refining a collective, rather than individualistic, story, through consensus practices, about how to model sustainability.

The Asaṅga ecovillagers' future orientation toward collapse stands in some contrast to the palpable living in history of the Cuban urban farmers. For them, recent memories of two economic and social collapses orient their stories. However, many of the practices they have chosen to avert future collapse or grow and regenerate from past collapse are similar to those of the ecovillagers, such as regenerative agriculture and more equitable and democratic forms of social engagement.

El Organopónico

El Organopónico urban farm is in a peri-urban area on the eastern side of the city of Havana, Cuba. It sits on roughly twenty-seven acres of land and is less than a mile away from the northern coast of Cuba (for more detail, see Ergas 2014, 2021). The stories that the urban farmers tell relate to their history of struggle through revolution and economic collapse. Common themes in these stories include the needs for organic urban agriculture, solidarity, community, and self-sufficiency. Each challenge necessitated regenerative change.

The stories here are descriptive of the time in which I conducted my research in Cuba, from the summer of 2010 through the winter of 2011, and may be changing. I cannot make claims about current conditions. At the time of this writing, Cuba's economy has been ravaged by a combination of the long-term US embargo against Cuba, the Trump administration's tightening of restrictions, and the ongoing COVID-19 pandemic, which crushed Cuba's most lucrative industry, tourism. The country is undergoing a mass exodus, as many Cubans are looking for economic opportunities elsewhere (Augustin and Robles 2022). Current economic conditions aside, the stories below describe some of the resilient features of Cuban culture.

A significant event that some Cuban farmers use to contextualize their stories is the communist victory of the Cuban Revolution that ended in 1959, which led Cuba to rely more on the Soviet Union. Many older farmers fondly remember how this victory offered educational and employment opportunities, as education at all levels became free and other social services were greatly expanded. When the Soviet Union fell in the early 1990s, Cubans were confronted with an ecological and economic collapse that lasted almost a decade, known as the Special Period in the Time of Peace. To address widescale hunger, Cuba radically altered its food production system to restore degraded ecosystems and meet human needs. At the time of my research, Cubans were celebrated globally for their innovative urban agriculture, which produces most of the vegetables consumed by the island nation, and their urban reforestation programs, which preserve biodiversity, water and soil quality, and coastal areas.

Revolutionary Changes

Billboards, murals, and commercials in Cuba commemorate the story of Cuba's 1959 revolutionary victory. After the revolution, opportunities arose for many women and for poor and rural Cubans. Social services, including free childcare, healthcare, and education at all levels, allowed impoverished Cubans, including women, to obtain advanced degrees and employment.

At the farm, the older generation who lived through the revolution recounted stories of gratitude for the opportunities of the revolution. However, Cubans who came of age during or after the Special Period in the 1990s expressed longing for more opportunity and material possessions. Expressing the youthful sentiment, a former English professor turned cab driver quipped about billboards, "We don't have any advertising here for products. Political propaganda is our McDonald's." Older-generation Cubans share gratitude for the revolution, similar to Guillermo's story at the farm:

> Look, I'm grateful. Why? A *guajirito* [farm boy] from Sierra Maestra—in Sierra Maestra the rebels, Fidel's people, came together and fought against tyranny. That's why they call it Sierra Maestra [Master Mountains]. . . . Then, I was a *guajirito* that was born in the country. The revolution gave me the opportunity to study; I studied and became an engineer. The revolution made me an engineer; I married an engineer. . . . She [the revolution] gave me a house, my wife, me, my two daughters, a scientist and another. She [the revolution] gave me two grandchildren. . . . I have the revolution to thank. Although there are things that, aware of them or not, are mistakes of the revolution, but sometimes things—people are more fixated on the bad than on the good. Here, you get seventeen years or twenty years, or thirty years, or forty years of studying and are not charged a penny. If you go to a hospital and you are in a hospital for twenty years, there at the hospital, they do not charge you a penny. When you retire, the state assures you a retirement, not very large, but it assures you something until you die. Before the revolution, people went hungry,

you know what I mean? After the revolution, no. Before the revolution, the only ones who bought meat were those who had money; the poor did not eat meat. In this revolution, bad or good, you eat something.

This story begins as an account of what the revolution did for him, but then the beneficiary becomes the universal "you," "people," and "the poor." The stories of the socialist revolution are those of collective support and equitable opportunity off and on the farm.

Community

Three sisters who worked together at the farm discussed the importance of community in an interview. The rest of the world clearly casts individual and community differently, as one of the sisters said: "Focusing on the collective is very important. It's bad to be like most people in the world who only care about themselves." Her twin chimed in, "Just going home and being isolated in your apartment in front of the TV isn't good for anyone. People need each other." Their older sister added, "Cubans live more collectively. You go say 'hi' to your neighbors, ask how they are, borrow some sugar, drink a coffee, sit and talk." A story of what one properly does, as opposed to what may be more commonly done, fleshes out the value of community.

The sisters' stories of community were consistent with other stories on the farm about the importance of cooperative labor. They rely on their *compañeros* to complete important steps so they can complete their own work to sustain the cooperative.

Compañero

Compañero means comrade, a nonhierarchical form of address, and is a common way that Cubans address each other, even strangers. The farm atmosphere was casual, and farmers referred to each other informally, calling each other "comrade." The president often told other workers, in jest, that I was his niece. When I used the formal "you" (*usted*), he insisted that he was not above anyone, nor was he that old, and thus I should use the informal "you" (*tú*). Thus, the president enacted nonhierarchical social relations with me, which is illustrative of their stories about more equitable social arrangements and commitments to cooperation.

Special Period Changes

After the Soviet Union collapsed, regular imports of petroleum needed for industrial agriculture to run machinery and develop petrochemical fertilizers and pesticides halted. As a result, most agriculture was converted to organic, much of which became urban. The government incentivized farmer cooperatives, or Basic Units of Cooperative Production (UBPCs), to expand employment and food production. Some agronomists saw this as an opportunity to promote agroecology and organic urban agriculture. Urban agriculture provided much-needed employment within cities during the economic downturn. Urban farms also presented opportunities for self-sufficiency and regeneration after crises, and the nations' post-revolution investment in education drove experimentation with and the dissemination of regenerative practices.

Organic Urban Agriculture

Cooperative workers share an attitude of appreciation for organic urban agriculture, which provides beautified and cleaned-up blighted urban areas, accessible food, and gainful employment for Cubans. On the farm, they use a regenerative form of organic agriculture called agroecology. Miguel Altieri, a prominent professor and researcher of agroecology, defines agroecology as "the application of ecological concepts and principles to the design and management of sustainable agricultural ecosystems" (Altieri 2009: 2). On his website, Altieri (2017) further explains that the goal of agroecology, beyond managing sustainable agroecosystems, is to ensure that they "are also culturally-sensitive, socially just and economically viable."

Interviewees shared in common stories about their farm work as beautiful and fulfilling: it allows them to help their community by providing nourishment, and provides workers with food and economic security. According to Iset, urban agriculture is an alternative to hauling food long distances. It's a job for people who are unemployed. It cleans the air, atmosphere, and environment in the urban centers, where there is a lot of movement and pollution and where the contaminants collect. It brings food to people. In the peripheral urban areas where there is land, why not use it for food?

Iset's description integrates a low mimetic contrast to the waste and pollution of the world beyond the community.

Another interviewee, who came out of retirement to work at the farm, explains her decision in concrete terms of proximity to home, healthy environment, and good pay:

> The first characteristic was that I am close to my house, the proximity to my house. I live three blocks from work. . . . It is a very healthy job, a healthy job, since I am in an environment, in a healthy environment of trees, in the open air. And in addition, it is well paid, well paid, and well paid. The collective is very good. I feel I'm in a good collective.

Two sisters shared a story about the good they are doing for the community. They said that they enjoyed their work because they get to see the literal fruits of their labor and "people need your work, and you know that you are helping others." Members' personal narratives about their healthy, community-oriented jobs reflect Cuba's distinct history of the need for community after the communist revolution and the Special Period, which required efficient means to feed the population after support from the Soviet Union collapsed. Yet the accounts they shared were generally present-oriented and modest, anything but grand and universal.

Worker Cooperatives

Collective good stories at the farm are materialized and reinterpreted through cooperative labor, democratic decision making, and wages and are (re)defined in monthly meetings. El Organopónico is a UBPC established during the Special Period, and, as a workers' cooperative, all members have ownership over the machinery, inputs like seeds or fertilizers, and the produce they grow. Cooperative members share stories about being part of a team that relies on the members at each farm sector—such as the nursery, fields, and market—equally to accomplish cooperative goals. While there is hierarchy at the cooperative—el Organopónico is led by a president who was voted into leadership, and each sector has a manager—all members are co-owners and invested in the farm's progress. Each member's equal value is reflected in their wages and their vote. Everyone meets monthly to vote on new proposals, membership, and equipment purchases, which pass by simple majority. These meetings also serve to hone identities as cooperative members, particularly when they vote on new members. A cooperative member explains:

> Here we, the workers, when someone comes to work with us, they are on a three-month probationary period. After three months, the assembly of cooperative members decides whether or not this person becomes a cooperative member. The vast majority who continue working are good, intelligent people, who almost always stay with us for a long time.

Cooperative members described all farm sectors as connected and as equally important to the survival of the cooperative. A plant nursery worker explained, "Here, everyone takes seriously the work that there is." An accountant further spoke of the meshing of all work: "So they [fieldworkers] can charge for the work they're doing, they need people behind the computer. So here, everyone pulls their weight, one thing leads to another." Their *compañeros* at each sector provide the necessary work that allows other stations to complete their work and contribute to the larger goals of the cooperative. The composting sector provides the soil for the starter plants, which are then transferred into the fields, which are then harvested and sold in the vending area, and the funds from the vending area are accounted for, turned into wages, and reinvested in the farm.

Cooperative members' stories about the equal value of members were materialized through wages. At the time of my fieldwork, farmers earned a decent wage by Cuban standards, and wages at the farm were capped and calculated based on years employed at the farm rather than output. Workers were paid the same regardless of sector or rank; they began at a standard minimum salary and earned a raise every five years. In times of surplus, profits were evenly distributed among members. One of the accountants explained, "The more years go by, the better off you feel because you earn more, you gain seniority, your salary increases."

While Cubans suffered economic hardship during and after the revolution and Special Period, their stories about the importance of investing in people and community were actualized as free education, food rationing, and healthcare, which accorded them an abundance of human resources. These resources included skilled doctors, scientists, engineers, and laborers with the ingenuity and creativity to solve the problems associated with their crises. Cubans' stories boast that Cuba has only 2 percent of the Latin American population yet produces 11 percent of Latin American scientists (Morgan 2006). Their actualized communitarian stories, which promoted regenerative agriculture, helped them through the economic hardships of the Special Period. These stories impart lessons for preventing and surviving future climate catastrophes in practical, forward-looking ways.

Discussion: Assessing Real Utopias

The great dystopian novelist Margaret Atwood famously stated, "Within every dystopia there's a little utopia" (Marchese 2013). Put differently, other dystopian novelists have proffered that someone's utopia is someone else's dystopia. Not all stories intended for good manifest as or create good, and one person's ideals need not appeal to everyone. It is certainly possible that some would find ecovillage life overcrowded, burdensome, or stifling, and Cuban farm life physically taxing and lacking enough remuneration. Conversely, within a dystopia, there is opportunity: the ability to recognize and object to the dystopian world; the ability to envision liberating alternatives; and the potential to create something new—indeed, the need for dreams and hope. On the other hand, practice with myriad potential utopian alternatives is necessary for us to appraise unintended consequences and ultimately find the most adaptive and mitigative strategies for climate survival.

From interviews with ecovillagers and Cuban urban farmers, I offer a sense of the non-sensational stories that inform their regenerative daily practices. Research suggests that more equitable and democratic practices as well as regenerative environmental relations are necessary for community resilience and adaptation. Either based on research, intuition, or both, ecovillagers and Cuban urban farmers share community-oriented stories about sustainability. Survival, to these actors, requires equitable collaboration, space for democratic decision making, and cooperative regenerative agriculture. These stories counter more pervasive—and grand—narratives of catastrophe, climate denialism, hopelessness, and individual bunker survival. Actualizing their collaborative stories, they enact culturally distinct versions of the more equitable and regenerative social and environmental relations needed to mitigate climate change. Despite existing in very different cultural, political, and geographical contexts, these two communal responses to apocalypse illustrate that equitable and environmentally conscious methods can be practiced almost anywhere but may need tailoring to fit local cultures and environments. These real utopian models are just two examples of many possible adaptive alternatives.

Ecovillagers share stories about how to avert collapse by practicing, modeling, and teaching sustainability. Community meetings are spaces where members build and sustain relationships and collective narratives by reaching consensus to handle conflict and ensure that everyone's voice is heard. In meetings, they share stories that solidify their community narrative identity as an eco-role model for the rest of the world. The crises of the revolution and Special Period inform Cuban cooperative farmers' stories about the importance of community and equality for survival. Poor Cubans and women share stories about how the revolution gave them opportunities for education and career advancement. While the Special Period required ingenuity and collaboration, Cuba's stories about investing in people and community aided in their creation of organic urban farmers' cooperatives. This community mindset is seen in farmers' stories about comrades and family, and their appreciation for everyone's contributions—enacted through equal pay between sectors, with extra pay for commitment and experience. Part of cooperative members' collective identity is everyone's investment in the success of the farm, which requires that they make decisions together on farm business. Both communities share stories about valuing the land as well and are committed to regenerative farming practices that maintain ecosystem and community health. For ecovillagers, permaculture is how many define sustainable social and ecological relationships. These stories inform resilient practices that are told in relation to surviving past and looming apocalypse.

I do not intend the stories explored in this chapter as prescriptive paths toward sustainability; instead, these examples of alternatives are meant to whet the appetite of those craving a different way. Based on the research on denialism and inaction—which suggests that wider audiences' access to these stories could empower them to act to counter climate change—and the research on the climate benefits of regenerative agriculture and more equitable social structures, the stories in this chapter offer different examples of effective and practical mitigative and adaptive strategies (Ergas 2021). Rather than prescribing liberatory paths, the purpose of the stories here is to remind readers that more sustainable and democratic alternatives exist and that for all to survive climate apocalypse, overconsuming, affluent, Western communities must reorient toward more adaptive practices. These "real utopias" may not necessarily be the visionary futures everyone wishes to live, but they are reminders of the possibilities.

NOTES

1 According to the *Oxford English Dictionary* (2023), the term "apocalypse" means "a disaster resulting in drastic, irreversible damage to human society or the environment, esp. on a global scale; a cataclysm." The term "collapse" generally refers to a de-complexification of sociopolitical-ecological systems (King and Jones 2021).
2 Constructions of race in Cuba and the United States are very different, and the Cuban respondents identified as either white or mixed. At the ecovillage, my respondents mostly self-identified as white, and a couple of people mentioned some parts Native American and Jewish ancestry.

REFERENCES

Altieri, Miguel. 2009. "Agroecology, Small Farms, and Food Sovereignty." *Monthly Review* 61 (3). https://monthlyreview.org.
Altieri, Miguel. 2017. "Miguel Altieri: Professor of Department of Environmental Science, Policy, and Management, Berkeley." UC Berkeley Department of Environmental Science, Policy, and Management website. https://ourenvironment.berkeley.edu. Accessed December 23, 2017.
Augustin, Ed, and Frances Robles. 2022. "Cuba Is Depopulating: Largest Exodus Yet Threatens Country's Future." *New York Times*, December 10. www.nytimes.com.
Callero, Peter. 2018. *The Myth of Individualism: How Social Forces Shape Our Lives*. New York: Rowman and Littlefield.

Campbell, B. J. 2018. "The Surprisingly Solid Mathematical Case of the Tin Foil Hat Gun Prepper: Or, 'Who Needs an AR-15 Anyway?'" *Medium*, April 20. https://medium.com.

Clarke, Lee, and Caron Chess. 2008. "Elites and Panic: More to Fear Than Fear Itself." *Social Forces* 87 (2): 993–1014.

Crippa, M., E. Solazzo, D. Guizzardi, F. Monforti-Ferrario, F. N. Tubiello, and A. Leip. 2021. "Food Systems Are Responsible for a Third of Global Anthropogenic GHG Emissions." *Nature Food* 2: 198–209. https://doi.org/10.1038/s43016-021-00225-9.

Eckstein, Barbara. 2003. "Making Spaces: Stories in the Practice of Planning." In *Story and Sustainability: Planning, Practice, and Possibility for American Cities*, edited by Barbara Eckstein and James A. Throgmorton, 13–36. Cambridge, MA: MIT Press.

Ergas, Christina. 2010. "A Model of Sustainable Living: Collective Identity in an Urban Ecovillage." *Organization and Environment* 23 (1): 32–54.

Ergas, Christina. 2014. "Barriers to Sustainability: Gendered Divisions of Labor in Cuban Urban Agriculture." In *From Sustainable to Resilient Cities: Global Concerns and Urban Efforts*, vol. 14, edited by William G. Holt, 239–63. Bingley, UK: Emerald.

Ergas, Christina. 2021. *Surviving Collapse: Building Community toward Radical Sustainability*. New York: Oxford University Press.

Ergas, Christina, and Matthew Clement. 2016. "Ecovillages, Restitution, and the Political-Economic Opportunity Structure: An Urban Case Study in Mitigating the Antagonism between Humans and Nature." *Critical Sociology* 42 (7–8): 1195–211.

Ergas, Christina, Patrick Greiner, Julius McGee, and Matt Clement. 2021. "Does Gender Climate Influence Climate Change? The Multidimensionality of Gender Equality and Its Countervailing Effects on the Carbon Intensity of Well-Being." *Sustainability* 13 (7): 3956. https://doi.org/10.3390/su13073956.

Ergas, Christina, Laura McKinney, and Shannon Bell. 2021. "Intersectionality and the Environment." In *Handbook of Environmental Sociology*, edited by Beth Schaefer Caniglia, Andrew Jorgenson, Stephanie A. Malin, Lori Peek, David N. Pellow, and Xiaorui Huang, 15–34. Cham, Switzerland: Springer.

Ergas, Christina, and Richard York. 2012. "Women's Status and Carbon Dioxide Emissions: A Quantitative Cross-National Analysis." *Social Science Research* 41: 965–76.

Frye, Northrop. 1957. *Anatomy of Criticism: Four Essays*. Princeton: Princeton University Press.

Gilman, Robert. 1991. "The Eco-Village Challenge: The Challenge of Developing a Community Living in Balanced Harmony—with Itself as Well as Nature—Is Tough, but Attainable." *In Context* 29: 10–14.

Haiven, Max, and Alex Khasnabish. 2014. *The Radical Imagination: Social Movement Research in the Age of Austerity*. London: Zed.

Holmgren, David. 2004. *Permaculture: Principles and Pathways beyond Sustainability*. Hepburn Springs, Victoria: Holmgren Design Services.

Intergovernmental Panel on Climate Change. 2018. "Summary for Policymakers." In *Global Warming of 1.5°C*, edited by V. Masson-Delmotte, P. Zhai, H. O. Pörtner, D. Roberts, J. Skea, P. R. Shukla, A. Pirani, et al. Geneva, Switzerland: World Meteorological Organization.

Kellstedt, Paul, Sammy Zahran, and Arnold Vedlitz. 2008. "Personal Efficacy, the Information Environment, and Attitudes toward Global Warming and Climate Change in the United States." *Risk Analysis* 28 (1): 113–26.

King, Nick, and Aled Jones. 2021. "An Analysis of the Potential for the Formation of 'Nodes of Persisting Complexity.'" *Sustainability* 13: 8161. https://doi.org/10.3390/su13158161.

Kozeny, Geoph, ed. 1995. "Intentional Communities: Lifestyles Based on Ideals." In *Communities Directory: A Guide to Cooperative Living*, 18–24. Rutledge, MO: Fellowship for Intentional Community.

Krosnick, Jon, Allyson Holbrook, Laura Lowe, and Penny Visser. 2006. "The Origins and Consequences of Democratic Citizens' Policy Agendas: A Study of Popular Concern about Global Warming." *Climate Change* 77: 7–43.

Marchese, David. 2013. "Doomsday Machine." *New York*, August 23. nymag.com.

McGee, Julius, Christina Ergas, and Matthew Clement. 2018. "Racing to Reduce Emissions: Assessing the Relationship between Race and Environmental Impacts from Transportation." *Sociology of Development* 4 (2): 217–36.

Merriam-Webster. 2022. "Utopia." Accessed January 3, 2022. www.merriam-webster.com.

Merriam-Webster. 2023. "Apocalypse." Accessed May 1, 2023. www.merriam-webster.com.

Morgan, Faith. 2006. *The Power of Community: How Cuba Survived Peak Oil*. Yellow Springs, OH: Community Solutions. www.communitysolution.org.

Norgaard, Kari Marie. 2009. "Cognitive and Behavioral Challenges in Responding to Climate Change." World Bank Development Economics World Development Report Team. Policy Research Working Paper 4940. Washington, DC: World Bank.

Norgaard, Kari Marie. 2011. *Living in Denial: Climate Change, Emotions, and Everyday Life*. Cambridge, MA: MIT Press.

Oxford English Dictionary. 2023. "Apocalypse." Accessed May 1, 2023. www.oed.com.

Presser, Lois. 2013. *Why We Harm*. New Brunswick: Rutgers University Press.

Riessman, Catherine Kohler. 1993. *Narrative Analysis*. Newbury Park, CA: SAGE.

Rushkoff, Douglas. 2018. "How Tech's Richest Plan to Save Themselves after the Apocalypse." *Guardian*, July 24. www.theguardian.com.

Solnit, Rebecca. 2009. *A Paradise Built in Hell: The Extraordinary Communities That Arise in Disaster*. New York: Penguin.

Ugelvik, Thomas. 2019. "The Tales Things Tell: Narrative Analysis, Materiality, and My Wife's Old Nazi Rifle." In *The Emerald Handbook of Narrative Criminology*, edited by Jennifer Fleetwood, Lois Presser, Sveinung Sandberg, and Thomas Ugelvik, 217–38. Bingley, UK: Emerald.

Whyte, Kyle. 2018. "Indigenous Science (Fiction) for the Anthropocene: Ancestral Dystopias and Fantasies of Climate Change Crises." *Environment and Planning E: Nature and Space* 1 (1–2): 224–42.

Wright, Eric Olin. 2010. *Envisioning Real Utopias*. New York: Verso.

PART II

Good in the Telling

5

Morality from the Mountaintop

*Comparing Philosophical and Narrative
Approaches to Increasing the Good*

PAUL JOOSSE

If the field of moral philosophy had a mission statement, it might be expressed as something like "Devising strategies for increasing goodness in the world." From Socratic yearnings for "the good life," to Augustine's depictions of the "City of God," to modernist calculations aimed at "maximizing utility" within society, philosophers are continually envisioning states of goodness and thinking up pathways to them.

Behind all such moral-philosophical approaches is the assumption that "good-making" is a task that is best approached with a thorough *thinking-through*. There is a basic optimism underlying this premise—believing that we can actively strategize our way toward ideal states, that philosophical programs, once put into action, might actually be carried out with success ("If only they would listen!"). All too frequently, however, philosophical systems struggle to find influence within the societies where they are devised. "Goodness" increases and abates in ways that are frustratingly independent of the quality of the thinking being done in book-lined offices or (depending on the tradition) by bearded sages on inaccessible mountaintops.

The goal of this chapter is not to criticize moral philosophy, still less to comprehensively summarize it. Instead, I want to review some common themes and arguments from the moral-philosophical tradition and advocate for *narrative* forms of their delivery. My claim is that, as carriers for moral arguments, narratives offer illustrative possibilities that are liable to make the arguments of moral philosophy more evocative and persuasive. Additionally, I argue that narrative devices can transmit moral messages and outline good-making processes in ways that philosophical argumentation can't. These devices avoid the didacticism and elitism of much philosophical writing, while also illustrating a broader truth: that our moral sensibilities are rooted first and most deeply within sociocultural—as opposed to individual-intellective—forms of knowledge. My central claim, then, is that while philosophy approaches the problem of good-making as an intellectual exercise, *storying* philosophical arguments helps us to actually accomplish what they aim to do—which is to do good.

By arrangement, the argument relies on an idealized and therewith somewhat artificial contrast between "philosophical" and "narratological" styles. And I've formed an awareness of these through admittedly limited exposure, first as a philosophy undergrad and later as a working sociologist—but always as a reader of stories. Of course, the examples I choose represent tendencies for which there are many exceptions. Some of the world's most celebrated novelists (Dostoevsky, Camus) are regularly referenced by philosophers, for example, and many self-identified philosophers regularly avail themselves of narrative and other literary devices while conducting their work.[1] Therefore, while what follows relies to a degree on caricature, I hope the reader can find something approaching truth within the contrast itself.

In what follows, I first describe a strategy for increasing goodness that has found its way into many moral arguments across the history of philosophy—what I call "category expansion." This strategy involves broadening the domain of ethical consideration to include heretofore excluded groups. Human rights discourse, for example, represents a categorical expansion beyond rights discourses that are grounded in more particularistic social categories such as community or family. By expanding the domain of ethical consideration, these philosophers argue, we can embrace others in our midst and advance "the good" in society.

Second, I describe two rhetorical tendencies that are characteristic of moral-philosophical thinking and writing and that (I argue) frequently stand in the way of actualizing good-making initiatives. These stylistic tendencies—toward didacticism and elitism—involve "telling us directly" and "telling us with authority." I suggest that, while these features may be well suited to the rarefied environments where philosophical debate takes place, narratives are different creatures in that they are advantageously adapted to the sociocultural spaces where good-making actually happens. Narratives tend to be better at *producing* good for that reason.

Third and finally, I draw on a speech by Martin Luther King Jr.—a master storyteller—to illustrate my argument. I show how King used story to advance the "category expansion" theme while avoiding the aforementioned stylistic tendencies that tend to hinder moral philosophy's capacity to activate good-making practices in the world. As the narrator-leader for a social movement that pursued racial justice in the United States, King did more to advance the good than any philosopher ever has.

King was a Baptist minister whose storytelling strategy involved promulgating a biblical allegory between Israelite slavery in Egypt and contemporary racial injustice in America. This story "worked" in its time to mobilize his constituency while also forcing America to move in the direction of reckoning with its "original sin" of slavery. By referencing this particular intersection between religion and progressive social change, however, by no means am I suggesting that Christian stories hold "the answer" to questions about racial injustice in any exclusive or necessitarian sense. On the contrary, contemporary manifestations of Christianity have often been aligned with forces that stand in opposition to racial justice—as indeed many did in King's day. My observation in this chapter is solely about the power of stories-*qua*-stories—that at one point in history, King creatively drew from an existing cultural-narrative substrate to advance "the good" within society.

Embracing the Other: Theories of Category Expansion in Moral Philosophy

One strategy for increasing the good that has appeared in various forms across the history of philosophy involves advocating for an expansion of categories for membership within an existing moral community. Who should be regarded as a full-standing moral agent within society? Who should have a say in societal arrangements? Who is worthy of protection from harm? A variety of philosophers have argued that moral advancement is something that we can achieve by expanding the "who" in answers to these questions.

An early example of this type of thinking is the work of the second-century stoic philosopher Hierocles, who believed that ethical concern is distributed diminishingly across a series of ever larger circles that nest within one another. At the tightest orbit of concern is the mind, which is most immediately preoccupied with satisfying individual needs and desires—with being "selfish." Within a sequence of increasingly larger circles of attention, we dwell in a prioritized state of concern for close family members (where ethical feeling is still very strong, but lacking some of the phenomenological immediacy that drives self-interest); community (the domain beyond familial responsibilities where "social welfare" becomes salient); and finally, "humanity" generally (for which the pull of concern is most vague and intermittent). Hierocles suggests that ethical development involves collapsing all wider circles as far as possible into that smallest region usually occupied by the self, thereby expanding the scope of ethical concern outward toward universalistic altruism.

Immanuel Kant similarly advocated for pushing outwards from the tendency to evaluate actions from within the horizon of one's own limited circumstances. Instead, his "categorical imperative"—one of moral philosophy's most well-known contributions—maintains that we should constrain self-interest by "act[ting] according to that maxim whereby you can, at the same time, will that it [i.e., the maxim] should become a universal law" (1785 [2012]). In essence, Kant advocates that we always leap categorically—from the "I" to the "All"—in our evaluations of the actions we take.

In the twentieth century, various philosophers sought to push theories of ethical expansion beyond even the human community. For example, in *Animal Liberation* (1973 [2015]), Peter Singer critiques what he calls "speciesism," arguing that progressive movements of the past have laid the groundwork for embracing animals as full rights-bearing members of society. He cites the derision levelled at the early women's movement as being analogous to the type of opposition faced by animal rights advocates today (1973 [2015]: 28). Aldo Leopold, perhaps the most influential pioneer in the field of environmental ethics, makes an argument that is similar to Hierocles's in that it proceeds through a succession of expansionary stages, but he stretches much further, toward a consciousness of the "biotic community" as a domain of responsibility that encompasses all life.[2]

One can readily see that the biggest impediment to expanding moral horizons in this way will be a failure of imagination. As we go about our lives, hierarchies, social reproduction, and monopolistic closure do much to keep us in our respective lanes, often with blinders on. For this reason, when category-expanding vanguardists arise and make proposals, they will tend to be written off as unserious and eccentric, as "idealists" in the pejorative sense of the term.

Because of this difficulty with imagination, philosophers have suggested that we need to sensitize ourselves to injustice around us by engaging in hypothetical place-switching with those who occupy other positions relative to us. In *A Theory of Justice*, John Rawls (1971 [2020]) developed an influential heuristic for this purpose, what he calls the "veil of ignorance":

> Somehow we must nullify the effects of specific contingencies which put men [sic] at odds and tempt them to exploit social and natural circumstances to their own advantage. Now in order to do this I assume that the parties are situated behind a veil of ignorance. They do not know how the various alternatives will affect their own particular case and they are obliged to evaluate principles solely on the basis of general considerations. (1971 [2020]: 118)

Ideally, such a veil of ignorance would enable us to generate designs for society without knowing in advance what our position within that society would be. A society can be said to be just when it is something that we would choose to actualize even if we stood at risk of being placed in the lowliest position within it. Do we want a society where one's range of potential positions includes that of the prince and the pauper? In the novel by that name, two boys, lookalikes, trade life circumstances with one another. Through the experience, the prince-turned-pauper gains an awareness of the intense class inequality of sixteenth-century England and the brutality of the justice system over which he reigns, and works to resolve these issues after returning to the throne. The story illustrates the persuasive power of imaginative place-switching, and how it can lead to an expansion of moral consideration toward as-yet excluded others.

There have been important cautionary objections to projects of category expansion, both from within the philosophical community and without. Nevertheless, a trajectory of progression does seem discernible, even if it is messy, in (for example) historical expansions of suffrage in the United States—from the non-propertied, to racialized groups, to women. These extensions hint at potential future motions toward the criminalized, to children, to noncitizens, and even to some form of democratic representation for non-humans in our midst. In the philosophical theory that underpins such expansions, the foundation for ethics is something that initially has little moral value, be it unthinking self-interest, in-group chauvinism, or uncritical anthropocentrism. But as all these thinkers suggest, such loci for concern can be extended outward to include others. As this expansion happens, our actions and decision-making processes accumulate moral weight, thereby increasing the good.

Stylistic Contrasts between Philosophical and Narrative Persuasion

When weighing the power of moral-philosophical work, we must also consider its strengths and weaknesses in rhetorical terms. In what follows, I assess two stylistic tendencies of moral philosophy—namely, toward *didacticism* and *elitism*. I contrast these with narrative's penchant for *polysemy* and *common ownership*.

Didacticism versus Polysemy

Philosophy is typically written didactically. That is, the philosopher usually intends to convey a specific message, working to ensure that the reader will come away with the same. For this reason, philosophical writing tends to prioritize the construction of "the argument" and the advancement of "the point." If there is any literary value to be found along the way in philosophical writing, this value is regarded as something that is at best an incidental, if suspicious, feature of the work.

This tendency appears most starkly in the "analytical" traditions of Anglo-American philosophy, but it also goes back much further to older, near-mathematical preoccupations with logic and argumentative structure. Syllogistic argumentation, for example, is an attempt to advance points in ways that are "sound" in the sense of completely disallowing alternative readings. All ornamentation is stripped away in an attempt to render a logical form that, because of its crystalline efficiency and transparency, cannot be denied. A different example of this penchant for logical parsimony is the radical doubt employed by René Descartes in his *Discourse on Method* (1637 [1999]). By systematically questioning everything until he arrives at a truth that (he believes) exists beyond all doubt, he seeks to produce unavoidable clarity at the foundation of his argument. His readers, he believes, cannot do other than accede to his line of thinking.[3]

Narrative illustration tends to operate in a very different manner. "What's the moral of the story?" is at best an entry-level question for literary interpretation. Stories that provide a clear "point" or moral therefore tend to be less celebrated by readers than those that invite multiple readings or those that, rather than hitting us over the head with didactic argumentation, contain wiles that work upon us more subtly. Rather than tracking linear paths toward a predetermined "point," the best stories contain thematic depths that we enjoy struggling to fathom. Rather than intending to impart singular messages, the best stories are generative and provocative, resulting in endless interpretation. In short, while didacticism is a virtue in philosophy, it tends to decrease the appeal of narratives.

Bakhtin (1929 [1984]) observed, for example, that Dostoevsky's novels, with their panoply of characters, allow for the airing of multiple lines of philosophical exploration, deepening and extending opposed views through their concomitant and contrasting airings within a single storyline. For Dostoevsky, however, the polyphonic approach is more than a simple means to air multiple lines of philosophical argumentation. Rather, Dostoevsky uses narrative context to temper rational argumentation, situating it alongside emotional, pistic, and aesthetic modes of human consideration. In *The Brothers Karamazov* (1879–1880), for example, Ivan's moral-philosophical perspective is presented as being undefeatable on logical-argumentative grounds even as, within the context of the novel itself, his arguments are overwhelmed by the humanity of the characters and their interactions with one another. As Kornelije Kvas (2019: 101) writes,

> The polyphonic novel and Dostoevsky's dialogicness of narration postulates the non-existence of the "final" word, which is why the thoughts, emotions and experiences of the world of the narrator and his/her characters are reflected through the words of another, with which they can never fully blend.

The strength of the polyphonic approach—and narrative polysemy generally—thus has little to do with the ability to land on a single "point" and make it "stick."

Elitism versus Common Ownership

Stories also have an ability to be *held in common* in a way that seldom obtains for philosophical writing and thinking. Purveyors of philosophical wisdom themselves often actively cultivate an air of exclusivity around their position and their work. In Plato's allegory of the cave, for example, everyone but the philosopher is consigned to see the world merely as shadows dancing on a cave wall. In Hegel's *Phenomenology of Spirit,* the first glow of self-awareness for the civilizational *Geist* appears in the mind of Hegel himself. Within Nietzsche's aristocratic ethic, a "people is a detour of nature to get to six or seven great men.—Yes, and then to get around them" (1886 [1992]: 277). These are just a few examples of the tendency on the part of philosophers to assume for themselves an elevated and exclusive vantage point. In stylistic terms, philosophical writing itself is often inaccessible, partly because it frequently requires a mastery of specialized language and knowledge of arcane historical-conceptual lineages, and because its texts demand rare powers of concentration. In its conceptual formulation, style, and presentational culture, then, we can say that philosophy is specifically *uncommon*.

Stories—if they are good stories—operate quite differently. Whereas philosophical writing demands active, intense concentration, stories immerse us in a world and hold us captive there. Whereas philosophical reading requires a careful tracking of where arguments fit within the history of ideas, narratives manifest within self-contained worlds that provide everything you need to follow along. Whereas philosophy requires a mastery of specialized jargon, narrative prose couches unfamiliar terms in contexts that assist us to understand their meaning, expanding our vocabularies, often without us even knowing it. In short, while philosophy requires hard work, stories sweep us away (Presser 2018).

Because stories capture us in their thrall, their path of dispersal through culture looks very different from that of philosophy. Like rhyme or melody, narrative plots function as a sort of mnemonic device, producing beats and tensions that resonate with our inborn need to anticipate completion, playing off our facility for pattern recognition. Thus, we remember stories, we recommend them, and in the act of telling and retelling, we achieve recognition and solidarity through them. For these reasons, stories have greater transmissibility and staying power than philosophical formulations, not only within our individual memories, but also (and perhaps especially) in wider cultural structures.

Storying the Good: Martin Luther King Jr. and the "I Have Been to the Mountaintop" Speech

So far, I have described a major theme—category expansion—that appears frequently in moral-philosophical attempts to increase goodness. I've also highlighted two stylistic contrasts—namely, didacticism versus polysemy and elitism versus commonality—that are salient to the persuasive power of philosophical versus narrative forms. In the remaining part of the chapter, I will integrate this thematic-stylistic analysis with an examination of Martin Luther King Jr.'s "I Have Been to the Mountaintop" speech, delivered at Mason Temple in Memphis in 1968.

It was King's last speech, delivered the day before his assassination. Typical of his public oratory, it had uncanny power. No retelling could substitute for direct viewing/listening, so I urge readers to access it for themselves.[4]

The occasion was an event supporting striking sanitation workers in Memphis. But in the speech, King spoke to a broad range of topics, from the politics of nonviolent direct action to the role leaders play in the movements they lead, to cautioning about the media's penchant for focusing on vandalism within the movement, to the utility of boycotts (Coca-Cola and Wonder Bread were current targets), to strengthening Black institutions, among other topics. For someone who by that time was widely recognized as being emblematic of the struggle for civil rights in its largest dimensions, King nevertheless remained very much "switched on" to the day-to-day operations of the movement in different locales.

But beyond these things, and above all, King told a story. His approach involved grand allegory, effecting a sense of symmetry and continuance with the biblical drama of liberation from slavery in ancient Egypt and the situation of Black citizens in midcentury America. Today it may be necessary to state the obvious, but for King and his audience, the characterological transpositions implied with this narrative overlay would have been immediately understood: Black Americans were the People of Israel, engaged in a righteous struggle for freedom. King was a modern-day Moses, a visionary leader, pointing toward the Promised Land. White oppressors were Pharaoh and the Egyptians, those who have committed the "sin of slavery" and who have perpetuated systems of oppression in a centuries-old project of nation building. By summoning this narrative and applying it the way he did in this speech (and in others, across his speaking career), King electrified contemporary understandings of the struggle for civil rights.

Undoubtedly, some of this power derived from the story's *scriptural* status. This was an ancient and holy tale, and it was being delivered by a charismatic Baptist minister from the pulpit. In this way, the allegory served to sacralize the claims of Black Americans, imparting moral authority to them as "God's chosen people." The application also opened up a fresh line of moral condemnation against White Americans, many of whom were Christian and would have been unnerved to find themselves positioned on the side of the villains in this familiar biblical tale.

Another important dimension of the speech's power, however, related to the simple fact that with this story, King was providing a *script*. Folkloric or traditional stories are teleological in that, by definition, everyone has heard them before and thus "already knows where they are going." The story of the Exodus fit into this category—as everyone knows, the "Promised Land" would be reached. But even in cases where there is a lack of such familiarity, stories are nevertheless telegraphic in the sense that they are set up with and impelled by narrative logics that listeners are meant to detect and follow, predictively. "Whodunit?" "Will they get back together?" These are by no means open questions. Rather, they are plot-figurational prompts that cast our minds down relatively narrow corridors of anticipation.[5] For King's story it was a different but no less familiar question: "Will they make it?" It is clear, here, that the answer is yes. With the scripted, forward-looking aspects of his biblical allegory, then, King was providing a sort of prophetic cipher that allowed his listeners to decode a plot that—they understood—was destined to arc toward redemptive justice.

Anyone conducting a sober examination of the asymmetries at hand would conclude that this arc was improbable. But for the genre within which King was working, this was all the better. Stacked odds were a *literary* necessity in this case—they were what made the plot interesting, inspiring, motivating. As a Christian reduction, King's story was a testament to the "mysterious ways" that God intervenes in human affairs. But the narrative's generic significance relates to the way that all "underdog" stories demand some form of extraordinary explanation (Joosse 2021). "Something else"—whether divine assistance, magical destiny, or the extraordinary qualities of a special character—must be buoying and propelling the protagonist along what is always an astonishingly unlikely course (Joosse 2018: 933). King makes reference to this "something" again and again in his speech, especially when ruminating on the difficulties faced by those engaged in the struggle against injustice:

> Something is happening in Memphis; something is happening in our world. And you know, if I were standing at the beginning of time, with the possibility of taking a kind of general and panoramic view of the whole of human history up to now, and the Almighty said to me, "Martin Luther King, which age would you like to live in?" I would take my mental flight by Egypt, and I would watch God's children in their magnificent trek from the dark dungeons of Egypt through, or rather across the Red Sea, through the wilderness on toward the Promised Land.

In these opening remarks, King describes the fate of his Memphian listeners as being somehow conjoined with that of the ancient Israelites. Speaking in this way, King was thus setting up for a bold claim. The triumph of the downtrodden against all odds almost never happens in real life—but it happens in stories all of the time. King was telling his listeners that this time, the story was real.

In the quote above, one can see how King's "panoramic view of the whole of human history" allows for a departure of sorts from the immediate concerns of the present, scaling up to a viewpoint from which the "grand plan" workings of God are more readily discernible. This move allows King to assert the primacy of a religious interpretive frame, speaking from a sort of sacred time that blurs between biblical and secular-historical realities. While this perspective is transcendent in the usual religious sense, we must at the same time recognize that it is transcendent in the *authorial* sense as well. That is, through this device of the "mental flight," King is able to address his listeners from the narrator's second-order location over and above the plot, prefacing the proceedings, selecting points for emphasis, and editorializing as he guides his audience's reception of the story he is telling.

After these opening remarks, King speeds quickly forward from this ancient Egyptian starting point, taking his listeners on a grand historical tour. The philosophical debates of Ancient Greece, the imperial expansion of Rome, the aesthetic innovations of the Renaissance, the ninety-five theses of the Reformation, the agonized vacillations of Lincoln prior to the Emancipation Proclamation, the desperate grappling of Roosevelt prior to the New Deal—King visits all of these on his journey, depicting them for his audience. But at each of these waypoints he is spurred onward, reciting the anaphora "But I wouldn't stop there." Until finally,

> But I wouldn't stop there [i.e., the New Deal era]. Strangely enough, I would turn to the Almighty, and say, "If you allow me to live just a few years in the second half of the twentieth century, I will be happy." Now that's a strange statement to make, because the world is all messed up. The nation is sick. Trouble is in the land. Confusion all around. That's a strange statement. But I know, somehow, that only when it is dark enough, can you see the stars. And I see God working in this period of the twentieth century in a way that men, in some strange way, are responding—something is happening in our world. And another reason I'm happy to live in this period is that we have been forced to a point where we're going to have to grapple with the problems that men have been trying to grapple with through history—but the demand didn't force them to do it. Survival demands that we grapple with them. . . . That is where we are today. And also in the human rights revolution: if something isn't done,

and in a hurry, to bring the colored peoples of the world out of their long years of poverty, their long years of hurt and neglect, the whole world is doomed. Now, I'm just happy that God has allowed me to live in this period, to see what is unfolding. And I'm happy that He's allowed me to be in Memphis.

The "strangeness" that King remarks on here relates to the notion that the "troubled," "sick," and "confused" present could be so charged with expectancy, that the current moment could in fact contain, if in concealed form, the arrival point for such an ancient and auspicious procession of events. By telling a story that begins with slavery in Egypt and culminates with the struggle for civil rights, King bestows significance and a sense of urgency to the "now"—*this* is the moment in the story we've been waiting for.

Another important aspect of the speech's power derived from the way that it narratively constructed King himself. That is, the crowd in Memphis was looking toward King not just as a beloved figure within the contemporary movement, but also as a central character within the grander religio-historical narrative that he was telling. They were gaining intimacy with King through the descriptions of *his* mental flight through history, *his* conversations with God, *his* process of formulating prophetic messages, and *his* ruminations on mortality. King does not shy away from the responsibilities implied by this narrative centrality, and nowhere is he more explicit about the personal-testimonial dimension of the story than in the final moments of his speech, where he uses the phrase "I have been to the mountaintop" to explicitly take on the mantle of Moses:

> I got into Memphis. And some began [to] . . . talk about the threats [to his life] that were out. What would happen to me, from some of our sick White brothers? Well, I don't know what will happen now. We've got some difficult days ahead. But it really doesn't matter with me now, because I've been to the mountaintop [*loud cheering*]. And I don't mind. Like anybody, I would like to live a long life. Longevity has its place. But I'm not concerned about that now. I just want to do God's will. And He's allowed me to go up to the mountain. And I've looked over. And I've seen the Promised Land [*growing cheers*]. I may not get there with you. But I

want you to know tonight that we, as a people, will get to the Promised Land! And so I'm happy, tonight. I'm not worried about anything. I'm not fearing any man! Mine eyes have seen the glory of the coming of the Lord!! [*roaring cheers*][6]

Again, the biblical allusions would have been eminently clear to all in the room: King, like Moses, is claiming special access to God, acting as an intercessor for his people. Like Moses, King is permitted to "climb the mountain" where God resides.[7] This vantage affords King, like Moses, a special and prophetic perspective, a direct line of sight to the "Promised Land" for which his people are destined, but which they cannot yet see.[8] Like Moses, King would die before seeing his prophecy fulfilled. And as it was with Moses, this tragic end was foretold (see Deuteronomy 32: 48–52 and Deuteronomy 34).

This reproduction of Moses in modern times served as its own form of evidence—literary evidence—for the remarkable "something" that was going on. The story was thus essential for this proof to have effect. Apart from the biblical narrative overlay, the proximity of the speech to King's assassination the next day could be written off as a tragic coincidence. As much as it was an outrage, King's murder was hardly surprising, given the ever-present threats to his life.[9] Instead, it was the *narrative* parallelism—culminating with his statement that he, like Moses "may not get there with you"—that lent a sense of the uncanny to events as they unfolded and that, after the killing, further served as a form of retrospective confirmation of the accuracy and authority of his prophetic vision. In short, it spoke to the truth of King's fiction.

Discussion and Conclusion

King's speeches are widely recognized as being consequential moments in America's ongoing "racial reckoning." In this sense, we can regard them, for the purposes of this chapter, as noteworthy bids to advance the good within society. With the above narrative description of King's "mountaintop" speech in hand, we can now turn back to the central aim of this chapter, which is to comparatively assess narrative versus moral-philosophical strategies of good-making.

As with the opening sections of the chapter, the analysis relates firstly to the theme of category expansion and secondly to the rhetorical contrasts of (a) didacticism/polysemy and (b) elitism/common ownership. I will deal with these in reverse order.

Elitism versus Common Ownership in King's Speech

At the outset we should note that, like the philosopher, King claims an elevated position for himself—a mountaintop perch from which he can see much farther than those he leads. But this initial similarity should not be allowed to obscure a more fundamental difference relating to the *source* of power in King's case as compared with that of the traditional philosopher. That is, the forms of expression that led to King's elevation did not involve displays of rarefied expertise or a mastery of abstruse material. (As someone who wrote a PhD dissertation on the philosophy of Paul Tillich, King certainly could have chosen this style of delivery.) Instead, King approached his audience by invoking one of the most immediately recognizable of stories—a story that they would have heard their entire lives (Shearing 2020). Thus, the sociocultural territory King was traversing here was, unlike traditional philosophical terrain, very much *common ground.*

The communal pre-presence of this narrative also meant that there was no need for King to engage in an exhaustive retelling. A phrase alone (which no doubt would have gone unnoticed by those "without ears to hear") was all that was needed to call to mind an entire universe of moral-political meanings. In this way, King's speech shows how commonly owned narratives can offer a shortcut to understanding and a direct line to the heart.

For the same reasons, the credibility of King's authority within the movement was also commonly owned. That is, the legitimacy of the mantle King was claiming resided within the *recognition* that his audience experienced when they were in his presence. As Carl Couch (1989: 268) noted in his examination, King

> did not seek leadership during the early stages of the civil rights movement. . . . Others began to think of him as their leader at the time . . .

[and] it was not until sometime later that he assumed the identity of the leader of the civil rights movement, [a role that] was the consequence of action initiated by others.

King, like Moses, was thus initially oblivious to the leadership role that was awaiting him (Moses was initially aghast at being asked to lead, protesting that he was "slow of speech, and slow of tongue"). As such, both King and Moses responded to their people's suffering (in the Durkheimian inversion, to "God's call") only with great reluctance (Exodus 3:9–4:17).

So, in these readings, neither of these storytelling leaders grasped after power or elite status.[10] Rather, as it had been with all charismatic leaders, their capacity to serve as a source for cultural meanings depended upon an interactional process of mutual recognition between leader and following (Joosse 2017). In the recording, one can hear that with every allegorical link King promulgated—between himself and Moses; between America's "racial sins" and bondage in Egypt; and between the "mysterious" interventions of God in both contexts—he was met by enthusiastic cheers of recognition from what was clearly a resonant audience. In short, like all storytellers, he was ever at the mercy of his audience. King's mountaintop speech thus demonstrates the salience of common ownership to the persuasive power of good-making initiatives.

Didacticism versus Polysemy in King's Speech

There is a danger when invoking well-known stories of sounding trite, or of having listeners' eyes glaze over. But as we've seen, King avoided the potentially pernicious effects of didacticism by exercising a light touch, making only choice, quick references to the story. This sparing treatment worked to conserve and concentrate the narrative's power, resulting in excited flashes of recognition each time it was conjured. This was no Sunday school lesson.

Unencumbered by demands of pedantic exposition, and confident that his audience would be right there with him, King was free to creatively engage with more of the story's polysemic affordances. Myths endure because of their ability to transcend their context of origination and mediate the present, lending a sense of significance to contemporary events. As we've seen, King's treatment was particularly effective at reanimating the Exodus story, bestowing it with a thrilling and politically subversive sense of immediacy. It is hard to overstate the importance of this feeling—that the story was *awake and breathing*—to movement morale. Normally, there is a tendency to regard "Bible times" as somehow bygone and beyond our grasp; to believe that miracles no longer happen and that spiritual logics have no bearing on the present; to think that God no longer intervenes in history, having somehow grown deaf to our prayers. For Christians living in a putatively secular age, this is a particularly dispiriting outlook. Part of King's power, then, derives from his dramatic repudiation of this sort of cultural deism. By invoking this biblical tale and applying it in the way he did, he was showing that the story of struggle between God's people and the forces of evil was *very much alive*.

This conviction, in turn, fostered a moral confidence that was crucial for the movement's efforts to assert its claims. The civil rights struggle was beset by objections on all sides, not only by unreconstructed racists who condemned the movement outright, but also, and perhaps most challengingly, by liberal Whites who were calling for patience and advocating for incrementalism in the pursuit of racial justice.[11] Petitioners of this sort invariably style themselves as well-meaning and reasonable—as "allies" who simply prefer a different, more prudent approach to effecting change. But King quashes all such motions with a revelatory moral statement pertaining to "Who's Who" in the story: "*We* are the Israelites," King is saying. "And *you* are Pharaoh."

This statement is striking in a saturnalian sense in that it constitutes a dramatic reversal of customary polarities within America's moral culture. While Americans reliably draw satisfaction from various portrayals of their nation—as a manifestation of reason, as a bastion of freedom, as a "nation founded on Judeo-Christian values"—King's story cut a decidedly different figure. This was America the Great Sphinx: fraught with contradiction, hewn in unfreedom, beastly, *ungodly*. The narrative alchemy at work here is thus clear: as King trained his narrator's eye on different actors and objects, he transfigured them. In this instance, all well-meaning half-measures and all "reasonable" compromises were revealed as hideous forms of complicity with America's moral failure. The only place for such motions was with Pharaoh, at the bottom of the sea.

All of this alchemy was possible because, like all biblical tales, the Exodus story makes itself endlessly available as a frame for interpreting the present. Drawing on the polysemic affordances of story, King was therefore able to creatively and consequentially intervene within America's moral culture, strengthening initiatives to advance the good.

Category Expansion and Increasing the Good in King's Speech

Finally, we can turn to category expansion. As described in the chapter's opening, this is one of moral philosophy's most timeworn "good-making" strategies. The civil rights movement itself can be interpreted as a collective push for category expansion, and one can surmise that most civil rights leaders would agree with the general thrust of the philosophy examined so far. In King's case, the most explicit and programmatic statements to this effect can be found in his "I Have a Dream" speech:

> When the architects of our great republic wrote the magnificent words of the Constitution and the Declaration of Independence, they were signing a promissory note to which every American was to fall heir. This note was a promise that all men—yes, Black men as well as White men—would be guaranteed the inalienable rights of life, liberty and the pursuit of happiness. It is obvious today that America has defaulted on this promissory note insofar as her citizens of color are concerned.

King's "mountaintop" speech contains a pithier formulation: "All we say to America is, 'Be true to what you said on paper.'" The basic criticism, then, is that America has not lived up to the categorical commitments made in its founding documents. America thus represents the ruinous effects of failed actualization, of category expansion stalled.

But therein lies the problem: actualization. As I mentioned in the opening, the contention of this chapter is that philosophical and narrative strategies can be distinguished from one another on the basis of whether they actually help to bring about good. When we consider philosophy as a comparator, the approaches surveyed so far seem for the most part uninterested in this question. If anything, there seems to be an unstated presumption of undeniability or automaticity to the processual aspects of category expansion in moral philosophy. This presumption starts with the point of origin for ethical movement—the rational thinking subject—which in the modernist conceit is universally self-same and naturally possessed by all. The subjective preconditions for realizing projects of category expansion are thus always automatically in place and at the ready. From this starting point, progress is thought to carry forward almost as a logical necessity. As described earlier, a consciousness of the argument *alone* is meant to compel humans, as rational agents, toward an agreement about the need to extend ethical consideration outwards. In this way, the argument itself is conceived as a powerfully transformative reagent. As an admixture to social discourse, it is thought to be sufficient for catalyzing social change.

This presumption of automaticity does not mean that philosophers who spark off such processes are above receiving credit, however. After all (so the thinking goes), considerable perspicacity is required to see moral needs before anyone else. And articulating society's ethical deficiencies is a significant intellectual achievement in its own right. What's more, moral congratulations are also in order: since these ethical extensions issue from those (the philosophers) who already possess moral standing and are then dispensed toward those who do not, they are by definition acts of generosity. Progress in these models is thus depicted as something that emerges out of a self-satisfied comradery of enlightened and eminently "reasonable" individuals who occupy an ethical vanguard and who engage in acts of rational benevolence.

Perhaps this description of philosophy—as a chummy and self-congratulatory bonhomie of togas and tweed—is uncharitable. But as mentioned earlier, I have chosen to err on the side of caricature in order to accentuate the central contrast. For its part, King's storied depiction of how change occurs is dramatically different. As a Black man who lived through the centenary of the Emancipation Proclamation, King was particularly well positioned to be skeptical of the notion that ideas alone are enough to instigate change. If there's any word that captures King's storied rendering of how change happens, it would be *struggle*. There is nothing inevitable or taken for granted in his vision.

One can see, for example, that within King's story, the demand for racial justice originates not with someone who already possesses status. Rather, it issues from those who suffer injustice. In this vision, those in positions of comfort are unlikely to be generous or benevolent when confronted with the differentials that constitute their privilege. Rather, the hands of the powerful must be forced, as happened with the Pharaoh.[12] King was cognizant of these things, and his interventions demonstrate the forceful, emotional power that can be unleashed with stories. Rather than inviting his audience to partake in dispassionate contemplation or intellectual exercise, and rather than offering an opportunity for self-congratulation, King uses a story to confront listeners—supporters and detractors alike—with a moral reality from which there can be no retreat.

The characterological transpositions in King's allegory can also be read as a form of place-switching, as per Rawls's "veil of ignorance" heuristic. But again, the style and process here are very different. Although his story involves dramatic forms of imaginative self-emplotment, these moves aren't done as a means of accessing empathic identification with "lower-placed" individuals, as in Rawls's philosophy. King and his fellow travelers hardly needed to summon hypotheticals or engage in thought experiments to imagine injustice. The very existence of a device like the one invented by Rawls thus speaks to the privilege of its user. Further, in the light of King's approach, the desire to relocate moralizing to some rationally distantiated "original position" outside society begins to look suspect, in so far as it threatens to divert attention away from all-too-real injustices in the here and now.

For all of these reasons, King frequently warns against over-intellectualization in his "mountaintop" speech. Witness, for example, his digression about the scriptural lead-up to the story of the Good Samaritan:

> One day a man came to Jesus, and he wanted to raise some questions about some vital matters of life. At points he wanted to trick Jesus, and show him that he knew a little more than Jesus knew, and throw him off base. . . . Now that question could have easily ended up in a philosophical and theological debate. But Jesus immediately pulled that question from mid-air, and placed it on a dangerous curve between Jerusalem and Jericho [the location of the Good Samaritan tale]. And he talked about a certain man, who fell among thieves [at this point King proceeds to tell the story of the Good Samaritan].

In King's view, therefore, all systems of thought—whether philosophical or theological—can very easily miss the point if they lose contact with the ethical demands that call out to us from life itself. A student of philosophy and systematic theology, King knew all about elevated settings of contemplation. He was aware of the enticements of philosophical debate, and so he warns about philosophical distraction, obfuscation, and the potential for philosophical preoccupations to become a lurking ground for bad faith. In his "mountaintop" speech, he makes sure to give credit to philosophy where it is due, even expressing great reverence for "Plato, Aristotle, Socrates, Euripides and Aristophanes, assembled around the Parthenon as they discussed the great and eternal issues of reality." But as we've seen, his story does not end in the company of these figures. He brushes quickly past them on his way to Memphis.

NOTES
1 Examples are Plato's allegory of the cave, Kierkegaard's meditations on the story of Abraham and Isaac, and the novels of Simone de Beauvoir.
2 In a section entitled "The Ethical Sequence," Leopold (1949 [1970]: 238–39) outlines his theory of expansion involving a move from individual-to-individual ethical relations, to individual-to-society relations, to a "land ethic" involving humanity's "relation to land and to the animals and plants which grow upon it."
3 *Cogito, ergo sum*—"I think, therefore I am."
4 The speech can be viewed at https://www.youtube.com/watch?v=-dgcMTn2lY8. Only audio is available for the majority of the clip, but the titular "I have been to the mountaintop" portion includes video from 41:38 onward.
5 The "twist" also depends on this phenomenon of narratively generated expectation, and is in this sense no less teleological. With respect to the "Whodunit?" question, for example, the answer always is "Someone you'd least expect"—a contradiction we invariably find quite pleasing.
6 Video for this section occurs at minute 41:19 here: https://www.youtube.com/watch?v=-dgcMTn2lY8&t=2178s.
7 In the biblical setting, others who so much as touched such sacred mountains were to be put to death.
8 In the biblical tale, Moses summits Mount Nebo, from which one can see the entire Jordan Valley.
9 Just before the "mountaintop" portion of the speech, King described the state of threat in which he was living, including his security team's worries about his plane the day prior. For more on the threats to King during his lifetime, see King Institute (2022).
10 For some criticisms of charismatic power, particularly its gendered dimensions as it has applied to King, see Joosse and Willey 2020.

11 For King's most pointed response to these arguments, see "Letter from Birmingham Jail" (1963b [1992]) and his "I Have a Dream" speech (1963a [2022]), where he condemns "the tranquilizing drug of gradualism."
12 In the Exodus narrative, Moses secures an agreement from Pharaoh for his people's freedom, only to have it revoked ten times.

REFERENCES

Augustine of Hippo. 426 [2009]. *The City of God*. Peabody, MA: Hendrickson.

Bakhtin, M. M. 1929 [1984]. *Problems of Dostoevsky's Poetics*. Edited and translated by Caryl Emerson. Minneapolis: University of Minnesota Press.

Buber, Martin. 1923 [1970]. *I and Thou*. Translated by Walter Kaufmann. New York: Scribners.

Couch, Carl J. 1989. "From Hell to Utopia and Back to Hell: Charismatic Relationships." *Symbolic Interaction* 12 (2): 265–79.

Descartes, René. 1637 [1999]. *Discourse on Method and Meditations on First Philosophy*. Indianapolis: Hackett.

Dostoyevsky, Fyodor. 1879–1880 [2003]. *The Brothers Karamazov*. London: Penguin.

Hegel, Georg Wilhelm Friedrich. 1807 [2018]. *The Phenomenology of Spirit*. Oxford: Oxford University Press.

Joosse, Paul. 2017. "Max Weber's Disciples: Theorizing the Charismatic Aristocracy." *Sociological Theory* 35 (4): 334–58.

Joosse, Paul. 2018. "Countering Trump: Toward a Theory of Charismatic Counter-Roles." *Social Forces* 97 (2): 921–44.

Joosse, Paul. 2021. "Narratives of Rebellion." *European Journal of Criminology* 18 (5): 735–54.

Joosse, Paul, and Robin Willey. 2020. "Gender and Charismatic Power." *Theory and Society* 49 (4): 533–61.

Kant, Immanuel. 1785 [2012]. *Groundwork for the Metaphysics of Morals*. Edited and translated by Mary Gregor and Jens Timmerman. Cambridge: Cambridge University Press.

King, Martin Luther, Jr. 1963a [2022]. "I Have a Dream." Speech delivered at the March on Washington, August 28, 1963. Available at "Read Martin Luther King Jr.'s 'I Have a Dream' Speech in Its Entirety," NPR, January 16, 2023, www.npr.org.

King, Martin Luther, Jr. 1963b [1992]. "Letter from Birmingham Jail." *UC Davis Law Review* 26: 835.

King, Martin Luther, Jr. 1968. "I've Been to the Mountaintop." Speech delivered at Mason Temple, Memphis, Tennessee, April 3. Available at American Rhetoric website, www.americanrhetoric.com (text) and YouTube, https://www.youtube.com/watch?v=-dgcMTn2lY8. Accessed December 18, 2022.

King Institute. 2022. "Martin Luther King, Jr.—Threats/Attacks Against." Martin Luther King, Jr. Research and Education Institute, Stanford University. https://kinginstitute.stanford.edu. Accessed December 18, 2022.

Kvas, Kornelije. 2019. *The Boundaries of Realism in World Literature*. Lanham, MD: Lexington.

Leopold, Aldo. 1949 [1970]. *A Sand County Almanac: With Other Essays on Conservation from Round River*. New York: Ballantine.

Mill, John Stuart. 1863 [2015]. *Utilitarianism*. London: Parker, Son, and Bourn.

Nietzsche, Friedrich. 1886 [1992]. *Beyond Good and Evil*. In *Basic Writings of Nietzsche*, translated by Walter Kaufmann, 179–435. New York: Modern Library.

Plato. 375 BCE [2007]. *The Republic*. Translated by Desmond Lee. New York: Penguin Classics.

Presser, Lois. 2018. *Inside Story: How Narratives Drive Mass Harm*. Berkeley: University of California Press.

Rawls, John. 1971 [2020]. *A Theory of Justice*. Cambridge, MA: Harvard University Press.

Shearing, Linda S. 2020. "Moses and Popular Culture." In *The Oxford Handbook of the Bible and American Popular Culture*, edited by Dan W. Clanton Jr. and Terry R. Clark, 31–45. New York: Oxford University Press.

Singer, Peter. 1973 [2015]. *Animal Liberation: The Definitive Classic of the Animal Movement*. New York: Open Road Media.

Twain, Mark. 1881 [2011]. *The Prince and the Pauper*. Berkeley: University of California Press.

6

"The Places I Could Go"

A Good Story of Probation

FERGUS MCNEILL

In some recent work, both alone and with others, I have explored how people who are or have been subject to penal supervision have chosen to represent and relate their experiences. This work has used both visual methods (Fitzgibbon, Graebsch, and McNeill 2017) and collaborative songwriting (Scott and McNeill 2021; McNeill 2018, 2019), generating a mixture of photographic, lyrical, and sonic representations. Pictures and songs—and the narratives that emerge in their production, exchange, and reception—also tell stories.

I have heard many stories of penal supervision. Often, though to varying degrees, these have been "bad stories," or at least stories of bad experiences. Accordingly, I have often framed my analysis within the context of other work—both ethnographic and interview-based—that has sought to expose and analyze the pains of probation (e.g., Durnescu 2011; Hayes 2015), rehabilitation (e.g., Cox 2017; Crewe 2011), and reentry (e.g., Miller 2021). For example, my development of the concept of the "Malopticon" was based on various engagements with "Teejay," a Scottish man more than a decade into lifelong parole. My conversations with Teejay centered first on making sense of a series of photographs he produced to represent his experiences, and then on cowriting a song together called "Blankface."[1] Referencing Bentham's famous Panopticon prison design, and Foucault's (1977) associated analysis on the *disciplinary* effects of surveillance, the idea of the Malopticon drew attention to how the apparatus of penal supervision provided not so much discipline (as in the Panopticon) as degradation and misrecognition. The Malopticon is an apparatus that sees its subjects badly, that sees them as bad, and that projects to wider society their badness (McNeill 2019). In the context of this book, we might consider the Malopticon to be a coercive penal-institutional apparatus for the coercive production, imposition, and projection of "bad stories" or even "stories of the bad." In other words, the Malopticon forces degrading and distorting stories upon its subjects.

However, a little while later, I used the experience of cowriting a second song, "Helping Hand," with "John," to refine my analysis (McNeill 2018). I noticed that John did not experience his parole supervision as "Maloptical," for three main reasons. Unlike Teejay, he found post-release supervision to be practically helpful (at least some of the time), morally legitimate (as part of a sentence that he felt deserved), and time-limited. Whereas Teejay was stuck on supervision for life and felt himself to be permanently degraded by his lifelong parole license, John was passing through the experience. His supervision story may not have been "good" exactly, but it was certainly much better than Teejay's.

Inspired by the contrasts between these two songs (and the associated stories of supervision), and for the purposes of this collection, I decided to trawl my research files for the most positive story of supervision that I have been told across quite a wide range of related research projects. I wanted to see what could be learned from a *very* "good story" of probation supervision. But before I come to the story "Mary" told me, it is necessary to explain the context in which she told it.

An Oral History of Scottish Probation: The Good, the Bad, and the Ugly

In 2008–2009, I undertook a small-scale study of Scottish probation in the 1960s, with the help of my colleague Beth Weaver. The study was motivated simply by curiosity about a largely forgotten period of probation history that preceded the major organizational restructuring instigated by the Social Work (Scotland) Act 1968 (see Kelly 2017). That act effectively abolished separate, locally organized Scottish probation services, transferring their functions to local authority social work departments, thus establishing the unusual context for "Justice Social Work" that endures in Scotland to this day. In the year or two preceding the study, conversations with veterans of 1960s probation had led me to question the "meta-story" of probation development offered in "official" sources of the period—essentially a history of steady evolution from a series of improvised and somewhat disordered local initiatives to the establishment of a social scientifically informed and increasingly professionalized service, available nationwide (see McNeill 2005).

Beth and I managed to trace and interview thirteen former probation practitioners and educators and twelve former probationers. The probationers included eleven men and one woman (Mary), ranging in age (at the time of the interview) from fifty-two to seventy. They were recruited through newspaper adverts and were then interviewed either at home, at the university, or by telephone, depending on their preference.[2] All the interviews were audio-recorded and transcribed in full. As is common in oral history research, the interviews were loosely structured and ranged in duration from just under twenty minutes to over an hour. Seven had been on probation for property offenses, two for violence or disorder, one for carrying an offensive weapon, and one for truancy. One could not remember the offense that led to probation. All the probationers came from the West of Scotland and nine of them had been on probation as juveniles (the median age at the time of the first order was 13.5 years). At that time in Scotland, probation was mainly used for juveniles, for first offenders, and for minor offenses (Arnott and Duncan 1970). The probation stories that the former probationers told might be described as ranging from the good to the bad to the downright ugly. While, as we will see below, some described very positive experiences indeed, one recounted experiences of physical abuse and another reported sexual abuse by a probation officer (McNeill 2010).

Our analysis of these stories led me to characterize 1960s probation as an experience that involved "helping, hurting, and holding," sometimes simultaneously (McNeill 2009). As well as outright abuse, the "hurting" aspect also referred (much like the more recent studies cited above) to the pains of supervision itself—often felt keenly where officers were judged to have betrayed probationers' trust or to have enforced orders unjustly (see McNeill and Robinson 2012). The "holding" aspect referred to the constraints of supervision and the experience of being subject to surveillance—not just directly from the officer but also by family members, police officers, and church leaders with whom officers sometimes liaised, creating dense networks of informal control. Surveillance could be experienced simultaneously as being both burdensome and supportive. The "helping" aspect referred to those positive experiences of supervision characterized by the kind concern and attention of officers doing all in their power to assist the probationers to improve their lives. Although some felt that officers had few resources at their disposal, the ways they used their skills and the sorts of virtues and qualities that they modelled to probationers were not, apparently, without impact.

In the "good stories," the combination of kindness and practical assistance had profound and positive consequences that altered life trajectories and not just offending careers. Most of those with more positive experiences of probation (and six of the twelve overall) went on to work or volunteer in caring roles themselves. As we will see below, Mary became a nurse; another became a justice social worker, another a lay member of the Children's Panel,[3] another a volunteer boxing coach, another a volunteer prison visitor, and another a welfare rights officer. These involvements in "generative" activities (Maruna 2001) may well owe something to the probationers' exposure to role models who enabled them to believe in who they might become.

This was a small-scale study and one that relied on memories of events experienced about fifty years previously, raising obvious questions both about generalizability to present-day practice and about reliance on recall of now-distant memories. Yet this half-century gap might also have been an asset. Unlike contemporary supervisees, the participants in our study were a long way removed from the forms of penal control they were discussing, and they were recruited directly by researchers rather than through probation services, meaning that both selection and social desirability effects might have been less likely to skew the findings (see Durnescu, Enengl, and Grafl 2013). Both the long time-gap and the mode of recruitment might also have encouraged people with more memorable and significant stories (positive or negative) to come forward, although one or two participants did relate experiences they themselves regarded as banal and unimportant. Importantly, the half-century gap also meant that participants were well placed to make their own judgment about the significance or insignificance of their probation stories, viewed through the long lens, as it were, of a mature life history.

From Oral History to Narrative Criminology

The editors of this volume and other collaborators have energized and refined narrative criminology both as a theoretical lens and as a methodological approach (see, e.g., Fleetwood et al. 2019). Since writing this chapter has involved a *post hoc* application of narrative criminological concepts and tools to an oral history interview, in the remainder of this section I briefly summarize those concepts and tools that I found most useful in this process.[4]

Presser has argued that criminologists must move beyond a focus merely on the *content* of narratives, "either as record or as interpretation," to paying careful attention to *how* they communicate and with what *effects* (Presser 2009, 2012). More recently, she has urged close attention to the *unsaid* in narratives (and other types of discourses), analyzing what omissions do, what interpretations they invite, and what they conceal (Presser 2023). Analyzing the unsaid matters in large part because it can help to reveal how omissions and silences produce and reflect the power relations that shape both stories and lives. It follows that no critical approach to narrative can set the unsaid aside.

Attending to the unsaid also connects to the role of *tropes* in narratives. Sandberg (2016) suggests that tropes often appear in the form of single words or phrases within narratives; they connect the story in question with wider cultural narratives and assumptions, reflecting and sometimes reinforcing dominant discourses. But since the connection is implied rather than explicit, tropes also leave room for audience interpretation and ambiguity. In this sense, there is an unsaid cultural hinterland that lies behind the tropes we find in stories, which those tropes tap into.

Tropes are only one of three overlapping and interconnected narrative forms that Sandberg (2016) identifies; the others are *life stories* and *event stories*. Accounts of temporality and causality are often considered definitive features of narratives: The stories we tell typically locate, contextualize, and relate events within sequences, with implications for how we understand how one event produces another. Summarizing crudely, *life stories* make sense of lives (and of the chronologies of life courses) and help to craft identities, while *event stories* account for episodes, rendering them significant or otherwise.

With respect to how we might analyze narratives, drawing on the work of Riessman (2008) and others, Sandberg (2022) distinguishes four approaches, three of which are relevant here. Thematic analysis focuses mainly on the content of narratives, on *what the stories are about*. Performative analysis examines *how stories are constituted and shared* in the telling; this includes attention to the context in which that performance is situated, and attention to *who is telling the story, to whom, and why?* Dialogical narrative analysis is more concerned with *which voices and whose voices can be found within stories*. With respect to both performance and dialogue, Gubrium and Holstein's (2008) approach to "narrative ethnography" demands attention to the *co-construction* of narratives in the complex interactions between stories' contexts, actors, and actions.

Evidently, when Beth and I first analyzed the oral history project interviews in 2009–2010, our approach was not informed by any of this literature. Rather, relying on oral history methods, we focused primarily on understanding the nature of 1960s probation. With hindsight, ours was a *thematic analysis* mainly concerned with the *content* of *event stories*, although to varying extents these were often contextualized within broader *life stories*, however briefly sketched.

In re-analyzing Mary's story below, I retain a focus on the thematic content of the interview, not least because that matters in thinking about what is "good" within this story. That said, drawing on the resources of narrative criminology, I also want to try to attend more carefully to the *unsaid*, to refer briefly to *tropes* in Mary's narrative, and to explore some of the *performative* and *dialogical* dynamics involved both in its *co-construction* (at the time) and in its telling to me. Though some have warned of the risks of narratives "distorting into clarity" realities that are complex, fragmented, and unsettled (Law 2010: 2), in this chapter, I am interested precisely in how Mary's clarification of her story—including in dialogue with me as her interviewer—works to make this a "good story" *for her*, and one that she thought it important to tell.

Before we proceed, it is important to acknowledge a problem with apparently "good stories" told by people who are or have been subject to state punishment. As Crockett Thomas et al. (2021) point out, drawing on Carolyn Steedman's (2000) work, these may often be "enforced narratives"—the sorts of story that poor and marginalized people have been compelled to offer in exchange for aid or clemency, ever since the development of the modern state. As such, they may tell us more about the institutionalized contexts of the stories' production than their narrators' lives or selves (cf. Fleetwood 2015). Mary's story is also interesting against this backdrop partly because, by the time of its telling to me, the storyteller was half a century away from these institutional forces. But it is also interesting because that telling also seems to reveal something important about how—even within institutional contexts shaped for and by penal forces—it might be possible for two differently situated people to negotiate the coauthorship of a good story. In other words, Mary's story may reveal something about how particular forms and styles of narrative engagement, even in penal spaces, might be good (and do good).

Mary's Story

In what follows, I have altered names and minor details to protect the anonymity of those involved. Mary is a pseudonym (as are all the names of people, places, and institutions used below), but I present her story in her own words as much as possible, leaving the core content intact and conveying as much possible *how* she told it.

The person who entered my office to talk about her time on probation wasn't who or what I was expecting at all. She could hardly have been more different from most of the people on probation or parole I had met when I was a social worker in the 1990s. Everything about Mary's self-presentation conveyed middle-class respectability. Indeed, she reminded me very much of older women I had seen at church every Sunday in my childhood. The resemblance was not just in how Mary dressed (i.e., smartly); it was also in the way she carried herself—with the same mixture of modesty, propriety, and self-assurance. Perhaps it was to protect this respectability that she had elected to meet me in the privacy of my university office.

At first, Mary seemed nervous—perhaps because at the heart of our conversation was something so starkly at odds with the respectability she embodied. Yet somehow, she also conveyed resolution and determination. She spoke quietly but clearly, and she kept her chin up and met my eye from time to time. It was clear to me that she had responded to the newspaper advert because she had a story that she wanted to tell, perhaps even a story that she felt she *should* or *must* tell. Even so, I did not get the impression that this was a well-rehearsed narrative; on the contrary, I suspect that she came because her story had been untold (or at least very rarely told). For Mary, now in her sixties, the interview was a chance to recognize and record a life-changing encounter she had experienced as a teenager, very likely breaking a long silence about her past.

In the early 1960s, shortly before her seventeenth birthday, Mary was placed on probation for two years. She and a friend had stolen some low-value items from a high-street shop. This was her second offense. A couple of years earlier, her parents had paid a fine after she had been charged with vandalism; she had been one of a group of young people who had broken a shop-front window.

By way of context, Mary explained that, having passed the qualifying exam, she had gained entry to a good local secondary school. She harbored ambitions of a career in journalism and dreamed of travelling the world. However, her home life was not happy. She was the second-eldest in a large family that, like many others, had moved from Glasgow's urban slums to its newly built peripheral public housing schemes in the two decades following the Second World War. She described her father as "a bit of a Jekyll and Hyde, you know, a weekend drinker who created havoc."

Despite her obvious academic ability and her ambitions, Mary's parents made clear that she would be leaving school at age fifteen to go out to work so that she could contribute to the family's income:

> So I thought, what's the point of me going, being at Hopeville High School, you know. I'm not—I'm going to have to leave when I'm fifteen. So I kind of rebelled a bit and I was a bit wild, I was a bit wild. Left school at fifteen, went to work in a machine factory, which was, to me was like a sweatshop—absolutely horrendous! You know, and I used to sit there and look about all these hundreds of machines and all these women, they were doing it, "piecework" it was called, and I thought, "God, no I can't, I can't do this, I can't do it!" Actually, I got the sack from there because I wasn't making anything, I was too busy. But, of course, I couldn't tell my mum and I used to pretend I was going to work, and I would go and sit

in the library until it was time to go home, and then I would go home. So I had a succession of jobs and I just didn't enjoy them, horrible, kept getting the sack or I just didn't go back, and then, as I said, I went into Bennett's one day. I pinched a lipstick, she pinched a scarf, and we were caught—ha, ha, ha!

Mary described what it was like going to court:

Horrible! It—actually—I was expecting judges with wigs and I was absolutely terrified, but it wasn't like that at all, actually, it was just a desk with I think about three people sitting at it. And I remember people to the right and to the left of me. My father was there too, and that's really all. That bit was kind of vague. . . .

FERGUS: And do you remember at all, and this is asking a lot, but do you remember . . . what the judge said to you at the time?
MARY: Yes, I remember that. He couldn't understand because I went to a good school. I remember him saying that, that because I went to Hopeville he couldn't understand why I had done this and—that bit stuck in my mind, about going to—he gave me a lecture and how it didn't look good on the school and blah, blah, blah, that part I remember.

Though she did not elaborate on what precisely made this experience so "horrible" (despite being less court-like and formal than she had expected), my impression was that what she recoiled from in the memory was the mixture of shame and embarrassment associated with it; her description of "people to the right and to the left" of her gives the impression of her being surrounded by their disapproving gaze.

Mary's first experience with probation was no better. She had to travel a long way from her peripheral housing scheme to a city center probation office, where she met a stern-sounding woman probation officer in her late thirties whom she described as appearing "very professional" and "well-dressed":

That was a bit of a trek—because at that time we'd moved to Holyhill, you know—to go down there, and I went down. It was one evening, it was evening—went down and was called in, and it actually didn't go very well. You know, I thought, "I don't like you." . . . From what I can remember about it, there was absolutely nothing, I just—I couldn't communicate with her, you know, it wasn't—you know, I would go in and "How are you?"—"Fine"— "How are things going?" She never asked how things were at home or anything like that, and "Are you working yet?" and "When are you going to find a job? I think it's time you found a job," you know, and it was things like that and I just couldn't communicate with her, I just couldn't communicate with her.

Fortunately, as it turned out, after about six months, this officer—whose name Mary could not recall—instructed her that her supervision was being transferred to another probation officer in a different office.

> MARY: And I had to go to there, oh I can't remember, two or three weeks' time or something like that. But she said the letter would be sent. So the letter came and I went to the office and I met Grace Carswell, and I can honestly say Grace Carswell turned my life around.
> FERGUS: Okay.
> MARY: We hit it off straight away, you know. She was really, really fantastic. And instead of having to, coming into town to the probation office, I ended up going to see her in a school, in a primary school which was just down the road, and she said I was to go once a week, she saw me once a week. And it was really good, you know. I was able to tell her about my home life, you know, and how miserable that I felt, and she asked me what I wanted to do with my life and, you know, we just hit it off, we just hit it off. And on the occasions, you know, she'd say occasionally to come to the office in town and I would go . . . and she'd take me to tea in town, it was called Miss Cranstoun's. Now, you must remember here I was a seventeen-year-old, terrible background, you know, I never had any money, and she would take me into this beautiful tearoom, you know, where all these well-dressed people were sitting and, with the cake-stand, the waiter coming and, you know, I'd be sitting—I was absolutely overawed—overawed with it! And I thought, "Gosh, she's brought me here!" you know, she's brought me here. So then—

FERGUS: Just a bit—what did that convey to you, that she'd brought you there? What did it mean to you?

MARY: I think it said that she liked me and, you know, and she listened to what I was saying. And also sitting there and looking round as well, and I thought, "I could be here too, I could do this as well," you know. "This is what I want to do, this is what I want to do."

FERGUS: Okay.

MARY: And then it got on we started talking about what, you know, well, she did ask me what I wanted to do and I had said to her, you know, I had always wanted to be a journalist and I had always wanted to travel, you know, and I told her I never got the opportunity. She knew all that.

FERGUS: Uh-huh.

MARY: And then we started talking about that, you know, I . . . left school at fifteen, absolutely nothing, absolutely nothing and no qualifications whatsoever. So she said to me about nursing, she said, "Do you ever think about nursing, Mary?" and of course I just laughed at her and I thought, "Gosh, no, no, no." And I said, "I wouldn't get into nursing, I don't have any qualifications." She was looking at it from the aspect because I wanted to travel and I think, when I look back, she was saying, "Here is your opportunity to travel." I also think, as well she knew, and I knew, that I had to get out of the environment that I was living in, you know, I had to get out of there or else nothing would have worked. So she encouraged me to write and I wrote to Heystoun Hospital . . . , so I wrote there and got the interview and thought, "Oh my God," and went for the interview and I was accepted. I was accepted . . . to do an enrolled nurse two-year course then, and I was absolutely delighted. My mother was not happy at all; she said I would last six weeks at it and of course she had to go and [get]—I think they called it a Provident cheque or something—a ten-pound Provident cheque because I had to get shoes and the wee fob watch and things like that.[5]

FERGUS: Yeah, yeah.

MARY: And so, I started at Heystoun Hospital and I think as well the good thing about it too was you had to live in, so I was away. I was away from home, I was away from all the fighting, I was away from

all that and I just went on from there. I did my general, I did my specialism, worked with [Indigenous peoples in different countries]—
FERGUS: Wow!
MARY: —and worked in [Asia] and—
FERGUS: So you got to travel!
MARY: I got to travel and really I can only say it was due to Grace, it was due to her. She got married—you know, she used to tell me things, you know, wee things—still very professional, but she would tell me wee things. She told me when she got engaged and things like that. She got married and then she got pregnant very quickly after she got married, but at that time too it was coming up to the end of my probation as well, and that was it. Really, I have never looked back.

As the ending of their story suggests, Mary and Grace were close in age; Grace was in her early twenties. Mary also described her as "much more outgoing, you know." But this wasn't the only difference between the two probation officers:

MARY: The first time I met her, she came out, she shook my hand, you know. She took me into the office, you know, she said did I want something to drink, much more outgoing—much more friendly—
FERGUS: Right.
MARY: She put you at your ease, whereas that first probation officer, oh my goodness! I would go in and just sit and she would just look at papers and she wouldn't say anything to me, and I would be sitting there and thinking, "This is an absolute waste of time! This is a waste of everybody's time!"

One other aspect of Mary's story is worth relating. This concerns a discussion between Mary and Grace about whether or not she should disclose her convictions during the process of applying to train as a nurse:

FERGUS: What was Grace's . . . advice about it?
MARY: Her advice was, "I can't tell you what to do if they—what I will say is—if they don't ask, if there isn't a reason for you to tell them,

don't tell them." And the interview—in fact, I actually didn't think I was going to get in, you know. Matron sitting in her big chair and I—and I must admit I found it very difficult as well when I did start because it was very, very disciplined and I just, I wasn't used to that, but I was determined, I was determined to get there.

Mary explained that her determination to secure her place to train as a nurse and to succeed in that profession was partly related to the opportunities that nursing provided, but also related to her loyalty to Grace: "I wanted to travel, but on the other hand I didn't want to let Grace down—that was another thing too, you know, because she had been so good, so helpful, and she was there for me, and I didn't want to let her down as well. Plus, I was thinking the places I could go." When I asked, she also acknowledged that she wanted to prove wrong her mother's prediction that she would fail.

Making Sense of Mary's Story

In this section, in order to analyze what is "good" in and about Mary's story, I attend to some of the key themes within it, but I also consider the role of tropes and, more generally, the importance of what went unsaid, both back in the 1960s and in the telling of the story to me. I also explore what seems to have been good about the ways in which Mary and Grace coauthored this story, and what good may have been done for and by Mary in telling it to me.

Class, Distance, and Proximity

Evidently, her account of her "terrible" upbringing sets the scene for Mary's escape and for her ascent. It also describes the low position (in the class structure) from which she engages with the authority figures in the story—the judge, the first probation officer, and the matron. In her description of these characters, she vividly conveys the social distance—indeed, the gulf in status—between them, referring both to these agents' stern manner and at times to their formal dress. They all seem distant, elevated, and judgmental (the three judges behind their desk, the probation officer looking at her papers, the "matron sitting in her big chair"), underscoring her lowly position as a subject of their power.

At the same time, what remains unsaid is how Mary also puts distance between herself and other working-class women in her story. Her mother, for example, is cast only as an obstacle to or brake upon her ambitions to study and to travel. Her description of the hundreds of women "at their machines" doing piecework conveys a mixture of pity and horror—specifically, horror that this might have been her fate. In contrast, her description of the "well-dressed" people being served by the waiter in the tearoom seems to communicate admiration and respect. They represent the kind of person she dreamed of becoming (and, for that matter, the kind of person she did become).

Her relationship with Grace Carswell is particularly interesting in this context. Grace was perhaps no less middle-class than the other authority figures, but she was younger and much closer in age to Mary. Perhaps most importantly, from her first meeting with Mary, it seems obvious that, rather than mobilizing the social distance between them as a modality of control, she immediately sought to narrow it. As Mary put it, Grace was "much more outgoing, you know. The first time . . . she came out, she shook my hand, you know. She took me into the office, you know, she said did I want something to drink, much more outgoing—much more friendly." Grace also shared information about her personal life with Mary—information about her relationship, her engagement, and her pregnancy—all of which doubtless contributed to the generation of proximity rather than distance between them.

If Mary's is a story of movement *away* from her kith and kin, then the significance of Grace's movement *toward* her seems obvious; in effect, Grace offers a hand to Mary, one that might pull her out of the lowly and troubled position in which she finds herself. In many respects this narrative invokes an earlier era of probation history, during which its connection with the middle-class paternalism of the "child-saving" movement was clear (see, e.g., Mahood 1995). What is interesting in Mary's telling of her story is the sense that, rather than being plucked from the supposedly vicious "lower classes" by a bourgeois savior, Mary depicts herself as reaching up, eager to grasp the offered hand. Indeed, it might be argued that, to some extent, Mary's story reflects both the "rescued girl" and the "rags to riches" tropes associated with Cinderella, with Grace appearing as the fairy godmother who recognizes Mary's qualities and potential and seeks to (magically) liberate her from the injustice of her tragic situation. At the outset of her story, her description of her father as a monstrous "Jekyll and Hyde" character immediately situates Mary as being in peril, connecting her story with fables and folktales.

Gender, Confinement, and Mobility

Parts of Mary's tragic situation are articulated (the drunken father, the unsympathetic mother), but others remain unsaid. For example, Mary says nothing explicitly about the material poverty that her large family presumably experienced, though—to a fellow Glaswegian—both the neighborhoods she mentioned and the description of her large family encode that presumption. Partly in what is said, and partly via the tropes mentioned above, Mary's account focuses more on the attitudes and behaviors of her parents. Their gendered and classed expectations (that she must work to bring in money) confine her, and frustrate her prospects of educational achievement at Hopeville High School and thus the possibility of escape and of social and geographical mobility.

For Mary, it was these constraining expectations that provoked her rebellion. The feeling of being trapped is represented vividly in Mary's account of the "sweatshop"; perhaps it is noteworthy that she immediately juxtaposes that scene with the scene in the library. Libraries are primarily places of stillness; they are quiet places filled with resources for imagining all sorts of movement; as such, they could hardly be more different from the dull repetition of the noisy factory. It is also notable that Mary relates how submission to a classed and gendered position was reinforced by the first probation officer, who made no effort to understand the context of her life or indeed her own hopes, asking only "Are you working yet?" and "When are you going to find a job? I think it's time you found a job."

Though she never articulates it directly, class and gender role violations may also have been implicit in the judgment Mary felt keenly from the judge who imposed the probation order. In her account, he said that he could not understand her conduct, which brought discredit to her "good" school. The judge's characterization of Mary perhaps suggests another trope, that of the spoiled girl who spurns opportunity and, in so doing, threatens the reputation and standing of her benefactor (in this case, the "good school"). This trope reflects the promotion of feminine modesty and submission in various fairy tales about ungrateful daughters, particularly princesses who come to grief by thinking too much of themselves. Though this imposed narrative only emerged in the interview in response to my invitation to elaborate on what the judge said, making it explicit helps Mary to set up its comprehensive rebuttal in her own evolving narrative.

Against this highly gendered context, and in stark contrast to the judge, Grace seeks to understand not just Mary's situation, but also her hopes and aspirations. Perhaps we can assume that Grace, a young woman who had charted her own path into the probation profession, may have taken (and communicated) a less traditional view of gender roles. In Mary's telling of the story, it certainly seems that Grace may have recognized something of herself (and perhaps her own struggles with gendered expectations) in Mary's situation. Certainly, Mary confided in Grace and, as a result, Grace understood the situation in which Mary felt trapped. Indeed, the way that Mary describes their encounters depicts them as coconspirators, plotting her escape from the confinements of her classed and gendered position; to put this another way, Mary presents the pair as working together on the project of coauthoring a different story for her. It seems important to consider how exactly Grace enabled this collaborative approach.

Rites and Recognition

The foundation of their relationship, and of this process of coauthorship, seems to lie in Grace's recognition of Mary as a person of value and worth. The first of Grace's actions that Mary relates, at least after acts of welcome, is listening. Before they can rewrite Mary's story, Grace seeks to understand it as it is, or, more importantly, as Mary wishes to tell it. This active listening forms the basis of the trust that developed between them (see Ugelvik 2022 for more recent examples of similar dynamics). Crucially, as Mary puts it, Grace's recognition of her extends beyond the story of who Mary was and into the story of who Mary wanted to become:

> I think—when I look back on it—I think Grace saw the potential there, you know? She did come to the house as well . . . and, you know, I told her what I wanted to do, and I did tell her about my home life as well, which of course she knew, you know. I sometimes think, did she see something there, you know?

In some respects, this is a simple statement, but it stands in almost diametrical opposition to the judge's construction of Mary, and of the potency of Maloptical *mis*recognition as experienced by Teejay (McNeill 2019). Whereas negative and degrading assessments and portrayals of him are formed, reified, and projected into a bleak future, Mary feels truly *seen* by Grace—perhaps, at this formative time in her life, only by her—and Grace sees her *as* good and projects this positive assessment into an imagined future that matches her highest hopes for herself. Indeed, Grace's recognition of Mary's potential is what allows them to set about cowriting a life story that, in the end, is full of movement and mobility.

Grace's recognition of Mary is also reflected in both mundane and exceptional actions and events, which include elements of ritual (see Maruna 2011). The metaphorical "hand up" that I mentioned in the preceding section begins as a simple handshake, a symbolic offer of hospitality rather than hostility, accompanied by being asked if she would like a drink (see Urie et al. 2019). These small acts of hospitality seem to have communicated worth, respect, and care to someone who, at that time, was not accustomed to such treatment, particularly from adults and authority figures. In narrative terms, they serve as small signs of Grace's virtues as the "good" probation officer, or even as Mary's rescuer.

But the most potent moment (and ritual) of recognition, and perhaps the most vivid scene in Mary's story, was the trip to Miss Cranstoun's tearoom. It is impossible, of course, to know what Grace intended in taking Mary to tea. But Mary's description suggests that doing so powerfully communicated Grace's recognition of her worth and potential: "Gosh! She's brought *me* here." To be liked, to be listened to, and to be deemed worthy of sitting (and being served) in this lofty company of middle-class tea drinkers—all of this served to underscore Mary's own determination to build a different life for herself. If Grace thought that Mary could belong here, Mary's determination to achieve that belonging was reinforced. The tearoom visit, in other words, and in stark contrast to what she experienced in the courtroom, was a status elevation ritual (Maruna 2011).

In narrative terms, this scene also depicts a key turning point (McAdams 2006). But the "turning" in question has little or nothing to do with turning away from crime (Maruna 2001). Rather, the scene serves to underscore Grace's virtue and generosity and to show how it cemented Mary's resolve and inspired her onward movement. It is interesting, in hindsight, that at this point in the interview I interjected to invite Mary to make the meaning of the event more explicit, to say the unsaid. Even then, Mary does not (perhaps could not) say clearly that she wanted to leave her working-class origins behind and become middle-class like Grace and the other people in the tearoom. Instead, she chooses words that emphasize not identity but rather action and desire: "I could *be* here, . . . I could *do* this as well. . . . *This is what I want to do*" (emphases added).

Silencing and Speaking the Past

Mary's story also makes clear that the first steps on that journey were perilous. She was beginning not just in a difficult (and by implication "lowly") position, but also from a discredited position. She faced a narrative problem. Though we might see her teenage offenses as trivial, they were enough to constitute a criminal record, and she had been forced to leave school without qualifications. Social mobility, then, was not going to come easily to her.

Indeed, Mary reported in the interview that one escape route—via enlisting in the army—had been blocked by her criminal record. Her second attempt—via training to become a nurse—might also have been blocked, were it not for the surprising advice that Grace offered in relation to the disclosure (or nondisclosure) of her criminal record: "I can't tell you what to do if they—what I will say is—if they don't ask, if there isn't a reason for you to tell them, don't tell them." Here, Grace encourages Mary to leave part of her story unsaid; she suggests silencing that part of her past that might most discredit her.

By the standards of today's probation practice, preoccupied as it is in many jurisdictions with the assessment and management of risk (Robinson and McNeill 2017), Grace's licensing of Mary's silence is striking. Then and now, it seems to underscore her positive assessment of and preoccupation not with Mary's offending but with her potential. It also communicates trust in Mary, rather than fear associated with any risk that she might pose. In Mary's telling of this part of her story, her swift listing of her career achievements—in Alaska, in Australia, and in India—serves to powerfully vindicate both the narrative risk that Grace took (in licensing silence) and Mary's nondisclosure. After the interview, she further underscored her story's happy ending, describing how she met her husband on her travels, and that they had settled back in Scotland, raising three children.

There is an irony perhaps in the fact that clearing Mary's path to a happy ending seems to have depended on following advice *not* to tell one part of her story at an important moment in her life, and perhaps subsequently. But, more recently, Gålnander (2020) has shown how and why women in Sweden also preferred to withhold concealable stigma (about their criminalized pasts) when possible, precisely because they feared prejudicial reactions from others. For Mary, this kind of editing—consigning past criminalization to the realm of the unsaid—was necessary in the process of constructing a narrative good enough to persuade the forbidding matron to give her a chance. At that interview, Mary needed to conform to the gatekeeper's expectations and requirements if she was to gain access to the opportunities that the matron could unlock. Mary's performance must have been convincing enough, perhaps partly due to Grace's gentle coaching. Surely the unsaid can and does do harm (Presser 2023). When it comes to good writing of stories, however, partiality also has its uses and its merits.

For Mary, perhaps part of the function of the research interview was to allow some narrative revision, to say the unsaid and reinstate the omissions in her story. Presumably, it was not just in the interview with the matron that she had to manage the concealed stigma of an unspoken and discreditable aspect of her past. As she progressed through her life, both professionally and personally, she may well have chosen to omit that part of her life story that cast her as an "offender" but also as a probationer. If so, the irony is that this might also have meant writing Grace out of her life story. Mary left me with a clear sense that she was telling this new, fuller version of her story not just because I offered circumstances that made it safe to do so, but also because she wanted Grace's pivotal role in her life to be articulated and recognized. What better, safer way to write Grace back into her story than to tell her tale to a professor in a university collecting probation stories?

Conclusion

Mary's story—and the manner and timing of its telling—reveals something about the power of class and gender-based expectations, concentrated through criminal justice processes (cf. Carlen 1988). But for her own determination and Grace's perhaps unusual approach, Mary's narrative trajectory might have ended in quite a different (and perhaps much more familiar) and negative way.

Instead, as a "rescued girl," "rags to riches" tale, Mary's story speaks of rising from adversity, escaping classed and gendered constraints, and escaping the clutches of criminal justice. More importantly, perhaps, it also reveals the possibilities that are opened up by practices of recognition and attentiveness. Even in penal contexts that seem, in general, more likely to enforce degrading and life-limiting narratives, being recognized, heard, and supported can sometimes create the relational conditions in which new narrative possibilities emerge and can be chosen. Centrally, Mary's story stresses the importance and power of recognition in bridging the distance between supervisors and supervised, so that dialogical spaces are created where new and better stories can be imagined and enabled. Grace's willingness and ability to create those conditions meant that she and Mary could coauthor the beginning of a different life story than the one in which she felt trapped. As a result, Mary understood their encounter as one that liberated her, thus playing a key part in enabling her to recognize and to realize her own potential, to live well, and to do good in the world.

But Mary's story also reveals the importance of what went unsaid, not just in her dialogue with me, but also by (and between) characters in her story, including via allusions to certain familiar tropes. Some of these tropes had the effect of elevating Mary to the role of the story's hero, while others implied judgment and degradation of her. One of the most important aspects of Grace's intervention was her licensing of Mary's editing and rewriting of her story, consigning discrediting episodes into the realm of the unsaid. Enabling these silences was an essential narrative device in Grace's co-construction with Mary of a blank page on which a different life story could begin to be written. But paradoxically, this also meant that, at least until the research interview, a dramatic turning point in Mary's story had to be omitted, and with it one of that story's key characters and coauthors: Grace. In telling her story to me, I think, Mary was seeking to put back on record that crucial part of her story, as well as paying her dues to her coauthor in the process.

NOTES

I'm very grateful to Robin Gålnander, Phil Crockett Thomas, Thomas Ugelvik, the editors, and two anonymous reviewers for very helpful comments on an initial draft version of this paper. I am grateful to the British Academy for funding this study (Award no: SG48403), and to Beth, now Professor of Criminal and Social Justice at the University of Strathclyde, for working with me on the project.

1. The song can be heard (and the lyrics read) here: https://voxliminis.bandcamp.com/track/blankface, accessed April 5, 2022.
2. The adverts contained this simple text: "Probation in the 1960s. Were you on probation in the 50s or 60s? As part of a research study I'd like to talk to you—confidentially—about your experiences. Please contact Professor Fergus McNeill, University of Glasgow."
3. The 1968 act also established the Scottish Children's Hearings system, in which a panel of lay members decides how best to promote the welfare of children and young people referred on grounds of care and protection and/or because of offending.
4. This section of the chapter draws on two previous papers: see McNeill (2009) and Crockett Thomas et al. (2021).
5. For working-class Glaswegians, "Provident cheques" were a common means of securing credit, in return for weekly repayments collected from the home.

REFERENCES

Arnott, Alison, and Judith Duncan. 1970. *The Scottish Criminal*. Edinburgh: Edinburgh University Press.
Carlen, Pat. 1988. *Women, Crime and Poverty*. Buckingham: Open University Press.
Cox, Alexandra. 2017. *Trapped in a Vice: The Consequences of Confinement for Young People*. New Brunswick: Rutgers University Press.
Crewe, Ben. 2011. "Depth, Weight, Tightness: Revisiting the Pains of Imprisonment." *Punishment & Society* 13 (5): 509–29.
Crockett Thomas, Phil, Fergus McNeill, Lucy Cathcart Frödén, Jo Scott Collinson, Oliver Escobar, and Alison Urie. 2021. "Re-writing Punishment? Songs and Narrative Problem-Solving." *Incarceration* 2 (1). https://doi.org/10.1177/26326663211000239.

Durnescu, Ioan. 2011. "Pains of Probation: Effective Practice and Human Rights." *International Journal of Offender Therapy and Comparative Criminology* 55: 530–45.

Durnescu, Ioan, Christine Enengl, and Christian Grafl. 2013. "Experiencing Supervision." In *Offender Supervision in Europe*, edited by Fergus McNeill and Kristel Beyens, 19–50. Basingstoke: Palgrave Macmillan.

Fitzgibbon, Wendy, Christine Graebsch, and Fergus McNeill. 2017. "Pervasive Punishment: Experiencing Supervision." In *The Routledge International Handbook of Visual Criminology*, edited by Eamonn Carrabine and Michelle Brown, 305–19. London: Routledge.

Fleetwood, Jennifer. 2015. "In Search of Respectability: Narrative Practice in a Women's Prison in Quito, Ecuador." In *Narrative Criminology: Understanding Stories of Crime*, edited by Lois Presser and Sveinung Sandberg, 42–68. New York: New York University Press.

Fleetwood, Jennifer, Lois Presser, Sveinung Sandberg, and Thomas Ugelvik, eds. 2019. *The Emerald Handbook of Narrative Criminology*. Bingley, UK: Emerald.

Foucault, Michel. 1977. *Discipline and Punish: The Birth of the Prison*. London: Allan Lane.

Gålnander, Robin. 2020. "'Shark in the Fish Tank': Secrets and Stigma in Relational Desistance from Crime." *British Journal of Criminology* 60 (5): 1302–19.

Gubrium, Jaber F., and James A. Holstein. 2008. "Narrative Ethnography." In *Handbook of Emergent Methods*, edited by Sharlene Hesse-Biber and Patricia Leavy, 241–64. New York: Guilford.

Hayes, David. 2015. "The Impact of Supervision on the Pains of Community Penalties in England and Wales: An Exploratory Study." *European Journal of Probation* 7 (2): 85–102.

Kelly, Christine. 2017. "Probation Officers for Young Offenders in 1920s Scotland." *European Journal of Probation* 9 (2): 169–91.

Kilbrandon Report. 1964. *Children and Young Persons Scotland*. Cmnd 2306. Edinburgh: Her Majesty's Stationery Office.

Law, John. 2010. *After Method: Mess in Social Science Research*. London: Routledge.

Mahood, Linda. 1995. *Policing Gender, Class and Family in Britain, 1850–1940*. New York: Routledge.

Maruna, Shadd. 2001. *Making Good: How Ex-Convicts Reform and Rebuild Their Lives*. Washington, DC: American Psychological Association.

Maruna, Shadd. 2011. "Reentry as a Rite of Passage." *Punishment & Society* 13 (1): 3–28.

McAdams, Dan. 2006. *The Redemptive Self: Stories Americans Live By*. New York: Oxford University Press.

McNeill, Fergus. 2005. "Remembering Probation in Scotland." *Probation Journal* 52 (1): 25–40.

McNeill, Fergus. 2009. "Helping, Holding, Hurting: Recalling and Reforming Punishment." Apex Scotland Annual Lecture, Signet Library, Edinburgh, September 8. https://pure.strath.ac.uk.

McNeill, Fergus. 2010. "Supervision in Historical Context: Learning the Lessons of (Oral) History." In *Offender Supervision: New Directions in Theory, Research and*

Practice, edited by Fergus McNeill, Peter Raynor, and Chris Trotter, 492–508. Cullompton, UK: Willan.

McNeill, Fergus. 2018. *Pervasive Punishment: Making Sense of Mass Supervision*. Bingley, UK: Emerald.

McNeill, Fergus. 2019. "Mass Supervision, Misrecognition and the Malopticon." *Punishment & Society* 21 (2): 207–30.

McNeill, Fergus, and Gwen Robinson. 2012. "Liquid Legitimacy and Community Sanctions." In *Legitimacy and Compliance in Criminal Justice*, edited by Adam Crawford and Anthea Hucklesby, 116–37. London: Routledge.

Miller, Reuben. 2021. *Halfway Home: Race, Punishment and the Afterlife of Mass Incarceration*. New York: Little, Brown.

Presser, Lois. 2009. "The Narratives of Offenders." *Theoretical Criminology* 13 (2): 177–200.

Presser, Lois. 2012. "Collecting and Analyzing the Stories of Offenders." In *Advancing Qualitative Methods in Criminology and Criminal Justice*, edited by Heith Copes, 44–59. London: Routledge.

Presser, Lois. 2023. *Unsaid: Analyzing Harmful Silences*. Oakland: University of California Press.

Riessman, Catherine Kohler. 2008. *Narrative Methods for the Human Sciences*. Thousand Oaks, CA: Sage.

Robinson, Gwen, and Fergus McNeill. 2017. "Punishment in the Community: Evolution, Expansion, and Moderation." In *The Oxford Handbook of Criminology*, 6th ed., edited by Alison Liebling, Shadd Maruna, and Lesley McAra, 868–88. Oxford: Oxford University Press.

Sandberg, Sveinung. 2016. "The Importance of Stories Untold: Life-Story, Event-Story and Trope." *Crime, Media, Culture* 12 (2): 153–71.

Sandberg, Sveinung. 2022. "Narrative Analysis in Criminology." *Journal of Criminal Justice Education* 33 (2): 212–29. https://doi.org/10.1080/10511253.2022.2027479.

Scott, Jo Collinson, and Fergus McNeill. 2021. "Sensing Supervision through Stories and Songs." In *Sensory Penalities: Exploring the Senses in Places of Punishment and Social Control*, edited by Kate Herrity, Bethany Schmidt, and Jason Warr, 35–52. Bingley, UK: Emerald.

Steedman, Carolyn. 2000. "Enforced Narratives: Stories of Another Self." In *Feminism and Autobiography: Texts, Theories, Methods*, edited by Tess Cosslett, Celia Luria, and Penny Summerfield, 25–39. New York: Routledge.

Ugelvik, Thomas. 2022. "The Transformative Power of Trust: Exploring Tertiary Desistance in Reinventive Prisons." *British Journal of Criminology* 62 (3): 623–38.

Urie, Alison, Fergus McNeill, Lucy Cathcart Frödén, Jo Collinson Scott, Phil Crockett Thomas, Oliver Escobar, Sandy Macleod, and Graeme McKerracher. 2019. "Reintegration, Hospitality and Hostility: Song-Writing and Song-Sharing in Criminal Justice." *Journal of Extreme Anthropology* 3 (1). http://dx.doi.org/10.5617/jea.6914.

7

Good Storytelling and the Fraught Promise of Intimacy

FRANCESCA POLLETTA, TANIA DOCARMO, AND
KELLY MARIE WARD

In an era of algorithmic marketing and microtargeted political messaging, personal storytelling has remained a powerful force for social change (Meyers 2016; Nicholls 2013; Swerts 2015; Trevisan et al. 2020). At least, that is how many advocacy groups and nonprofits see it. Groups fighting for reform regularly tell the stories of people affected by the issue they target. People who were once homeless tell their personal stories to legislators. Those released from prison tell their stories to journalists. Women who have had abortions tell their stories to potential donors. Trans teens tell their stories in professionally produced YouTube videos and Facebook posts. Narrative consultants and a narrative how-to literature seek to identify the "five essentials," "four elements," or "three ingredients" of effective storytelling (Polletta et al. 2021).

Some communications strategists use a distinctly economic language in talking about personal storytelling. They urge nonprofits to build "story banks" filled with poignant accounts of people affected by poverty, climate change, or a lack of healthcare, stories they can supply to journalists in short order (Goodman 2009). They talk about "demand-side" and "supply-side" issues in the provision of digital stories (Rockefeller Foundation 2014). They urge advocacy groups to "centralize the management [of storytelling] to optimize [story] distribution" (Trevisan et al. 2020: 154).

But many advocacy groups, and indeed, many communications strategists, emphatically reject what they call a "transactional" or "extractive" approach to advocacy storytelling. The advocates, strategists, and foundation executives we interviewed faulted such an approach for treating storytellers simply as the producers of valuable objects that are then taken from them and circulated in remote networks. An immigrant rights advocate and an antipoverty advocate both criticized stories becoming a kind of "currency." Many decried the commodification of stories. All agreed that stories that treated their tellers or protagonists as only victims were exploitative and unethical.

Such stories were also unnecessary, interviewees insisted. It was possible to tell stories that both empowered *and* persuaded. Indeed, authentic stories did both. No one wanted to tell a story about themselves as a victim, and no one wanted to hear that kind of story, interviewees reasoned. Audiences responded to stories of hope, resilience, and fortitude. They wanted to connect emotionally with people's dreams and aspirations, not their suffering. They wanted to hear stories of agency, not stories of victimhood. And those were the stories that the survivors of injustice wanted to tell.

Professionals' argument for personal storytelling is a compelling one. But we are not convinced that it has overcome the tension between storytelling as empowering and storytelling as persuasive. *Representing* people as empowered is not the same as empowering them, although advocates sometimes seemed to suggest that it was. Emotionally affecting a remote audience is not the same as having an egalitarian relationship with them, though professionals suggested that too. Underpinning the discourse of advocacy storytelling is what we call a fantasy of intimate connection: a belief that sharing personal experiences will create a relationship of egalitarian intimacy between people separated by differences of geography, power, and experience (Polletta 2020). We call it a fantasy because in advocacy communication, the sharing was rarely mutual. The person affected by the issue told her story; the audience was not expected to do so. We call it a fantasy, second, because intimacy is not the same as equality. The person affected by the issue was empowered to tell her story—as long as she did so in a way that resonated with the audience.

Yet this fantasy appeared frequently in the practical discourse of advocacy storytelling: in how-to manuals and online guides, workshops on narrative advocacy and blog posts by narrative strategists, and in practical talk about personal storytelling by activists, communications strategists, leadership trainers, and foundation executives. Indeed, some of the same how-to guides that used the economistic language we cited above also talked about narrative intimacy as a bulwark against exploiting storytellers (Rockefeller Foundation 2014). One might suspect that slick media consultants would have a tendency to remake storytellers' needs to suit their audiences. But media consultants by no means had a monopoly on this discourse, nor was any other group—grassroots organizers, say—completely immune to it. This is what we mean by a discourse of personal storytelling: an institutionalized way of talking and thinking about how stories work, one that was produced and reproduced in multiple settings and that, like language, marked its users as competent through its correct usage (Foucault 1980; Polletta et al. 2021; Warr 2020).

Yet we also heard alternatives to this discourse: different ways of talking and thinking about personal stories' role in advocacy. We heard ones that, in our view, better accomplished the task of balancing tellers' empowerment with audiences' persuasion. In the alternative we highlight here, advocates were forthright about the need to persuade remote audiences. But they did not subordinate the needs of tellers in the process. Critically, we argue, they did not assume or strive for a relationship of intimacy between storyteller and audience. Progressive activists, we conclude, need to identify not only the components of good *stories*, but also the practices associated with good story*telling*. We aim in this chapter, then, to contribute both to an understanding of how popular and professional beliefs about storytelling shape stories' impact, and also to an understanding of the conditions for the kind of stories that challenge existing arrangements of power (Fleetwood et al. 2019).

Storytelling in Professionalized Advocacy

Advocates have always told personal stories. Nineteenth-century abolitionists told personal stories of their escape from slavery. Twentieth-century temperance activists recounted their personal struggles with alcohol; civil rights activists described the brutality they experienced at the hands of southern sheriffs; radical feminists told the stories of their abortions; and gay men and lesbians told the stories of their coming out as homosexual (Polletta 2006). The intersection of feminism with self-help and therapeutic self-actualization movements in the 1980s led to a surge of personal storytelling in those movements—along with a predictable backlash. For critics on the right, stories of personal victimization discouraged people from taking responsibility for their own choices (Hughes 1993). For critics on the left, victim stories required a posture of supplication, thereby diminishing tellers' sense of agency and power (Minow 1993; Wolf 1993). At the same time, the personal storytelling associated with South Africa's Truth and Reconciliation Commission and other transitional justice initiatives came under fire by sympathetic critics. Asking people to publicly relive their stories of suffering at the hands of a brutal regime with no hope of criminal prosecution and outside a therapeutic context might well re-traumatize them, critics argued (Crowe 2015; Fletcher and Weinstein 2002; also see Walklate 2016 on another shift during this period, from stories of victimhood to stories of trauma; and Shuman 2005 on appropriated stories).

These criticisms were familiar to the people we interviewed, and indeed, were sometimes made by them. Advocacy storytelling today has heeded the lessons of those earlier experiences, interviewees maintained.[1] Several developments were probably behind storytelling's renewed popularity in the 2000s. Wins on same-sex marriage and losses on abortion rights convinced left-leaning strategists in the United States that political progress required changing the "hearts and minds" of an indifferent public (Callahan 2014; Harold 2014; McQueen 2013). Personal storytelling seemed capable of doing that. At the same time, an industry of public interest communication firms was emerging, with special expertise in producing messages that would cut through the barrage of Internet-mediated information to which people were subjected. As nonprofits increasingly included advocacy in their remits, public interest communicators developed expertise in the kinds of messages that would generate public attention (Polletta et al. 2021). The development of crowdsourcing software allowed large advocacy organizations to solicit the stories of thousands of their members, stories that could then be developed and edited by professional staffers (Trevisan et al. 2020). Foundations initially turned to storytelling to report on their projects, but then began to fund the groups they worked with to receive training in storytelling, with the idea that this would assist in their advocacy and fundraising efforts (Siska 2005). Today, there are whole consultancies devoted to training groups on how to tell their stories, and countless workshops, webinars, handbooks, and blog posts advising advocacy groups on how to use personal storytelling in their fundraising, legislative, and media work (Polletta et al. 2021).

To make sense of the contemporary discourse of advocacy storytelling, we interviewed sixty-two people who, variously, funded narrative advocacy, recruited storytellers, coached them on how to tell their stories, and produced their stories for use online or in other media. Interviewees were staff members of activist and nonprofit groups, foundation executives, and communication, strategy, and leadership development consultants who worked with activist groups. The stories interviewees helped produce were used in fundraising, policy advocacy, and public consciousness-raising. Stories were often delivered in person (in speeches to potential donors, legislative testimony, and interviews with journalists), but they were also written up in brochures, ads, articles, and blog posts. Some were produced as online videos. The issues interviewees targeted included homelessness; the rights, variously of sex workers, people with disabilities, undocumented immigrants, drug users, and trans people; reproductive choice and justice; economic justice; environmental justice; labor; climate change; sex trafficking; and police brutality. In addition to interviewing people in the business of personal storytelling, we also read the recent how-to literature on personal storytelling in advocacy, which appeared in published handbooks, in articles in nonprofit and foundation periodicals, on websites, and in blogs. Our collaborator Jessica Callahan analyzed forty-five online stories that our interviewees rated as especially effective. The four of us participated in several workshops and webinars designed to train advocates in effective storytelling (see Polletta et al. 2021 for more on our data and methods).

By no means did all interviewees imagine stories working the same way. Some interviewees articulated quite different ideas about storytelling over the course of an interview. We first sketch a discourse about advocacy storytelling that was voiced by many of our interviewees and that appeared in the how-to guides, workshops, and blog postings with which advocates were familiar. Certainly the discourse would be recognizable to most people involved in advocacy storytelling. The discourse was coherent, but there were also interesting elisions in it, and we highlight these. Then we contrast this discourse with other ways of thinking about advocacy storytelling that appeared in our interviews.

Stories Build a Relationship

Advocates, strategists, communications consultants, and foundation executives often said that successful stories forged a bond with the audience. Told well, personal stories enabled storytellers to connect emotionally with the audience; our interviewees used phrases such as "allows somebody to really connect with an individual" (an anti-trafficking advocate); "connect with a person" (a human rights advocate); "connect emotionally" (an anti-homelessness advocate); "gets to emotional connectedness" (an antipoverty advocate); "connect . . . with people" (a women's rights advocate). That connection, ideally, should last past the moment of hearing or seeing the story. Stories should help to forge a relationship. As an antipoverty organizer explained, stories provided "an opening for a relationship." "Storytelling [is a] medium of relationship," an anti-trafficking advocate explained. "That's the whole point of telling a story: just to deepen a relationship." The relationship created through storytelling would lead donors, legislators, and ordinary people to act on behalf of the cause. In telling stories, "you're trying to engage a community of people around your work, to become your advocates," as an anti-trafficking advocate put it.

The goal was that audiences would become "your advocates," not your "benefactors." Parties to the relationship that advocates sought were not equal in terms of wealth or influence, but their joint commitment to the cause would equalize them. The relationship should be based on empathy, not pity. "The best stories are when the audience will have some level of personal connection to it," an anti-trafficking advocate explained, but then emphasized, "It doesn't just have to be someone sharing all of the gory details of their abuse. . . . [It should not be] a relationship of pity between the audience and the person who was abused." People should tell their stories in a way that led audiences to have the same "respect [for them] that they hold for themselves and they hold for decision makers," an immigrant rights advocate explained. The relationship should benefit the teller as much as the audience and the cause. It should be "empowering."

That was a tall order. How does one create empathy when parties are separated by distance and experience? And how does one create anything like equality when one party has money and sometimes political influence and the other does not? How does one get audiences to care about another person's suffering without encouraging that person to seem to be a victim, lacking agency and power? Interviewees, and the broader discourse on storytelling, answered those questions in two ways. One was that storytelling as a communicative form was intrinsically equalizing. The other was that stories that were authentic to their tellers just happened to be ones that appealed to audiences. We discuss each of these in turn.

Stories Build a Reciprocal Relationship

Interviewees, like the countless briefs for storytelling available now, emphasized the fundamentally human quality of storytelling. Interviewees explained that people "are hardwired for storytelling," that people had been telling stories for thousands of years, and that we are "storytelling animals." How-to guidelines cited research on readers' altered brain patterns to argue that people are "wired" to remember stories (Working Narratives n.d.; Grounded Solutions Network 2015), that "narrative is basic to what it means to be human" (Narrative Initiative 2017), and that people are "narrative animals" (Bioneers 2017). There was rarely any distinction made in these briefs between telling stories and hearing them. The needs of speakers and those of the audience meshed: as much as audiences naturally wanted to hear the stories of those affected by the issue, those affected wanted to tell their stories. Storytellers, in this view, were not being forced to do something that was foreign or unappealing to them. Moreover, if everyone lived in and through the stories they told and heard, then storytelling required no natural talents; it was inherently egalitarian. With a little coaching, anyone could tell a persuasive story.

Storytelling, as our interviewees had it, was egalitarian not only in the sense that it was a form available to all, but also in the sense that it was inherently reciprocal. When an interviewee said that humans are "kind of campfire people," the image was one of stories traded among a group rather than that of a performer speaking to a passive audience. Often the imagery invoked was of an intimate encounter. In the same vein, advocates often described people "sharing" their story rather than telling it (Grounded Solutions 2015; Hattaway Communications 2014; Narrative Initiative 2017; Working Narratives n.d.). Rather than a "transactional" relationship, in which tellers were treated simply as the producers of valuable objects that were then taken from them and circulated as a form of political currency, the relationship between teller and audience was understood as reciprocal.

In most advocacy contexts, though, storytelling was not reciprocated. Some groups, especially those involved in grassroots organizing, did have trainers, members, and those new to the organization share their stories as a form of leadership development. And some advocacy websites had a "Share Your Story" tab in which visitors could describe their own connection to the issue. But in most cases, the storytelling went in one direction. Storytellers only rarely met their audiences, let alone exchanged stories. The people who told their stories in congressional hearings, at gatherings of potential donors, and in YouTube videos rarely came to know the people to whom they told their story. A blurb on a handbook for narrative advocacy observed that "when two people sit down to tell stories from their lives and to listen, something happens" (Working Narratives n.d.)—but the storytelling featured in the book was to remote audiences.

This, then, was a first interesting elision in the contemporary discourse of storytelling. Stories would create a relationship between teller and audience, but the relationship was an imagined one. Although in reality, only one party engaged in self-disclosure, in the imagined relationship, they both did.

Stories Build an Intimate Relationship

If advocates encouraged tellers to connect with their audiences more than the reverse, they did not advise tellers to mold themselves to the audiences' needs. Interviewees were clear that storytellers should be honored, protected, and listened to. It was too easy to forget that "the people who are sharing those stories are the owners of those stories," an Indigenous rights advocate insisted. "This is still your story. You made this, it belongs to you." "An object of compassion is still an object," another advocate complained. Storytellers should be recognized as the subjects of their stories. That meant ensuring that tellers understood and agreed to the purposes to which their stories would be put. It meant stopping journalists from asking questions that were considered too intrusive and making sure that people were emotionally ready to tell their stories. But it also meant ensuring that tellers portrayed themselves in ways they wanted to be portrayed. "Authentic" stories—interviewees often used the term—were tellers' own (see also Bioneers 2017; Bridgespan Group n.d.; Meyer Foundation 2014; Rockefeller Foundation 2014).

This did not mean that tellers' stories should be spontaneous or unpracticed. After all, few people can tell their stories in a coherent and meaningful way on demand. We all tend to meander, to fixate on details that are tangential to the story's narrative line, and to skip over ones that are actually essential. "You do have to craft stories," a trainer explained. She had had experiences where, because a member of the activist group (in this case, sex workers) "rambled on and didn't find their own story," the reporter interviewing them "took whatever they wanted from their story. Whatever fit that reporter's angle." One could argue that the rambling version *was* the group member's own story. What the interviewee meant, we believe, was that the story did not make the point that the group wanted to make.

How, then, could one craft tellers' stories or train them to craft their own stories while still ensuring that the stories remained the tellers' own? A storytelling trainer maintained that it was a matter of degree: "When you asked me that question of when do I think it's wrong to craft, I think it's wrong to *overly* craft." There was a more common answer, though, and it involved a second elision to which we want to draw attention. In the contemporary discourse of advocacy storytelling, it just so happened that the stories that tellers wanted to tell were the stories audiences wanted to hear. It was a misconception to think that authentic stories were "very difficult scenarios," said an organizer who worked with low-income people. "That, for me, is a very important piece to really work on. That it's not actually about trauma, it's about agency." An anti-trafficking advocate noted, "I think particularly the picture of the girl being rescued and being completely helpless, it's a very negative picture in trafficking because it kind of gives the impression of they're just needing complete and utter help and there's nothing we can really do, nothing they can do to help themselves. Which of course is really unhelpful for them." "If we continue to tell that story of ourselves as the victims, even if we don't mean it, even if it's a subconscious thing, it still reinforces where we are in the story. So I would say that actually works against collective liberation," said a storytelling trainer. An anti-trafficking advocate recounted that his group had "really shifted gears to not telling the individual rape stories . . . [but instead a] story about an individual girl's move towards the future, what her hopes and dreams were, what she was becoming, what she's learned about herself, and moving further away from salacious details that quite frankly are personal and belong to that particular survivor." Anti-trafficking advocates in particular, but others too, insisted that victim stories were disrespectful to the subject of the story. "[I want to find] storytellers, the clients, who are able to speak from a position of power instead of a position of victimization and vulnerability," said one.

The strategy was ethically motivated: the point was to avoid exploiting the storyteller. Yet interviewees also pointed out that such storytelling was effective in persuading audiences of the urgency of the cause. An anti-trafficking advocate explained, "Part of the healing process is not to carry guilt and shame because of what's happened to you. And when a girl is able to do that freely, then that's a win-win. It helps the organization, it helps not just the organization, it helps the cause." A children's rights advocate insisted, "You don't have to rely on the sad pathetic pictures of starving children to generate people's interest and concern. When you see people being empowered, then they feel happy to be able to give money." A human rights activist observed, "If the stories are developed with more emphasis or focus on the challenge, it comes out like a pity story or a victim story. And I don't think it works much for—people wouldn't want to share it anyway."

Note how the last interviewee shifted from saying that victim stories were unappealing to the audience to saying that they were unappealing to the teller (who "wouldn't want to share it anyway"). An anti-trafficking advocate made the same shift when describing the importance of conveying "hope" and "how important it is to not just smack people over the head, punch them in the face with this awful message. That's not enough, and it also doesn't serve a client very well either. It reinforces all these ideas about pity that we can have toward people in a different culture." Donors admired organizations that portrayed survivors with dignity, one advocate observed. Interviewees often used aesthetic terms. One wanted to tell "beautiful stories of redemption," and another worried that negative images "strip people of their agency"—as if positive images would give them agency.

The point of telling stories of resilience and hope was to honor the teller's dignity and agency. But it was also to appeal to audiences who were inspired by stories of overcoming. Representing victims as hopeful gave audiences hope, and when one represented victims as empowered, as a drug legalization advocate promised, "then you"—meaning the audience— "also get empowered." Professionals repeatedly alluded to a possible tension between an instrumental commitment to using the story and an ethical one to not "using" the storyteller. But they also cast that tension as solved: telling stories ethically also happened to be what made them effective.

Modulated Suffering and People Who Are Just Like You

We found the same slippage between what was good for the audience and what was good for the teller in how advocates and consultants talked about suffering. Advocates occasionally encountered well-meaning fundraisers who urged them to push storytellers to cry, they said. But they retorted not only that doing so was unethical, but that it was unnecessary. A filmmaker recounted, "I definitely have worked with some organizations who are all about making their subjects cry on camera because they feel like that's what's going to get the best total response. I push back and say no, it's if your audience cries at the story, not necessarily if your subject cries." Indeed, too much emotion on the part of storytellers could backfire, alienating audiences rather than affecting them emotionally. An anti-trafficking advocate described a situation in which a survivor broke down in tears during a fundraising event in a private home. "We walked out of there with zero dollars, the entire event," he commented. "And it was because it was emotionally moving but it was really awkward." Another anti-trafficking advocate observed, "It's not that tears are always a bad thing, but . . . you have to be intuitive in those moments to know if it's okay or not." The goal was that survivors are "able to own that past and they present it like it's a scar, not like it's a gaping open bleeding oozing wound. . . . The best storytelling is scars."

The point of modulating tellers' emotional performances was to treat them with respect, to avoid a voyeuristic presentation of victims overcome by pain. But the resulting performance also avoided discomfiting audiences. Possibly, it made the performance even more engaging, because audiences knew that at any moment the teller might dissolve in tears. This was suggested by our analysis of a collection of videos that interviewees rated as effective. They were mainly YouTube videos, produced by advocacy organizations to raise consciousness as well as funding for causes including anti-homelessness efforts, anti-trafficking, reproductive justice, and aid to refugees. In analyzing the videos, we were struck by the absence of strong emotions in the people featured. For example, in a video produced by an anti-homelessness organization, a young man described his homeless childhood as a series of adventures (Film and Family Homelessness Project 2014). His account of living in cars and under bridges was interspersed with rap lyrics and images of dragons. In a matter-of-fact tone, and betraying no sadness or resentment, he recounted being turned down for jobs and finding it difficult to fall asleep in indoor spaces as a result of his chaotic upbringing.

A video produced by the Center for Reproductive Rights (2015) and picked up by multiple media sites featured the actress Jemima Kirke, famous from the television series *Girls*, recounting the story of her abortion. In an affectless tone, she described discovering she was pregnant and deciding to have an abortion. The only point at which she showed some emotion was when she wryly laughed before saying that she did not have enough money for the abortion and had to borrow it from her boyfriend. In a video aimed at ending the war in Syria, a White Helmet rescuer described finding a two-week-old infant in the rubble of a bombed building (Syria Campaign 2014). When the interviewer asked him whether he had seen the infant's family since then, he said no, with a knowing laugh, there was no time. The camera then lingered on his face as he seemed to process, as the audience was encouraged to do, the fact that there were so many lives to save and so many lives already lost.

In other videos too, the storyteller was shown either struggling to restrain his or her emotions or speaking in a surprisingly flat tone. The audience was invited to interpret the meaning of the tight grin or the shaky voice. Again, the same thing that, according to advocates, made storytelling ethical—that tellers were discouraged from performing their suffering—was also what made it effective.

Perhaps surprisingly, advocates suggested that stories that were easy for audiences to identify with were also more authentically the teller's own. For example, an article in the *Nonprofit Quarterly* advised storytellers to "ensure others can see themselves in the story" as one of the "five ways for nonprofits to tell an ethical story," elaborating, "We can all be inspired to give money or time because we see our own moments of need reflected in our neighbors' stories." *Ethical* storytelling required that the audience see itself in the story. Similarly, a how-to guide on storytelling quoted the executive director of a center serving religious minorities: "We never want to 'other' our clients" in their storytelling, the director said. "We want people to relate." Casting clients as similar to audiences was a way of treating them respectfully, in this view. "Asking people to tell their stories is ultimately not about you; it's about the storyteller, since this is a very personal process for most," a storytelling guide counseled, emphasizing, like our interviewees, the importance of being true to the storyteller. "*If, however, you take the time to listen fully and authentically, you are likely to hear stories that reflect both your key messages and messages that will resonate with your audiences*" (our emphasis). Again, stories' authenticity—or, in this case, the ability to listen to stories authentically—would bridge the needs of audience and teller (Marple 2014; McCambridge 2013).

Risks of the Discourse of Advocacy Storytelling

We have argued that the contemporary discourse of advocacy storytelling made the needs of storytellers and their audiences similar. Tellers wanted to be represented as hopeful and agentic, according to this discourse, and audiences wanted those protagonists. Tellers wanted to present "scars, not wounds," that is, to modulate their emotions, and audiences did not want to be made uncomfortable by effusive expressions of grief. Tellers wanted audiences to see themselves in their stories, and audiences wanted the same thing.

However, in each case, we have argued that it was the *discourse* of storytelling that matched storytellers' needs with those of their audiences more than anything storytellers had communicated to professionals. Certainly, the discourse made some sense. Who would want to be represented as a victim? Who would want to perform one's suffering on demand, possibly over and over again? There may have been real benefit to the victims of injustice in recognizing their own agency and developing a sense of hope about the future. On the other hand, if the overriding criterion of good storytelling was, as advocates maintained, that people tell stories that were their own, that were *authentic*, then one might imagine tellers sometimes wanting to dwell on the ways in which they were victimized. Tellers might also have wanted to express emotions of pain, anger, indignation, and confusion. The discourse of advocacy storytelling did not much acknowledge those kinds of desires (see Presser 2018 on the "not said" in storytelling).

Several interviewees struggled with that omission, however. One interviewee had done a filmmaking project with Latina teenagers who were mothers. The young women told a variety of stories, she said—some happy, some not:

> [They were] difficult stories that maybe they hadn't told before, like grief around their mother's death or stuff about sexual violence. . . . Still the executive director, when she saw them, she was very critical. And she said, "You know, these are not the kinds of narratives that we want to put out there. These are victim narratives. We want to show the positive aspects of what our girls do." . . . [She wanted] to stay away from stereotypes or negative portrayals of all the trauma and drama that these girls have gone through. But that's kind of ignoring the reality of their experiences.

A development consultant who argued for telling stories of empowerment also remarked, "But I suppose the other side of that, though, is a lot of the work we do isn't always about success stories. Sometimes we do a lot and at the end of the day, things are still really difficult." The two options of victimization or resilience—or, as the filmmaker put it, "narratives that are either problem-saturated and oppressive or relentlessly upbeat"—did not encompass storytellers' experiences.

Again, it may have made sense strategically to represent those who suffered from injustice as agentic and hopeful, if that was what was needed to compel people to support them. The problem, though, was in treating the effort to empower and a representation of people as already empowered as the same thing. Doing so obscured trade-offs that advocates might have wanted to consider before making. Had they distinguished tasks of empowering victims from persuading audiences, advocates still might have asked victims to tell their stories in ways that emphasized their hope, resilience, and similarity to their audiences. But they also might have acknowledged the sacrifice that storytellers made in doing so (Allen 2004). Alternatively, they might have recognized that empowerment did not necessarily depend on forging emotional intimacy with the audience. In the next section, we explore this possibility.

Alternatives: Stories Build Agendas, Organizations, and Political Consciousness

It is tempting to attribute the problems we have described to the professionalization of advocacy. In this view, media-savvy communications consultants run roughshod over the desires of storytellers in their bid to craft a story that will go viral. Certainly, it makes sense that people charged simply with producing persuasive stories rather than working directly with the people affected by the issue would be less likely to attend to the needs of stories' tellers, and more likely to treat tellers' agency as something to be represented aesthetically rather than promoted practically. But we resist a characterization of professionalized storytelling as by definition bad. For one thing, even the most grassroots, nonprofessionalized groups have to do the work of persuading remote audiences. They too have to make their case to outsiders, whether to gain funding, to attract media coverage, to mobilize supporters, or to win favorable policy. Doing so requires crafting stories strategically. In addition, though, we found this discourse of intimacy-producing storytelling voiced by many people, including some in grassroots organizations. And we heard challenges to it from professional communications consultants.

We also heard alternatives: approaches to storytelling that did not strive to forge intimacy with a remote audience. Some of these approaches involved inward-facing advocacy tasks rather than communicating with outside audiences. The filmmaker we quoted a moment ago was frustrated by the nonprofit executive's view of stories because her own views came from the educator Paolo Freire's ideas about participatory learning. As she saw it, sharing one's experience with sympathetic but critical others was a way to begin to identify the structural forces shaping those experiences. Stories in this approach were material for group members' political education. An advocate who worked on issues of poverty, women's rights, and reproductive justice explained that the experiences shared by teenage mothers in her group became the basis for the group's agenda. When the young women recounted the injustice of high school athletes not being penalized for school absences to attend games whereas they were penalized for missing school to care for their children, the group decided to fight for policy change on that issue. Storytelling was empowering insofar as it translated politically unrecognized needs into group goals. In the public narrative strategy developed by activist Marshall Ganz (2011), and used by several of our interviewees, learning to tell the story of "us" and the story of "now" is as important as learning to tell one's own story. It builds the solidarity and purpose that are necessary to act collectively.[2]

One risk of the more familiar discourse of narrative advocacy, then, is that it leads us to think of storytelling as only about public persuasion, rather than also about these other critical tasks of advocacy. That said, storytelling for public persuasion remains important, and almost all the advocates we interviewed struggled with the pressure to supply stories for journalists, policy makers, funders, and the public that were simple rather than complicated, and that touched and inspired. They often provided those stories. Some advocates also treated storytellers as more than their stories, however. In faith-based organizing, interviewees said, it was common practice to have a few people affected by the issue tell their personal stories in public meetings with policy makers. After their testimonials, several other people affected by the issue presented the group's demands or described the importance of the policy reform they were seeking. The next time the group met with policy makers, though, the people who had earlier told their personal stories would move up the ladder of leadership to presenting the group's demands.

For example, Braunstein (2017) describes a faith-based organizing group training a woman to recount her struggles with healthcare in a public meeting the group had planned with a health official. The first few times the woman tried her story out with the group, she emphasized her own needs more than those of people like her. She knew that her story was supposed to be an example of the kinds of problems others were facing, but she kept getting stuck on wanting to get help for her particular issues. After months of training, however, she delivered her story to the official clearly, authoritatively, and in a way that communicated that hers was one of many such stories. "Afterward," Braunstein writes, "she beamed as she posed for pictures alongside other members of the working group" (165). Her satisfaction—indeed, her sense of empowerment—came from the audience's applause and the praise she received from her fellow organizers, not from any feeling of intimate connection with the official. Similarly, an interviewee who worked with people with hepatitis

C said that people in his group who told their stories of illness publicly were also asked to master a great deal of technical information so that they could "engage in debate with any kind of scientist or pharma rep." The power here came from mastering and delivering a story effectively as part of the process of fighting for reform.

Organizers in the undocumented student Dreamer movement trained participants to tell the kinds of stories that would appeal to Americans who were ambivalent about immigration. Such stories emphasized the fact that immigrants had not chosen to come to this country, that they were therefore "innocent," and that they were hardworking and high-achieving. But organizers also provided opportunities for Dreamers to tell their stories in their own way to an audience of peers (Nicholls 2013; Swerts 2015). One member of a Chicago-based Dreamer network said,

> When we were in [the group], all sitting around that table and talking about our statuses and our stories, I was like, I've finally found a group where people know what frustrations I'm going through and can actually identify with them. And I don't have to explain what it feels like because they know. And they know how frustrating it is, and some of them have already dealt with it and can actually help, and some of them are just starting to go through it. . . . That was beautiful and probably the best feeling I've ever had. (Swerts 2015)

Several features of the storytelling this Dreamer describes distinguish it from the kinds of stories that typically are told to public audiences. In this context, the teller did not have to do the difficult emotional work of explaining what it felt like to be undocumented, because her audience already knew. She could express "frustrations"—presumably anger, indignation, and other emotions that might, in another context, alienate an audience that was being asked to give money or support. And she got "help" from her fellow activists—perhaps practical help, but also emotional understanding and support from people who had experienced the same thing. None of these things was likely possible when she told her story in public settings.

Indeed, the personal stories that Dreamers told at rallies, to politicians, and to the media were carefully crafted and rehearsed. There were guidelines for how to tell one's story, and organizers carefully selected the people whose stories best fit the point they were trying to make. One activist explained, "I try hard to be both entertaining and politically interesting, so I . . . have told it so many times that I know which parts of my story shock people, and I know where the, like, 'Oh' comes, and I also know which parts to highlight . . . depending on the point that I am trying to make" (Swerts 2015: 353). Another said of lobbying politicians, "I've learned how to talk to them now . . . and present our case, and make them sympathize and work in favor of us" (356).

Dreamer activists were gimlet-eyed about how they used stories to elicit empathy and support in their audiences. Intimacy came from the peers with whom they genuinely exchanged stories, while empowerment came from the satisfaction of performing their story effectively to a public audience. An advocate for trans youths described a similar setup. When the young people she worked with told their stories publicly, they found themselves the subject of often prying media coverage. The group established a separate site where they could tell their stories to each other away from public scrutiny.

More generally, in these alternative approaches, activists understood personal storytelling differently than in the more familiar discourse, in at least two ways. Telling one's personal story was only one step in an activist trajectory. In community organizing, people who told their personal stories at one public meeting then went on to present the group's demands at another one. In Freirian popular education, people who told their stories first in individual terms went on to explore their experiences in more structural terms. Where personal storytelling was used to identify issues that the group wanted to work on, the people who told and heard those stories then strategized an agenda for action. Storytellers in each case were treated as more than their stories. This was not only in the sense that they were recognized as having lives and dreams outside their experiences of injustice, but also in the sense that telling their story was a step toward further political understanding and leadership.

These approaches were different, second, in treating empowerment and persuasion as different tasks. Both were necessary, and stories *could* do both, but did not necessarily do so. Underpinning this belief was a very different imaginary than one of intimate connection. In this imaginary, the powerful and the powerless rarely shared interests. Advocates did not rule out the possibility that storytellers might connect emotionally with their audiences, that policy makers might be persuaded by their accounts, or that donors might throw in their lot with the cause. But they did not assume common interests, let alone intimate bonds.

Conclusion

Good stories touch us. They lead us to identify emotionally with the story's protagonist. We may admire her or feel that she is almost something like a friend. Our relationship to the story's protagonist, who may be the story's teller, often feels like an intimate one. So it is perhaps unsurprising that many advocates have come to see personal storytelling as about creating that experience of intimacy—connecting emotionally, as our interviewees put it.

The risk, we have argued, is in assuming that that experience is reciprocal. Certainly, it may be reciprocal. A person may share her story with a stranger and feel heard and understood. The sense of emotional connection may be mutual. And that sense of connection may be empowering to the teller. But in most instances of advocacy storytelling, only the teller shares her experiences. Her story is not reciprocated. The audience is relatively anonymous. And often, the teller has been coached to tell her story in a way that gives the audience an experience of intimate connection. In our view, providing that sense of connection is not the same as an egalitarian relationship. And that experience is unlikely to be empowering. Instead, storytelling professionals are put in the awkward position of counseling people who have been homeless or had an abortion or been sex-trafficked that their stories are most authentic—that their stories are most *theirs*—when they display just the right amount of suffering mixed with resilience and hope that are easily related to by remote audiences.

What *is* often empowering, we have suggested, is the experience of telling a story effectively. To be sure, encouraging the people affected by an issue to *perform* their stories risks seeming calculated and even manipulative. It seems inauthentic. But this is because of the fantasy of intimate connection that accompanies advocacy storytelling today, in which audiences have the privilege of being inspired without being discomfited. Abandoning that fantasy does not mean surrendering the capacity of personal stories to empower their tellers. And it does not mean surrendering stories' capacity to persuade otherwise indifferent audiences. It does mean recognizing that those are different tasks, though, and may require different kinds of storytelling.

The larger point is that what makes for a good story depends on what the purposes of the story are. The stories that women told about their abortions in the 1960s and those that gay men and lesbians told about their homosexuality in the 1970s were not about eliciting empathy from an indifferent audience. They were about breaching the silence, about defying the shame of stigma (Polletta 2006). The stories that AIDS sufferers told on federal research review panels in the 1980s were not about securing empathy or expressing defiance; they were about educating scientists with the goal of finding a cure (Epstein 1996).

That the stories Black people told in an interracial dialogue group studied by Katherine Cramer Walsh (2007) elicited empathy and identification on the part of white participants was *not* good. Black participants' personal stories led white participants to tell their own personal stories about how they treated all their friends as the same, or to express bromides like "Under the skin we're all the same" in a way that denied real difference in their experience. White members of the group began to understand that difference only after Black members stopped them from too quickly identifying with the stories they heard and instead challenged them to recognize that their experiences were not the same.

In sum, treating stories as effective insofar as they create in the audience a warm glow of identification and empathy with the story's protagonist discourages us from recognizing other ways in which stories, and other forms of talk, can be politically effective.

NOTES

Thank you to the editors for immensely helpful comments on prior versions of this chapter, to the Open Society Foundations for supporting the research on which it is based, and to the many advocates who took the time to talk to us about their work.

1 The lines between grassroots social movement organizations, professional advocacy organizations, and nonprofit service organizations have become increasingly difficult to draw (see Polletta et al. 2021). Still, we focus here on a *professionalized* discourse of narrative advocacy, articulated by people who are paid to elicit, produce, and disseminate stories, rather than on stories of resistance that are crafted, often jointly, by ordinary people (see Sandberg and Andersen 2019).

2 Telling the story of us, for Ganz (2011), means naming the values of the group on behalf of whom we act. Telling the story of now means articulating why we must act now, and how we must act to be effective. Public narrative, as Ganz uses it, thus includes strategy along with self-expression.

REFERENCES

Allen, Danielle S. 2004. *Talking to Strangers: Anxieties of Citizenship since Brown v. Board of Education*. Chicago: University of Chicago Press.

Bioneers. 2017. "Social Change Campaign Strategy: The Importance of Storytelling." https://bioneers.org.

Braunstein, Ruth. 2017. *Prophets and Patriots: Faith in Democracy across the Political Divide*. Berkeley: University of California Press.

Bridgespan Group. N.d. "Why Nonprofits Need to Be Great Storytellers: An Interview with Andy Goodman." www.bridgespan.org. Retrieved May 15, 2019.

Callahan, David. 2014. "A Closer Look at Atlantic's End Game—And Where It's Putting the Biggest Money." *Inside Philanthropy*. www.insidephilanthropy.com.

Center for Reproductive Rights. 2015. "Jemima Kirke Shares Her Story about Ending a Pregnancy." YouTube. https://www.youtube.com/watch?v=m1DhscWRT9w.

Crowe, Kate. 2015. "Sexual Assault and Testimony: Articulation of/as Violence." *Law, Culture and the Humanities* 15 (2): 401–20.

Epstein, Steven. 1996. *Impure Science: AIDS, Activism, and the Politics of Knowledge*. Berkeley: University of California Press.

Film and Family Homelessness Project. 2014. "American Refugees: The Beast Inside," created by Amy Enser and Drew Christie. Youtube. https://www.youtube.com/watch?v=nwg8nZFhBEE.

Fleetwood, Jennifer, Lois Presser, Sveinung Sandberg, and Thomas Ugelvik, eds. 2019. Introduction to *The Emerald Handbook of Narrative Criminology*. Bingley, UK: Emerald.

Fletcher, Laurel E., and Harvey M. Weinstein. 2002. "Violence and Social Repair: Rethinking the Contribution of Justice to Reconciliation." *Human Rights Quarterly* 24: 573–639.

Foucault, Michel. 1980. "Two Lectures." In *Power/Knowledge: Selected Interviews*, edited by Colin Gordon and translated by Colin Gordon, Leo Marshall, John Mepham, and Kate Soper, 78–108. New York: Pantheon.

Ganz, Marshall. 2011. "Public Narrative, Collective Action, and Power." In *Accountability through Public Opinion: From Inertia to Public Action*, edited by Sina Odugbemi and Taeku Lee, 273–89. Washington, DC: World Bank.

Goodman, Andy. 2009. "A Bank That Always Builds Interest." *Free-Range Thinking*, April. www.thegoodmancenter.com.

Grounded Solutions Network. 2015. "Storytelling for Advocacy." https://groundedsolutions.org.

Harold, Steph. 2014. "Four Ways to Create Culture Change around Abortion." *Rewire*. https://rewirenewsgroup.com.

Hattaway Communications. 2014. "Digital Storytelling for Social Impact." www.hattaway.com.
Henry, Nicola. 2009. "Witness to Rape: The Limits and Potential of International War Crimes Trials for Victims of Wartime Sexual Violence." *International Journal of Transitional Justice* 3 (1): 114–34.
Hughes, Robert. 1993. *Culture of Complaint: The Fraying of America*. New York: Oxford University Press.
Marple, Kate. 2014. "Five Ways for Nonprofits to Tell an Ethical Story." *Nonprofit Quarterly*, October 22. https://nonprofitquarterly.org.
McCambridge, Ruth. 2013. "Pity Charity: When 'Storytelling' Is Abuse." *Nonprofit Quarterly*, November 22. https://nonprofitquarterly.org.
McQueen, Ann. 2013. "Compton Foundation: Art as a Strategy for Change." Americans for the Arts. http://animatingdemocracy.org.
Meyer Foundation. 2014. "Stories Worth Telling: A Guide to Strategic and Sustainable Nonprofit Storytelling." www.meyerfoundation.org.
Meyers, Diana T. 2016. *Victims' Stories and the Advancement of Human Rights*. New York: Oxford University Press.
Minow, Martha. 1993. "Surviving Victim Talk." *University of California Los Angeles Law Review* 40: 1411–45.
Morrissey, Janet. 2017. "To Sell Themselves to Donors, Nonprofits Are Turning to the Pros." *New York Times*, September 10. www.nytimes.com.
Narrative Initiative. 2017. *Toward New Gravity: Charting a Course for the Narrative Initiative*. https://narrativeinitiative.org.
Nicholls, Walter. 2013. *The DREAMers: How the Undocumented Youth Movement Transformed the Immigrant Rights Debate*. Palo Alto, CA: Stanford University Press.
Polletta, Francesca. 2006. *It Was Like a Fever: Storytelling in Protest and Politics*. Chicago: University of Chicago Press.
Polletta, Francesca. 2020. *Inventing the Ties That Bind: Imagined Relationships in Moral and Political Life*. Chicago: University of Chicago Press.
Polletta, Francesca, Tania DoCarmo, Kelly Marie Ward, and Jessica Callahan. 2021. "Personal Storytelling in Professionalized Social Movements." *Mobilization: An International Quarterly* 26 (1): 65–86.
Presser, Lois. 2018. *Inside Story: How Narratives Drive Mass Harm*. Berkeley: University of California Press.
Rockefeller Foundation. 2014. "Digital Storytelling for Social Impact." https://rockefellerfoundation.org.
Sandberg, Sveinung, and Jan C. Andersen. 2019. "Opposing Violent Extremism through Counter-Narratives: Four Forms of Narrative Resistance." In *The Emerald Handbook of Narrative Criminology*, edited by Jennifer Fleetwood, Lois Presser, Sveinung Sandberg, and Thomas Ugelvik, 445–66. Bingley, UK: Emerald.
Shuman, Amy. 2005. *Other People's Stories: Entitlement Claims and the Critique of Empathy*. Urbana: University of Illinois Press.
Siska, Darlene M. 2005. "Story Time." *Chronicle of Philanthropy* 17 (22): 35–37.

Swerts, Thomas. 2015. "Gaining a Voice: Storytelling and Undocumented Youth Activism in Chicago." *Mobilization: An International Quarterly* 20 (3): 345–60.
Syria Campaign. 2014. "The Heroes and the Miracle Baby." Youtube. https://www.youtube.com/watch?v=6hoVDhENotI.
Trevisan, Filippo, Bryan Bello, Michael Vaughan, and Ariadne Vromen. 2020. "Mobilizing Personal Narratives: The Rise of Digital 'Story Banking' in US Grassroots Advocacy." *Journal of Information Technology and Politics* 17 (2): 146–60.
Walklate, Sandra. 2016. "The Metamorphosis of the Victim of Crime: From Crime to Culture and the Implications for Justice." *International Journal for Crime, Justice and Social Democracy* 5 (4): 4–16.
Walsh, Katherine Cramer. 2007. *Talking about Race: Community Dialogues and the Politics of Difference*. Chicago: University of Chicago Press.
Warr, Jason. 2020. "'Always Gotta Be Two Mans': Lifers, Risk, Rehabilitation, and Narrative Labour." *Punishment & Society* 22 (1): 28–47.
Wolf, Naomi. 1993. *Fire with Fire: The New Female Power and How it Will Change the 21st Century*. New York: Random House.
Working Narratives. N.d. *Storytelling and Social Change: A Strategy Guide*. https://narrativearts.org. Accessed August 7, 2023.

8

Youth Narrating the Future

Climate Change Activism as a Civil Rights Movement

ROBIN KUNDIS CRAIG

Introduction: Youth and Climate Change

> "There is no Planet B." "There is no Planet Blah." Blah, blah, blah. Blah, blah, blah. "This is not about some expensive, politically correct, green act of bunny-hugging or" blah, blah, blah. "Build back better" blah, blah, blah. "Green economy" blah, blah, blah. "Net Zero by 2050" blah, blah, blah. "Net Zero" blah, blah, blah. "Climate neutral" blah, blah, blah.
>
> They are clearly not listening to us. And they never have. Just look at the numbers. Just look at the statistics. The emissions are still rising. The science doesn't lie. (Greta Thunberg, Youth4Climate Summit, September 28, 2021)

COP26 was the twenty-sixth Conference of the Parties to the United Nations Framework Convention on Climate Change, which took place in Glasgow, Scotland, from October 31 through November 12, 2021. If this conference had a theme, it was "blah, blah, blah." Greta Thunberg's rallying phrase encapsulated youth's frustration with the seemingly endless climate change negotiations that had yet to generate sufficient action to mitigate the global existential threat that has emerged from adherence to a fossil fuel–based economy. More impressively, however, these three words became *the* measure of the conference's success (or lack thereof). As the negotiators headed home, the entire world asked, *Was* COP26 anything more than more "blah, blah, blah"? (O'Sullivan 2021; Shefrin 2021; Vives 2021).

Greta Tintin Eleonora Ernman Thunberg was still only eighteen years old when she set the terms for evaluating COP26's efficacy in combatting climate change.

* * *

The fact that climate change is a narrative event is not news. Notably, scholars in many disciplines have examined the narrative aspects of climate change (Craig 2016; Murphy and Lawless 2012). In popular culture, fictional narratives about climate change have become so common that the genre has its own moniker, "cli fi" or "CliFi" (e.g., Martin 2018).

Beyond fiction, climate change narratives are birthed in *many* contexts (e.g., science and politics as well as fiction) and operate at multiple scales, from the individual to the cultural. Cultural narratives provide the worldview lenses through which individuals in a culture make sense of their experiences, including new experiences like that of climate change. For example, in *The End of Sustainability*, Melinda Harm Benson and I identified four climate change cultural narratives unproductively operating at the societal scale within the United States, which we referred to as climate change doesn't really exist, it isn't us, technology will save us, and it's the end of the world as we know it. We argued that the United States needed a new cultural narrative to more effectively deal with climate change and offered the resilient trickster as our candidate replacement (Benson and Craig 2017).

Young people, however, occupy a different narrative position vis-à-vis climate change than adults and hence can potentially create worldview-changing new cultural narratives about it. Janet Currie and Olivier Deschênes (2016: 3) identified four themes that govern this differential positionality, emphasizing that "climate change will fundamentally alter Earth's climate system in many ways that threaten children's physical and mental wellbeing" and that "today's children and future generations will bear a disproportionate share of the burden of climate change, which will affect child wellbeing through many direct, indirect, and societal pathways." In this emphasis, Currie and Deschênes tellingly reveal that adult climate change narratives inferentially position youth (and future generations) as non-subjects and non-agents with respect to climate change. They are instead, first, the silent *objects* of contemporary climate change policies—the people upon whom those policies will ultimately act. Second, relatedly, youth and future generations are the disproportionately affected *victims* both of climate change itself and of current adults' incapacity and/or unwillingness to act. As Currie and Deschênes (2016: 4) summarize, "Children are largely left out of discussions about appropriate responses to climate change but they ought to be central to these debates because they—as well as future generations—have a much larger stake in the outcome than we do."

As this chapter will detail, young people *are* becoming central to the climate change discussion, narrating in both political and legal arenas their own stories of what climate change means and the drastic action necessary now to achieve the futures they prefer. Admittedly, the lines between "adult" and "children" are fuzzy in this context. Lawsuits often take significant time, and participants who were clearly children—younger than age eighteen—at the start of a lawsuit may be young adults—ages eighteen to mid-twenties, sometimes even early thirties—by the end of it. Acknowledging, therefore, that these terms are imprecise, this chapter uses "adults" to refer to the generations currently holding political, social, and economic power but who are unlikely to still be alive when the worst impacts of climate change (on its current trajectory) start to become serious realities in, roughly, the 2050s and 2060s. The terms "youth" and "young people," in turn, refer, admittedly sometimes clumsily, to the generations who currently lack the traditional forms of power, status, and ability to effectuate policy directly but who are increasingly likely to still be alive when climate change impacts become truly devastating on a global scale. This chapter will reserve "child," "children," and "young adult" for direct quotations and for discussions where either greater precision is important or the youth narrator self-identifies to one term.

The increasingly active participation by young people in shaping climate change *cultural* narratives offers an important counterbalance to the still-pervasive adults' figuring of youth as passive and particularly vulnerable climate change victims (Sanson and Burke 2020: 345; Burke, Sanson, and van Hoorn 2018; Ebi and Paulson 2007; Leister 2020; Tanner and Seballos 2012; Trott 2019). As one example of this paradigm's pervasiveness, psychologists and parents alike are concerned not only about the potential impacts of climate change itself on young people's well-being, but also about the destructive effects of *stories* about climate change that youth hear and then fret about (Burke et al. 2018; Rousell and Cutter-Mackenzie-Knowles 2020). Notably, climate narratives can harm youth psychologically and emotionally exactly because these young people feel powerless to effect any change even as they simultaneously fully accept what climate science tells them about their likely seriously impoverished futures (Burke et al. 2018: 3). As a result, climate change narratives become a "'stressor' for young people, even when the impacts are vicarious rather than direct" (ibid.).

In other words, the paradigmatic narrative adults tell each other about youth and climate change is one of disempowerment and victimization and the emotional stress young people experience as a result. However, child psychologists and therapists also recognize that taking action—that is, becoming subjects of climate narratives and agents of climate change policy—is an important psychological coping tool for youth (Burke et al. 2018; Hicks and Holden 2012; Ojala 2012a, 2012b; Trott 2019). A shift in attention from youth as the vulnerable victims to climate policy agents is thus warranted, both to promote young people's psychological well-being and to acknowledge their increasing authorship of climate change narratives (Kelsey and Armstrong 2012; Leister 2020; Ojala 2012a, 2016; Rousell and Cutter-Mackenzie-Knowles 2020; Trott 2019).

While many adults still figure climate empowerment as a self-interested gift from adults to the youth being empowered (Trott 2019; see also Rousell and Cutter-Mackenzie-Knowles 2020; Schreiner, Henriksen, and Hansen 2005), these young people increasingly use their own initiative to act with respect to climate change, and researchers are beginning to acknowledge that youths construct their own narratives about climate change (Tanner 2010; Trott 2019). Moreover, while it is perhaps less surprising that youth agency can inspire climate action within families (Hartley et al. 2021; Lawson et al. 2019) and communities (Ojala 2012b; Trott 2019), youth-led narration is also starting to make a real difference to national and international climate change law and politics. Young people are bringing lawsuits against governments in courts around the world, petitioning legislatures and agencies, and chiding national leaders to force and cajole governments into actively addressing climate change (Burke et al. 2018; Leister 2020). These political and legal efforts have evolved into something more than just psychological coping mechanisms for the youths involved; they have become serious mechanisms for political and legal change, particularly regarding climate change mitigation.

Given those real-world impacts, it is time to examine more closely the phenomenon of youths telling their own stories about climate change. This chapter looks first at young people who have motivated political change, focusing on Greta Thunberg. It then looks at the young plaintiffs who have brought their stories to courts around the world, increasingly catalyzing court orders that force nations to reduce greenhouse gas emissions. This chapter reveals that youth have exploited their differential positionality vis-à-vis climate change to offer stories to the world, permeated with a deep respect for climate science, of how climate change is already affecting them and their futures, requiring action *now*.

In particular, youth plaintiffs have carried their demand for action into legal forums that require them to articulate recognized legal claims. Adults have generally chosen to demand climate action largely through environmental claims. In the United States, for instance, climate change lawsuits tend to sound in public nuisance (e.g., American Elec. Power Co. v. Connecticut, 564 U.S. 410, 415 (2011); Native Village of Kivalina v. ExxonMobil Corp., 696 F.3d 849, 855–56 (9th Cir. 2012)), to invoke the public trust doctrine (e.g., In re Maui Elec. Co. Ltd., 506 P.3d 192, 196 (2022)), or to try to fit climate change within the Clean Air Act (e.g., Massachusetts v. EPA, 549 U.S. 497, 528–30 (2007)). In contrast, youth activists choose human rights causes of action.

This choice is more than just a legal strategy; it articulates a different cultural narrative of what climate change *means*. To adults, particularly in the Global North and West, climate change is often about impacts to the physical world, making climate change an environmental law problem, as numerous "Save the Polar Bear" campaigns attest. To youth activists, in contrast, climate change is about what is happening to them and their futures, an eroding of their lives and well-being that constitutes present existential harm and gives them common cause with many in the Global South. Notably, these young activists have also exploited a cause of action that underscores their distinct positionality as climate change narrators: the United Nations Convention on the Rights of the Child. In their hands, courts and tribunals became the metaphysical cauldrons in which their individual stories transmute into a new cultural narrative, refiguring climate change policy as a quest for human rights and global justice.

Greta Thunberg and Youth-Led Climate Politics

In 2018, at the age of fifteen, Greta Thunberg skipped school every Friday to sit outside the Swedish Parliament with a hand-painted sign, demanding action on climate change, her self-styled climate change school strike (Woodward 2020). Her protest sparked an international movement in a way that few children's protests have ever done (ibid.). On September 20, 2019, she led the largest climate protest in history (Baker, Perper, and Watson 2019). Children around the world walked out of school, inviting adults to join them—which the adults did, by the hundreds of thousands, accumulating millions of protesters globally.

Thunberg and other youth climate activists are narrating climate change, telling their story of why climate change action matters to the generations who will have to live with its increasingly severe consequences. In so doing, they are both asserting their own status as agents in addressing climate change *and* changing the legal terms of climate change activism. Regarding their agency, for example, if the psychologists tell stories of climate change politics creating child victims, youth activists figure themselves as climate heroes taking on the forces of evil (heroes, after all, get injured too). As one example, in August 2021, Thunberg and Ugandan youth climate activist Vanessa Nakate called the United Kingdom a "climate villain" for continuing to approve new licenses for offshore oil and gas drilling and for hiding emissions from shipping. Authors of books for young people also fit Thunberg's story into an archetypal "hero" or fairy tale quest narrative. This trend is perhaps most obvious in Zoë Tucker and Zoe Persico's 2019 *Greta and the Giants*, in which the giants destroying Greta's forest world are the adults perpetuating a resource-intensive carbon-based lifestyle.

In addition, the young activists know what weapons need to be wielded to stop the climate monsters—or with more of a fairy tale resonance, to turn the giants back into good people. Most prominently, these activists come from the generations of "digital natives" who grew up using social media to communicate with each other—and whose communicating peers are global, not just the kids down the block or classmates (Lusk 2010). In their online lives, they form and join far-reaching communities that offer support and inclusion (ibid.)—and, as Thunberg and her colleagues have proven, the means to coordinate action. Indeed, the increasing number of books for youth that tell these activists' stories emphasize these digital natives' social networking skills. For example, in the juvenile nonfiction book *Who Is Greta Thunberg?*, Jill Leonard (2020: 4) stresses that "like so many teenagers born in the twenty-first century, Greta understood the power of social media. She posted a photo of herself holding her sign on Instagram and Twitter. She contacted a few Swedish newspapers to tell them about her strike to call attention to climate change. Sure enough, a couple of local newspapers sent reporters." Similarly, Valentina Camerini (2019: 8) notes, "On the sixth day of the strike, Greta suggested to everyone that they should talk about the protests on their social networks. That way, people who couldn't join the protesters would be able to show their support with a message, a like, or a share."

By using these tools, the youth climate activists have inverted the normal power dynamic between adults and young people. In the face of adult inaction, they hold protests and file lawsuits. Instead of being content to accept whatever protection adults offer them, these youths take responsibility for their own futures. For example, Camerini (2019: 68–69) dramatizes the moment in 2018 when Thunberg accused the members of the United Nations of acting like children. According to Thunberg,

> Since our leaders are behaving like children, we will have to take the responsibility they should have taken long ago. . . . We have to understand what the older generation has dealt to us, what mess they have created that we have to clean up and live with. We have to make our voices heard. (Carrington 2018)

Perhaps more importantly, these youth activists also appear to have convinced at least some adults that they are necessary and vital drivers of climate action. In 2018, for example, UN Secretary General António Guterres announced, "Our younger generations will have to help drive, and complete, the work we start today. We need to harness their energy, invention and political power to raise climate ambition" (Carrington 2018).

Notably, these activists have often transformed their personal suffering into climate action. Thunberg herself suffered from climate change-induced depression (at age eleven) but emerged from it (with her parents' help) to realize that she could take her future into her own hands (Giannella 2019; Winter 2019). She is also acutely aware that she narrates the need for climate change action from an uncommon perspective. In her own book, *No One Is Too Small to Make a Difference*, she embraces her positionality both as a child and as a person with Asperger's Syndrome to drive home the message that the science of climate change demands action now, because "the climate and the biosphere don't care about our politics and our empty words for a single second. They only care about what we do" (Thunberg 2019: 2–3). She credits her Asperger's Syndrome with giving her a clarity of vision about climate change hypocrisy that most adults seem to lack:

> I think in many ways that we autistic are the normal ones and the rest of the people are pretty strange. They keep saying that climate change is an existential threat and the most important issue of all. And yet they just carry on like before. If the emissions have to stop, then we must stop the emissions. To me that is black or white. There are no grey areas when it comes to survival. Either we go on as a civilization or we don't. (Thunberg 2019: 6)

She considers her autism's "black and white" perspective on the world to be a "gift" that allows her to pursue climate activism instead of normal socializing (28).

Her positionality as a child, in turn, empowers her to remind the politically empowered adults around her that her future is very different from theirs. Addressing "all of you who choose to look the other way every day because you seem more frightened of the changes that can prevent catastrophic climate change than the catastrophic climate change itself," she announces that "your silence is almost worst of all" because "the future of all the coming generations rests on your shoulders. Those of us who are still children can't change what you do now once we're old enough to do something about it" (Thunberg 2019: 3–4). However, she and the other youth activists can still be the active narrators of the story that climate science is telling:

There is one other argument that I can't do anything about. And that is the fact that I'm "just a child and we shouldn't be listening to children." But that is easily fixed—just start to listen to the rock-solid science instead. Because if everyone listened to the scientists and the facts I constantly refer to then no one would have to listen to me or any of the other hundreds of thousands of schoolchildren on strike for the climate across the world. (Thunberg 2019: 30–31)

But in relating the truth of climate science, the young activist's narrative operates simultaneously as an accusation: Adults can afford to ignore climate science because *they* won't have to really live with the consequences.

The supposed victims have thus become the attacking plaintiffs, both figuratively and in real courts. It is in these courtrooms, moreover, that youth activists are actively changing the cultural narrative of what climate change means—and why adults must act.

Youth-Led Climate Litigation

Plaintiff Jaime B. . . . is a 14-year-old citizen of the US and a resident of Flagstaff, Arizona. Jaime is a member of the Navajo Nation. . . . Jaime and her Mother had to move from Cameron to Flagstaff because of water scarcity. Jaime and her extended family on the Reservation remember times when there was enough water on the Reservation for agriculture and farm animals, but now the springs they once depended on year-round are drying up. Jaime and her Mother were not able to sustain living on the Reservation because of the costs of hauling water into Cameron for themselves and their animals. . . . Participating in sacred Navajo ceremonies on the Reservation is an important part of Jaime's life, and climate impacts caused by the acts of Defendants are starting to harm the ability for Jamie and her tribe to participate in their traditional ceremonies.
—Complaint, *Juliana v. United States*

Litigation is a narrative act with real-world consequences—the one great truth that emerges from both the musical and movie versions of

Chicago's otherwise ethical farce of a criminal trial. Even in civil litigation, both plaintiffs and defendants (or their lawyers) strive to tell compelling stories of why they *deserve* to win, as well as why they are legally entitled to win. This reality is particularly true in climate litigation, in which significant cognitive biases and substantial investment in the status quo fossil fuel economy challenge plaintiffs' abilities to effectively narrate climate change as a real and immediate legal problem deserving a real remedy (Nosek 2018).

Thus, when youth climate activists take to the courts, they seek to create a compelling story of how the defendants—usually their own governments—are wronging them. The superb rhetorical tactic they have tended to choose is to turn their climate change-induced harms into human rights violations. Four examples, presented in chronological order, illustrate this youth-led transformation of climate change from an environmental problem into a global human rights and justice cultural narrative.

Our Children's Trust Litigation in the United States

In the United States, under the umbrella of Our Children's Trust (OCT 2022a), youth plaintiffs have litigated climate change with the federal government in *Juliana v. United States* (OCT 2022b) and pursued climate action in state courts, state legislatures, and state agencies in all fifty states (OCT 2022c). These lawsuits most generally seek to establish that the federal and state governments have a trust duty to protect the plaintiffs' futures from climate change.

The Our Children's Trust litigation has become most widely known through the two lawsuits litigated in Oregon. In *Chernaik v. Kitzhaber/ Brown*, 475 P.2d 68 (Or. 2020), the state court litigation, the youth plaintiffs argued that the State of Oregon has a duty under the state public trust doctrine to combat the effects of climate change. The Oregon state courts—including, as of October 2020, the Oregon Supreme Court—all decided against the plaintiffs, narrowly defining Oregon's public trust doctrine in the process to exclude both the atmosphere and an affirmative governmental trust duty to protect youth and future generations as trust beneficiaries (ibid., 77–78). However, in *Juliana v. United States*, 217 F. Supp. 3d 1224 (D. Or. 2016), the federal court litigation, the plaintiffs successfully argued to the US District Court for the District of Oregon that they have a constitutional right to a stable and life-supporting environment, based on the same principles the US Supreme Court used a few years earlier to find that the Constitution mandated marriage equality (ibid., 1250).

That victory was short-lived, but it illustrated the potential power of the federal courts to address the climate civil rights issue as decisively as they had taken on "separate but equal" racial discrimination or limitations on gay marriage. After the United States' convoluted procedural maneuvers that resulted in two trips to the US Supreme Court, the US Court of Appeals for the Ninth Circuit dismissed the case on January 17, 2020, on standing grounds, while still acknowledging that most of the youths' argument is true (*Juliana v. United States*, 947 F.3d 1159, 1169–73 (9th. Cir. 2020)). Importantly, the Ninth Circuit validated the current harms that the youth plaintiffs are experiencing as a result of climate change: "Jaime B., for example, claims that she was forced to leave her home because of water scarcity, separating her from relatives on the Navajo Reservation. . . . Levi D. had to evacuate his coastal home multiple times because of flooding. . . . These injuries are not simply 'conjectural' or 'hypothetical'; at least some of the plaintiffs have presented evidence that climate change is affecting them now in concrete ways and will continue to do so unless checked" (ibid., 1168). Moreover, "The plaintiffs' alleged injuries are caused by carbon emissions from fossil fuel production, extraction, and transportation" (ibid., 1169).

The problem was that the court lacked constitutional authority, at least according to two of the judges, to force the rest of the federal government to do anything to redress the harms (ibid., 1170). Dissenting Judge Staton decried this disempowerment of the courts to help future generations, complaining that "it is as if an asteroid were barreling toward Earth and the government decided to shut down our only defenses. . . . Plaintiffs bring suit to enforce the most basic structural principle embedded in our system of ordered liberty: that the Constitution does not condone the Nation's willful destruction" (ibid., 1176).

While legally the *Chernaik* and *Juliana* cases are defeats, they nevertheless showcased young people's narratives of climate change harms, making clear that youth experience climate change both as an existing real harm (e.g., being forced to move) and as a continual threat to their future ability to thrive—to live where they want, to practice the culture they grew up in, to be free of psychological and physical stress. The complaints in these cases are often usually long—not always the smartest strategy with busy judges—precisely to ensure that the youth plaintiffs can tell their stories of injury and activism. These cases are thus forums where the youth plaintiffs tell adults stories about how climate change harms them, arguably violating their rights to life and liberty. The courts' unwillingness to act, as Judge Staton's dissent underscores, reinforces the "child hero versus giant" narrative emerging from the activists' more political endeavors: the youth plaintiffs are taking on a big legal system that, at least in the United States, has not (yet) been willing to budge.

United Nations Committee on the Rights of the Child

On September 24, 2019, sixteen young climate activists ranging in age from nine to seventeen years old, and including Greta Thunberg, submitted a complaint, known as a "communication," to the United Nations Committee on the Rights of the Child (Communication 2019). This eighteen-person committee runs and monitors the Convention on the Rights of the Child, which came into force in 1990. The complaint targeted Argentina, Brazil, France, Germany, and Turkey. It asked the committee to find "that climate change is a children's rights crisis," "that each respondent, along with other states, has caused and is perpetuating a climate crisis," and "that by recklessly perpetuating life-threatening climate change, each respondent is violating the petitioners' rights to life, health, and the prioritization of the child's best interests, as well as the cultural rights of the petitioners from indigenous communities" (ibid., 7 ¶ 33).

On October 8, 2021, the committee issued its decisions against the respondent countries (UNHRTB 2021). It relied heavily on the plaintiffs' own stories of their experiences with climate change to conclude that they were, in fact, experiencing violations of their rights under the convention. These violations took the form of plaintiffs' worsening asthma from wildfire smoke and heat-related pollution; their contraction of vector-borne diseases such as malaria and dengue fever, which are expanding and intensifying in response to climate change; their exposure to extreme heat waves and drought; the Indigenous plaintiffs' risk of losing their subsistence way of life; the risk that the plaintiffs from the Marshall Islands and Palau face of losing their homelands; and the plaintiffs' suffering of climate anxiety (ibid., 12 ¶10.13).

In five separate opinions, one for each nation, the committee ultimately dismissed the complaint because the youth plaintiffs had not exhausted their domestic remedies first by filing lawsuits within the defendants' national courts—underscoring the importance of national-level lawsuits. Nevertheless, in finding that nations foreseeably injure the rights of young people everywhere by failing to curb their greenhouse gas emissions, the committee offered a powerful statement that climate change burdens youth with unjust harm. It also validated the unique positionality of children to use the convention to assert their rights to a productive future.

More importantly, by prompting these decisions, the youth plaintiffs transformed their individual stories of climate change's impacts on their lives into a collective narrative of how adults' failure to stop climate change was violating the rights of children everywhere. Climate change is now, legally, a human rights issue, backed by a powerful new cultural narrative: by refusing to act to stop climate change, governments are foreseeably harming real people, especially youth and future generations, and are violating their rights to life, freedom, health, and homelands as certainly as if those nations were committing genocide.

Youth Litigation Internationally

The number of climate change cases filed around the world nearly doubled between 2017 and 2020 (UNEP and Sabin Center 2020: 9), with youth activists bringing many of them, and judges are increasingly forcing nations to address climate change as a result. The human rights narrative remains the key to these successes.

Our Children's Trust's work extends internationally, from the *Urgenda* decision in the Netherlands to a constitutional amendment in Norway to constitutional climate litigation before the Supreme Court of Pakistan (OTC 2022d). The *Urgenda* decision from the Supreme Court of the Netherlands was a clear victory for youth everywhere, because the court concluded that the European Convention on Human Rights imposed enforceable obligations on the Dutch government to reduce greenhouse gas emissions (UNEP and Sabin Center 2020: 15).

Germany soon followed. In February 2020, a group of German youth argued that the nation's statutory target of reducing Germany's greenhouse gas emissions by 55 percent from 1990 levels by 2030 was not stringent enough to prevent major harms from climate change, violating the plaintiffs' human rights under Germany's constitution (Sabin Center 2022). On April 21, 2021, the Federal Constitutional Court agreed, striking down major portions of the law as incompatible with fundamental human rights—especially the rights of future generations. Specifically, it concluded that "one generation must not be allowed to consume large parts of the CO_2 budget under a comparatively mild reduction burden if this would at the same time leave future generations with a radical reduction burden . . . and expose their lives to serious losses of freedom" (ibid.).

The Federal Constitutional Court thus made explicit the importance of youths' and future generations' positionality to human rights in a climate change world. Climate change unfolds over time, and future generations will see their rights—to life, to freedom, to culture—erode in ways that are qualitatively and quantitatively different from the climate change experience of current decision makers. Thus, in addition to hearing youths' stories of climate change harms as collective human rights violations, courts also must be cognizant that government inaction is already creating future narratives of harm in order to justly evaluate the human rights implications of that government inaction.

European Court of Human Rights

The decision of the Netherlands and Germany regarding climate change human rights may soon be extended to the entire European Union. In September 2020, after Portugal experienced its hottest July in ninety years, four youth and two young adults from Portugal filed a lawsuit, *Duarte Agostinho and Others v. Portugal and Others*, in the European Court of Human Rights against thirty-three countries (see Sabin 2022b). They alleged violations of the European Convention on Human Rights, noting that "Portugal is already experiencing a range of climate change impacts including increases in mean and extreme high temperature" and heat waves, which in turn cause "wildfire, heat stress, and severe health impacts from ozone and particulate matter" (Complaint 2020: 7–8). "In 2017, wildfires came very close to [plaintiff] Catarina's home as well as [plaintiffs] Cláudia, Marim, and Mariana's family home. . . . . They also made [plaintiffs] Sofia and André anxious and upset" (ibid., 7). Thus, again, the youth plaintiffs (and their lawyers) packaged individual stories of actual risks from wildfire, future harms from heat waves and air pollution, and fears regarding climate change into a narrative of pervasive human rights violations resulting from governments' failures to reduce greenhouse gas emissions.

On October 15, 2020, the Court fast-tracked the case, then one month later required the nations to respond to the youths' complaint (Garden Court Chambers 2020). "The Court granted the complaint priority on the basis of the 'importance and urgency of the issues raised'" (ibid.). When the governments sought a reversal of the fast-tracking, the Court refused, and the nations filed their defenses on August 14, 2021. This is the first climate change case the Court of Human Rights has allowed (notably, the Court dropped "The People's Climate Case" in March 2021 [DW News 2021]), and it has attracted numerous intervenors on the plaintiffs' side, including the European Commissioner for Human Rights, Amnesty International, the Union of Concerned Scientists, and the European Center for Constitutional and Human Rights (ESCR-Net 2021).

Duarte Agostinho initially caused much excitement, because "on June 30, 2022, the Chamber of the European Court of Human Rights relinquished jurisdiction in favor of the Grand Chamber. The case is now going to be examined by the ECtHR's Grand Chamber of 17 judges on account of the fact that the case raises a serious question affecting the interpretation of the Convention" (Sabin Center 2024). However, on April 9, 2024, the European Court declared the application inadmissible, dismissing the case. It found no grounds for extraterritorial jurisdiction over the non-Portugal defendants, and the plaintiffs had failed to exhaust their domestic remedies against Portugal (ibid.).

Nevertheless, the Court's insistence on fast-tracking the case and the elevation to the Grand Chamber both demonstrate that the cultural narrative of climate change as a human rights issue is expanding into ever larger legal forums—from the relatively limited Committee on the Rights of the Child to individual nations to the entire European Union. The efficacy of this new cultural narrative derives from the special positionality of youth with respect to climate change, and in two ways. First, as climate change narrators, young people face the prospect of living (or not) through increasingly worsening conditions, and they make this future real to adults through their firsthand narratives of the harm and fear that climate change has already inflicted upon them. Second, these youth activists are uniquely enabled to fit those climate stories into the protections accorded them under the Convention on the Rights of the Child, the most widely adopted human rights treaty in the world; every United Nations-recognized nation except the United States has ratified this convention. The legal adoption of this cultural narrative is therefore potentially global.

Conclusion: Why Are Youths' Climate Narratives "Good Stories," and Do They Matter?

Sometimes a narrative is a good story because it encourages others to change how they view a problem. The youth climate activists' individual stories of how climate change is altering their lives are, as a collective, becoming a larger tale—a cultural narrative—of what climate change is really "about." These young people's legal narrative acts, moreover, resonate through both of Francesca Polletta's (2006: 2–3) political storytelling values.

First, storytelling has value for disadvantaged groups seeking to bring about cultural change, and "even before movements emerge, the stories that circulate within subaltern communities provide a counterpoint to the myths promoted by the powerful" (Polletta 2006: 2–3). Youth activists used their differentially positioned experience of climate change to create a different cultural narrative about climate change, using their facility with social media to share that narrative among themselves before presenting it to adult-run legal forums. Cultural narratives are the deep and structuring myths that a society tells itself about its origins, values, and purposes (Benson and Craig 2017: 7–10). Change the cultural narrative, even a little, and you will likely change how a society behaves, so this youth-driven shift to a good story of protecting human rights is potentially game-changing.

But, as Polletta acknowledges, the story comes with risks as well (Polletta 2006: 3). From one perspective, the youth activists' climate change stories are as scary and depressing as any of the most darkly visioned CliFi tales. These children and young adults tell tales of how climate change is already differentially harming the world's children in a variety of specific ways, and how they will suffer from those harms—asthma, heat stroke, water insecurity, food insecurity, increased disease, loss of culture, loss of homeland, refugeeism, loss of hope, and mental health problems—for much longer and to a greater intensity than the adults who currently make the world's climate decisions.

However, these youths' very positionality as narrators, together with their savvy use of social media, is changing the entire framing of climate change politics, moving climate change out of the realm of environmental law and policy and into the realm of human rights and justice. Moreover, "stories are differently intelligible, useful, and authoritative depending on who tells them, when, for what purpose, and in what setting" (Polletta 2006: 3). These youth activists' stories, unlike those of similarly situated adults, bring a moral force that climate politics have heretofore largely lacked: *We are your children and grandchildren, and you are hurting us, eviscerating our dreams, destroying our future.* So, despite the pain, theirs is a good story because it can move adults to real change—most obviously now in the court decisions, but also more subtly through changes in the larger cultural conversations about climate change. Climate change policy is no longer about saving the polar bear, the coral reefs, or even the planet. It's about saving humanity's future, a future that has real faces.

Have these stories mattered? Yes. The victorious lawsuits, and the press and social media coverage that goes with them, are the most obvious evidence of this claim. Only children can fully invoke the Convention on the Rights of the Child, and those rights now extend, at least in the United Nations, to the transboundary impacts of climate change. Germany and the Netherlands are under court orders to revise their national climate policies. However, the social movement component of the youths' activism is arguably also making a real difference (Development News 2019; Hartley et al. 2021). For example, after standing-room-only speeches in April 2019, Thunberg apparently helped to inspire the United Kingdom's Parliament to enact new climate legislation (Alter, Haynes, and Worland 2019)—a phenomenon that the *Guardian* dubbed "the Greta Thunberg effect" (Watts 2019). In the wake of Thunberg's September 2019 speech to the United Nations, New Zealand became the fifth country to enact a national law to achieve net zero carbon emissions by 2050 and also reductions in methane emissions, joining Thunberg's native Sweden as well as France, England, and Scotland (Fleming 2019). In survey research conducted every year since 2008, communications researchers have documented that adult concern about climate change in the United States has been increasing since 2015 (Marris 2019: 472). "About one-quarter of the adults in the 2018 survey thought that the most important reason to act on climate change was 'to provide a better life for our children and grandchildren.' That response suggests that youth activists remind adults why they care about the environment in the first place" (ibid.). Similar findings have been documented in the United Kingdom, Portugal, and Australia. In interviews conducted by Hartley et al. (2021: 4), "four central themes emerged around adult responses to youth activism. Informants reported that young people were inspiring, that they wanted to support young people, that they viewed young people as able to provide leadership for local action, and that young people could effectively challenge the establishment." In a plot twist, therefore, these responses suggest that youth climate storytelling has worked not just to refocus the climate change debate from environmental protection to human rights and justice but also to effectuate a transfer of rhetorical leadership in climate change politics from adults to youth.

Narrating climate change from the positionality of youth climate leaders gives them greater moral authority, commanding adults to listen to their stories and accusations (Marris 2019: 472). While youth protest has a long history (Elsen and Ord 2021), "the latest generation of protestors is louder and more coordinated than its predecessors," and "the movement's visibility on social media and in the press has created a feedback loop" (Marris 2019: 471).

However, the actual story that these youth climate activists tell is also critical to their success. As the lawsuits most sharply demonstrate, these activists' collective narrative changes climate change's narrative paradigm from environmental disaster to global justice (Marris 2019): *Adult perpetuation of climate change is actively hurting me, violating my rights as a child and my rights as a human being.* Through their stories, the failure of climate change policy becomes a civil rights movement—like the US civil rights movement of the 1950s and 1960s, a social movement seeking to force the establishment to recognize and enforce the legal and social rights of the disempowered—where an important part of progress is simply listening to the stories of the formerly voiceless. "This important connection between climate justice and social justice is regarded as one of the key foundations of the global youth climate movement" (Elsen and Ord 2021: 2). This new human rights narrative is more effective in generating broad support than the traditional environmental narrative (ibid.; Marris 2019: 471–72). In part, "their struggle is directly linked to the wider fight for social justice," and it can be adapted to particular situations in individual locations. However, this narrative is also revolutionary, highlighting the need to look more broadly than environmental policies to address climate change. Youth activists call for systemic change to correct deep-seated and long-standing injustices, including racism, sexism, and the legacies of colonialism, aligning these young "climate activists with social movements such as *Black Lives Matter*" (Elsen and Ord 2021: 2).

Thus, while Thunberg and her fellow activists have spurred real legal and political change with respect to climate change, perhaps the most potent and long-lasting impact of their individual stories of harm will be the new cultural narrative of climate change they induced. So long as climate change is "about" the environment, it is much easier to ignore or deprioritize. By making it clear through their individual stories that climate change is "about" unjust harm to children—that is, injustice—the youth climate activists offer a broader and, by all available evidence, more compelling cultural narrative, one capable of changing "the mindset of the culture from which the system arises" and bringing about "significant shifts in ideas, mindsets, and values" (Pigott 2021).

Hopefully, the adults in power will listen more attentively.

NOTE

The author thanks participants at the 2021 AALS Environmental Law Section Works in Progress Workshop for their comments and suggestions.

REFERENCES

Alter, Charlotte, Suyin Haynes, and Justin Worland. 2019. "TIME 2019 Person of the Year: Greta Thunberg." *Time*. https://time.com.

Baker, Sinéad, Rosie Perper, and Sara Kiley Watson. 2019. "Photos Show Huge Climate-Change Protests around the World, Which Have Spread across Continents as Millions Strike to Demand Action." *Business Insider*, September 20. www.businessinsider.nl.

Benson, Melinda Harm, and Robin Kundis Craig. 2017. *The End of Sustainability: Resilience and the Future of Environmental Governance in the Anthropocene*. Lawrence: University of Kansas Press.

Burke, Susan E. L., Ann V. Sanson, and Judith Van Hoorn. 2018. "The Psychological Effects of Climate Change on Children." *Current Psychiatry Reports* 20 (35). https://doi.org/10.1007/s11920-018-0896-9.

Camerini, Valentina. 2019. *Greta's Story: The Schoolgirl Who Went on Strike to Save the Planet*. London: Simon and Schuster.

Carrington, Damian. 2018. "'Our Leaders Are Like Children,' School Strike Founder Tells Climate Summit." *Guardian*, December 4. www.theguardian.com.

Communication to the Committee on the Rights of the Child, *Sacchi et al. v. Argentina, Brazil, France, Germany, & Turkey* (Communication No. 104/2019). 2019. https://childrenvsclimatecrisis.org.

Complaint, *Duarte Agostinho and Others v. Portugal and 32 Other States*. 2020. https://climatecasechart.com.

Craig, Robin Kundis. 2016. "Learning to Live with the Trickster: Narrating Climate Change and the Value of Resilience Thinking." *Pace Environmental Law Review* 33: 351–96.

Currie, Janet, and Olivier Deschênes. 2016. "Children and Climate Change: Introducing the Issue." *Future of Children* 26 (1): 3–9.

Development News. 2019. "Is Youth Activism Creating Change?" *iD4D*. https://ideas-4development.org.

DW News. 2021. "EU Top Court Drops Families' Climate Action Case." Deutsche Welle, March 25. www.dw.com.

Ebi, Kristie L., and Jerome A. Paulson. 2007. "Climate Change and Children." *Pediatric Clinics of North America* 54 (2): 213–26.

Elsen, Felix, and Jon Ord. 2021. "The Role of Adults in 'Youth Led' Climate Groups: Enabling Empowerment." *Frontiers in Political Science: Youth Activism in Environmental Politics* 3: art. 641154. https://doi.org/10.3389/fpos.2021.641154.

ESCR-Net. 2021. "Amicus Reaffirms States' Human Rights Obligations to Adequately and Effectively Address the Climate Crisis." May 12. www.escr-net.org.

Fleming, Sean. 2019. "These Are the Countries That Have Made Their Climate Commitments Law." *World Economic Forum*, November 13. www.weforum.org.

Garden Court Chambers. 2020. "European Court of Human Rights Is Fast-Tracking a Climate Case against 33 European States Brought by 6 Portuguese Youth." November 30. www.gardencourtchambers.co.uk.

Giannella, Valentina. 2019. *We Are All Greta: Be Inspired to Save the World.* London: Lawrence King.
Hartley, Jenna M., Katelyn M. Higgins, M. Nils Peterson, Kathryn T. Stevenson, and Megan W. Jackson. 2021. "Perspective from a Youth Environmental Activist: Why Adults Will Listen to Youth in Politics." *Frontiers in Political Science: Youth Activism in Environmental Politics* 3: 636583. https://doi.org/10.3389/fpos.2021.636583.
Hicks, David, and Cathie Holden. 2012. "Remembering the Future: What Do Children Think?" *Environmental Education Research* 13 (4): 501–12.
Kelsey, Elin, and Carly Armstrong. 2012. "Finding Hope in a World of Environmental Catastrophe." In *Learning for Sustainability in Times of Accelerating Change*, edited by Arjen E .J. Wals and Peter Blaze Corcoran, 187–200. Wageningen, Netherlands: Wageningen Academic Publishers.
Lawson, Danielle F., Kathryn T. Stevenson, M. Nils Peterson, Sarah J. Carrier, Renee L. Strnad, and Erin Seekamp. 2019. "Children Can Foster Climate Change Concern among Their Parents." *Nature Climate Change* 9: 458–62. https://doi.org/10.1038/s41558-019-0463-3.
Leister, Linn Lindström. 2020. "The Voice of the Young in a Climate Emergency: Changing the Narrative from Children as Helpless Victims to Active Agents of Change." B.A. thesis in Human Rights, Malmö University. www.diva-portal.org.
Leonard, Jill. 2020. *Who Is Greta Thunberg?* New York: Penguin Workshop.
Lusk, Brooke. 2010. "Digital Natives and Social Media Behavior: An Overview." *Prevention Researcher* 17: 3–6. Available at https://teachandtechassign3.weebly.com.
Marris, Emma. 2019. "Why Young Climate Activists Have Captured the World's Attention." *Nature* 573: 471–72. https://doi.org/10.1038/d41586-019-02696-0.
Martin, Emily. 2018. "What Is Cli-Fi? A Beginner's Guide to Climate Fiction." *BookRiot*, May 3. https://bookriot.com.
Murphy, Brenda L., and Jo-Anne Muise Lawless. 2012. "Climate Change and the Stories We Tell." *Journal of Canadian Studies* 46 (2): 196–220.
Nosek, Grace. 2018. "Climate Change Litigation and Narrative: How to Use Litigation to Tell Compelling Climate Stories." *William & Mary Environmental Law & Policy Review* 42: 733–803.
Ojala, Maria. 2012a. "Regulating Worry, Promoting Hope: How Do Children, Adolescents, and Young Adults Cope with Climate Change?" *International Journal of Environmental & Science Education* 7 (4): 537–61.
Ojala, Maria. 2012b. "How Do Children Cope with Global Climate Change? Coping Strategies, Engagement, and Well-Being." *Journal of Environmental Psychology* 32 (3): 225–33.
Ojala, Maria. 2016. "Preparing Children for the Emotional Challenges of Climate Change: A Review of the Research." In *Education in Times of Environmental Crises: Teaching Children to Be Agents of Change*, edited by Ken Winograd, 210–18. New York: Routledge.
O'Sullivan, Kevin. 2021. "Climate in 2021: Beyond the 'Blah, Blah, Blah' of Cop26." *Irish Times*, December 24. www.irishtimes.com.

Our Children's Trust/Youth v. Gov (OCT). 2022a. "Securing the Legal Right to a Safe Climate and a Healthy Atmosphere for All Present and Future Generations." www.ourchildrenstrust.org.
Our Children's Trust/Youth v. Gov (OCT). 2022b. "Juliana v. US." www.ourchildrenstrust.org.
Our Children's Trust/Youth v. Gov (OCT). 2022c. "State Legal Actions." www.ourchildrenstrust.org.
Our Children's Trust/Youth v. Gov (OCT). 2022d. "Global Legal Actions." www.ourchildrenstrust.org.
Pigott, Anna. 2021. "Young Climate Activists Have Far More Power Than They Realize." *Conversation*, October 26. https://theconversation.com.
Polletta, Francesca. 2006. *It Was Like a Fever: Storytelling in Protest and Politics*. Chicago: University of Chicago Press.
Rousell, David, and Amy Cutter-Mackenzie-Knowles. 2020. "A Systemic Review of Climate Change Education: Giving Children and Young People a 'Voice' and a 'Hand' in Redressing Climate Change." *Children's Geographies* 18 (2): 191–208. https://doi.org/10.1080/14733285.2019.1614532.
Sabin Center for Climate Law, Columbia University. 2022. "Neubauer et al. v. Germany." https://climatecasechart.com.
Sabin Center for Climate Law, Columbia University. 2024. "Duarte Agostinho and Others v. Portugal and 32 Other States." http://climatecasechart.com.
Sanson, Anne V., and Susie E. L. Burke. 2020. "Climate Change and Children: An Issue of Intergenerational Justice." In *Children and Peace: From Research to Action*, edited by Nikola Balvin and Daniel J. Christie, 343–62. Cham, Switzerland: Springer Open. https://doi.org/10.1007/978-3-030-22176-8.
Schreiner, Camilla, Ellen K. Henriksen, and Pål J. Kirkeby Hansen. 2005. "Climate Education: Empowering Today's Youth to Meet Tomorrow's Challenges." *Studies in Science Education* 41 (1): 3–49.
Shefrin, Hersh. 2021. "COP26 Produced More Than Blah, Blah, Blah: But How Much More?" *Forbes*, November 24. www.forbes.com.
Tanner, Thomas. 2010. "Shifting the Narrative: Child-Led Responses to Climate Change and Disasters in El Salvador and the Philippines." *Children & Society* 24 (4): 339–51. https://doi.org/10.1111/j.1099-0860.2010.00316.x.
Tanner, Thomas, and Fran Seballos. 2012. "Action Research with Children: Lessons from Tackling Disasters and Climate Change." *IDS Bulletin* 43 (3): 59–70. https://doi.org/10.1111/j.1759-5436.2012.00323.x.
Thunberg, Greta. 2019. *No One Is Too Small to Make a Difference*. New York: Penguin.
Trott, Carlie D. 2019. "Reshaping Our World: Collaborating with Children for Community-Based Climate Change Action." *Action Research* 17 (1): 42–62. https://doi.org/10.1177/1476750319829209.
Tucker, Zoë, and Zoe Persico. 2019. *Greta and the Giants*. Minneapolis: Francis Lincoln Children's Books.

United Nations Environment Programme (UNEP) and Sabin Center for Climate Change Law. 2020. *Global Climate Litigation Report: 2020 Status Review*. Nairobi, Kenya: United Nations Environment Programme.

United Nations Human Rights Treaty Bodies (UNHRTB). 2021. "UN Treaty Database, CRC-Convention on the Rights of the Child: Session 88." https://tbinternet.ohchr.org. Accessed August 9, 2023.

Vives, Xavier. 2021. "Opinion: Was COP26 Mostly 'Blah Blah Blah'? Yes, and Here's Why That's OK." *MarketWatch*, November 18. www.marketwatch.com.

Watts, Jonathan. 2019. "The Greta Thunberg Effect: At Last, MPs Focus on Climate Change." *Guardian*, April 23. www.theguardian.com.

Winter, Jeanette. 2019. *Our House Is on Fire: Greta Thunberg's Call to Save the Planet*. New York: Beach Lane Books.

Woodward, Aylin. 2020. "Greta Thunberg Turns 17 Today. Here's How She Started a Global Climate Movement in Just 18 Months." *Business Insider*, January 3. www.businessinsider.com.

9

The Gift of Survivor Stories

Recognizing the Political Promise of Sexual Violence Narratives

TANYA SERISIER

Stories of sexual violence have become highly significant in contemporary public cultures, especially since the global explosion of testimony inspired by #MeToo in 2017. These are quintessentially bad stories, of violence and trauma, put to good ends—educating society about the reality of sexual violence and seeking to galvanize prevention efforts and support for survivors. While these narratives remain subject to political contestation, and survivors continue to face shame and stigma, in societies such as the United Kingdom, the necessity of survivors telling their stories has come to be largely taken for granted. They are understood as a boon to other victims of violence, and to society in general, particularly women.

This chapter considers the cultural and epistemological revaluation of survivor narratives initiated by second-wave feminists in the 1970s. While historically these stories had been seen as either valueless or dangerous, feminists reconceptualized them as offering insight into the realities of gendered power and even, potentially, its undoing. Seen in this way, survivor narratives were understood as both a unique burden carried by survivors and a precious gift that they offered to other women and to society more broadly. This gift had historically been rejected by societies determined to cover up the realities of sexual violence. The task, therefore, for feminists was to first constitute a group or "counterpublic" able to offer an adequate reception of these stories, and then to force wider social recognition of their value (Salter 2013). The current cultural status of survivor narratives is therefore the outcome of what Kaitlynn Mendes (2016) describes as the "discursive activism" of feminist and survivor movements. These movements have taken these bad stories and made them some of the most politically efficacious narratives of the last fifty years. This wider story, of cultural reckoning with sexual violence, has itself become one of the most prominent good stories told by and about the feminist movement.

My account of this cultural shift focuses on both the epistemological revaluation of survivor narratives and the constitution of an audience for them. I argue that these processes are key to understanding how feminists and survivors turned bad personal stories into a key instigator of political change. Consideration of these processes can also, I suggest, offer insight into the complexities and ambiguities of discursive strategies for change. To be heard, feminists and survivors have tended to present and circulate stories with culturally recognizable and discrete narrative patterns. It is far easier to achieve social recognition for stories that draw on or reproduce existing tropes of sexual violation and innocence, and these tropes are heavily shaped by racial and class biases about both victims and perpetrators. Such an approach has been highly successful in generating recognition for survivor narratives in general. There remains, however, significant unevenness in the reception of individual stories, with only certain narratives being generally recognized as valuable social gifts. I am therefore particularly interested here in which survivor stories do and do not get treated as good stories and why.

The chapter begins with the epistemological basis of the feminist revaluation of these stories, examining how survivor narratives, and survivors, were reconceptualized as bearers of truth in the 1960s and 1970s. In the next section I consider how social space was made for these stories. I trace the processes by which feminists themselves learned to receive the gift and burden of survivor stories and, furthermore, insisted on this process within wider public cultures. Finally, I consider how narrative conventions and cultural tropes of good stories shape which survivor narratives are able to be received as gifts. I conclude by asking how we might think differently about the relationship between narrative and discursive practices, sexual violence and survival. I suggest that we need to learn to recognize and receive a wider variety of accounts as valuable gifts, ultimately by lessening the demands placed on survivors to tell "good stories."

The Burden of Truth and Gift of Narrative

The 1970s marked a key turning point in the second-wave feminist revaluation of survivor narratives, particularly in the women's liberation movement in the United States. Activists in the 1960s and 1970s used small consciousness-raising groups to question their understanding of problems in their lives that they might have previously dismissed as individual or trivial. Exemplified in the slogan "The personal is political," the practice of group consciousness-raising was founded on the epistemological and political position that individual experiences shared by multiple women had political significance that required collective analysis. Reflecting on this process in their movement publication *Rape: The First Sourcebook for Women*, Noreen Connell and Cassandra Wilson (1974: 3) write, "Rape as an issue didn't arise because feminist leaders decided it was 'the issue' or because it was a designated topic on a consciousness-raising list. Instead, it became an issue when women began to compare their experiences, and realized sexual assault was common." A foundation of individual narratives produced the collective political conviction encapsulated in the theme of the New York Radical Feminists' 1971 conference, that "rape is a political crime against women."

This conviction in turn led feminists to consider more closely the political significance and value of the insights of group members who had experienced rape, and to see this experience as profoundly transformative. As Susan Griffin (1979: 53) writes in *Rape: The Power of Consciousness*, "It strikes me now that one of the untold burdens of the survivor of rape is what she has come to know. She has been left holding the truth.... For her the world has changed. And in this understanding, she is isolated, because for us who have not been raped the world remains the same. We keep the fact of rape at the periphery of consciousness and do not let it bear on our vision." In this understanding, stories of sexual violence are burdensome because they reveal a deep, even world-changing truth. A survivor's experience, and her analysis of it, changes her conception of herself, her relationship to the world, and, particularly, the visceral individual and collective impacts of gendered oppression and violence. It reveals a profoundly disturbing truth that the world does not want to recognize, and that is even perhaps unobtainable by those who have not experienced this violation. Therefore, they and their allies must fight to have it heard.

I have previously described this understanding of survivor narratives as a feminist variation on the classic quest narrative, where a "hero ventures forth from the world of common day into a region of supernatural wonder (x): fabulous forces are there encountered, and a decisive victory is won (y): the hero comes back from this mysterious adventure with the power to bestow boons on his fellow man (z)" (Campbell 2008: 23). In the feminist version, it is sexual violence that removes the rape survivor from the world of the everyday, casting her into a realm of previously concealed truth. She must face the forces not only of structural violence but of silencing, stigma, and shame in order to bestow the boon of her story and its truth on her fellow women, and society more broadly. Like the hero, she is isolated by her status, and her burden can only be relieved through the power of collective narrative and sharing stories (Serisier 2018b).

In this revised quest narrative, not only does the survivor transform herself into a heroine, but her experience of sexual violence is transformed from being solely a burden that she carries into a boon, or gift, that she bestows on other survivors and on society, particularly women, more broadly. This is a different understanding to the classic formulation of autobiographical stories as constituted by a narrative transaction between the teller and their audience (Lejeune 1989). In the conceptualization of the feminist quest, the focus is on what the teller has to offer rather than on a mutually beneficial relationship. This is not to say that the teller does not or cannot receive anything from an audience willing to listen and believe her. As I have written about previously, for many tellers of survivor narratives, the benefits of a receptive audience are significant (Serisier 2018b). However, I suggest here that seeing story as gift emphasizes the positive revaluation of previously devalued stories and recognizes that survivor narratives remain narratives of trauma, which are both difficult to tell and difficult to hear. The conception of stories as a gift does not lose the relational element of the concept of transaction. Gifts must be recognized and received in order for gift-giving to be successful. And, as I discuss below, for narratives that are difficult, or that challenge established conventions of what makes a good story, learning to receive these gifts is a crucial and ongoing element of the epistemological revaluation performed by feminists in relation to survivor narratives (Ahmed 2000).

The significance of the epistemological shift that feminists sought to undertake can be fully understood only in comparison to the way that women's accounts of sexual violence have historically been denied and denigrated and the women who tell them "tainted" as liars and fantasists (Gilmore 2017). Juries in rape trials in the 1970s still adhered to variations on seventeenth-century jurist Matthew Hale's famous warning that rape was "an accusation easily to be made and hard to be proved, and harder to be defended by the party accused, tho never so innocent" (Ferguson 1987: 89). Alfred Kinsey, the well-known sexologist and advocate of progressive sexual values, joked that in many cases the difference between rape and a good time was if a girl's parents happened to be awake when she arrived home in a state of disarray (Brownmiller 1976). These prominent examples reflect wider cultural and social patterns that systemically rejected the truth-value of women's experiences. The vast majority of women who told stories of sexual violence found themselves subject to disbelief, blame, or overwriting of their accounts by others, including family, friends, and partners. These experiences, also shared in consciousness-raising groups, were considered to be as politically meaningful as sexual violence itself (Connell and Wilson 1974).

As feminist critics have noted, the history of Western discourse is one of "obsessive erasure" of survivors' speech, and particularly their insights into the structural violence and social significance of rape. This erasure is, however, accompanied by the "obsessive inscription" of dominant institutional and social narratives, which insisted historically that rape was rare, committed by criminal strangers, and usually enabled by the poor choices of women who put themselves in dangerous situations, such as being out in public late at night, or socializing with the wrong types of men (Higgins and Silver 1991: 1).

Where rape was seen to have a meaning beyond pure criminality or the irresponsibility of victims, it was mobilized in the service of dominant discourses, particularly around race. In the United States, where anti-rape feminism as we recognize it today first emerged, rape narratives were a key part of racial politics, through the "myth of the black rapist," a white supremacist narrative that portrays Black men as insatiably violent and sexual, and particularly dangerous to white women

(Davis 1983). These narratives were used to justify both legal violence such as wrongful imprisonment and extralegal violence like lynching directed against Black communities. Speaking of this context, Nellie McKay (1991: 253) describes the "white woman's 'word'" as a "sword of Damocles over all black people." Stories of rape were therefore not entirely taboo or devoid of political meaning, but the narrative framings available and the conditions under which stories were considered worth listening to were highly circumscribed. There was no room for the profound truth of rape as a key aspect of gendered oppression as described by feminist authors such as Griffin.

The stories arising from the white-dominated feminist spaces of the 1960s and 1970s were, however, not the first attempt to construct counter-narratives that addressed the role of rape as a tool of structural oppression and domination. In the nineteenth century, women such as Harriet Jacobs (2000) included testimony about sexual violence experienced at the hands of owners and overseers as part of their memoirs of the evils of slavery. These testimonies were vital to abolitionist politics. As Danielle McGuire (2010) has shown, this tradition of African American women testifying to and organizing against sexual violence as a tool of racial terror, particularly in the southern Jim Crow states, continued into the twentieth century and the civil rights movement with the testimony of women such as Recy Taylor. Leftist organizations such as the Communist Party joined campaigns for the release of the wrongfully imprisoned Scottsboro Nine, nine young African American men who were convicted of raping two white women on the basis of testimony that one of the women later recanted (Duru 2004). This history of injustice was recognized in key cultural texts such as *To Kill a Mockingbird*, in which the hero of the novel, Atticus Finch, is a white lawyer who faces social ostracism for defending a Black man falsely accused of raping a white woman (Lee 2010).

Feminist counter-narratives of the 1960s and 1970s were distinct from previous discursive contestations over sexual violence because they ascribed a unique significance and meaning to sexual violence's role in gendered oppression, and to the unique insights of survivors into this oppression. The overall story told by feminists often failed to draw on insights from these earlier contestations. But they did achieve remarkable success in making their case that survivor stories constitute a privileged form of knowledge that should be recognized and valued, at least in the abstract. The cultural impact of #MeToo was perhaps the culmination of this logic, but it was only the most prominent example of an increasingly accepted cultural logic around the value of survivor speech.

This is not to say that survivors do not continue to face shaming and stigma or that individual narratives are not routinely and regularly silenced or "tainted" with doubt and disbelief (Gilmore 2017). But these attacks generally still acknowledge the overall value of survivor narratives while arguing that a particular individual example should not be granted credence, or that collectively, as in the case of #MeToo, things have gone "too far," so that stories that are only about bad dates or other trivial topics are included under the auspices of survivor speech (Serisier 2022). This dynamic can be seen in the proliferation of responses to the defamation trial brought by Johnny Depp against Amber Heard in response to her allegations of domestic violence. Analysis of the vast amounts of social media commentary on the trial shows that Heard was commonly accused of both lying and undermining the narratives of other victims and survivors by doing so (Whiting et al. 2019).

These conflicts point to the fact that there is more to the political efficacy of survivor narratives than the speaking survivor. She must have an audience who is willing to hear and value the truth she offers. While much feminist epistemological thinking has focused on the role of survivors and their speech, the presence of a community of listeners in enabling and allowing stories to be heard and taken seriously has been equally as crucial for cultural and political change. It is to this I turn in the following section.

Making Counter-Publics, Making Stories Count

Feminist epistemologies such as that offered by Griffin have focused on the individual role and figure of the survivor, her knowledge and her story. However, both feminist politics and narrative practices are inherently collective and relational. As Connell and Wilson make clear in *Rape: The First Sourcebook for Women*, the practice of coming together in consciousness-raising groups was as crucial for developing new ways of thinking about and understanding rape as the role of individuals in telling their stories. Similarly, in his meditation on storytelling, cultural theorist Walter Benjamin (2002: 149) writes of the "community of listeners" who act as the "web in which the gift of storytelling is cradled." In feminist consciousness-raising groups of the 1970s, and in online equivalents like the #MeToo hashtag today, narrative practices are similarly relational and reciprocal. The audiences to any story are themselves potential tellers, with experiences that resonate and amplify those that have come before. So the public speak-out held by the New York Radical Feminists in 1971 arose from consciousness-raising sessions, which themselves were prompted by reading a story in a feminist 'zine from Boston (Brownmiller 1999). Even where audiences do not themselves become tellers, they provide the cultural space for stories to be heard, granting them what Leigh Gilmore (2017: 5) describes as "adequate witness," an audience who will listen to these stories without "deforming" them by doubt or "substituting different terms of value for the ones offered by" the survivor herself. It is not entirely the case that feminist communities or movements of the 1970s gave survivors the ability to speak. Rather, it created a community of listeners that was able to give those stories a fair hearing and, by that means, change the political possibilities of the stories themselves (Plummer 1995).

Even among feminists, survivors did not automatically receive adequate witnessing. As Sara Ahmed (2000) has written, learning to receive the stories of others as gifts can be difficult, especially when these stories may seem threatening or seem to provide unwelcome truths. An example of these difficulties, and of the process of learning, is provided by Susan Brownmiller, author of the foundational text *Against Our Will*, in her autobiographical accounts of that time. Indeed, she opens her famous book with a "personal statement" that acknowledges that she writes as someone who had "changed her mind about rape" (Brownmiller 1976: 9). She recounts that when members of her consciousness-raising group first suggested discussing rape, "I fairly shrieked in dismay." To Brownmiller, the definition of rape was clear: "Rape was a sex crime, a product of a diseased, deranged mind. Rape wasn't a feminist issue" (8). Brownmiller writes that, like many leftists, she believed that rape was political only when it was a case of false and racist allegations made by white women against Black men. Gradually, however, as she listened to the stories told by other members of her group, she was, she writes, "forced by my sisters in feminism" to face "a new way of looking at male-female relations, at sex, at strength and at power" and to acknowledge her own vulnerability (7).

As Susan Griffin writes, the experience of rape has the effect it does in part because it forces recognition of the structural nature of gendered violence, a recognition that most of us keep at the periphery of consciousness. Fully attending to the stories of survivors forces a similar reckoning, as that burden of knowledge comes to be shared by the audience and the speaker. The stories make the world seem less pleasant and safe than it was before. But they also offer insight that is essential for understanding the world as it really is, and for combating the realities of gendered violence and its causes. Taking on this burden can therefore be, as in the case of Brownmiller, politically galvanizing, if one has the capacity and skills to listen. Because Brownmiller was already part of the community of listeners and storytellers that make up a consciousness-raising group, she was able to receive the stories, despite her reservations. In turn, these stories not only "changed her mind" about rape but convinced her to devote the next five years of her life to writing a book about rape in order to change other people's minds.

Feminists such as Brownmiller, however, did more than use their changed conceptions of sexual violence to act as a small community of listeners. They sought to generalize the possibilities for hearing and responding to survivor narratives in order to reproduce their own personal and collective understandings socially. They wanted rape to be understood generally as not simply a feminist issue, but a social problem of gendered oppression and structural violence. They sought to make rape itself, and not only cases where rape allegations were politicized as tools of racism, a political and social concern. In her 1976 book *Against Our Will*, Brownmiller (1976: 15) famously described rape as "a conscious process of intimidation by which *all men* keep *all women* in a state of fear." Later in the book she finessed this by describing rapists as the "shock troops" of patriarchy, working to uphold male rule by keeping women in a state of submission and fear (209). *Against Our Will*, which became a *New York Times* bestseller and saw Brownmiller achieve celebrity author status, was emblematic of the feminist determination to politicize mainstream understandings of rape.

It is for this reason that Michael Salter (2013) has characterized feminists as a "counter-public" in relation to sexual violence. Drawing on

Fraser (1990: 67), he notes that counter-publics comprise "parallel discursive arenas" that "invent and circulate counter-discourses" to represent the identities and needs of marginalized groups more adequately (Salter 2013: 227). It is only within the context of these counter-publics that stories were able to be heard and the reconceptualization of women as survivors with valuable experience could occur. The use of speakouts, protests, and publication of texts such as *Against Our Will* is part of this. And so is feminist engagement with dominant institutional spheres such as the law, in both law reform and public trials, and media, from fictional characterizations of sexual violence to the promotion of survivor narratives in news, talk shows, and, more recently, hashtag and other social media campaigns. Survivor narratives in public spaces not only push an alternate agenda but also seek to teach or inspire others to replicate the process of learning to receive these narratives as gifts, and thereby change the cultural valuation attached to them.

Over time, the discursive space claimed by feminists on this issue has expanded. In turn, feminist understandings of rape as a key aspect of women's oppression have become increasingly accepted. In *Against Our Will* Susan Brownmiller (1976) is already able to reflect on these changes. She writes that when feminists began to draw attention to the politics of rape through survivor experiences, they were treated as a "joke" by the wider world. However, well before the publication of her book, she notes, "the world out there had stopped laughing." Indeed, the commercial success and critical attention paid to the text itself demonstrate the extent of this shift by the mid-1970s. Feminist conceptions of rape as a socially significant form of gendered violence that deserved to be taken seriously were put forward in numerous cultural sites in the 1980s, from television talk shows to fictional films such as *The Accused*, starring Jodie Foster and Kelly McGillis, to media attention paid to select rape trials and calls for legal reform. At the heart of these cultural interventions sat narratives of survivor experience, whether recounted directly for audiences on talk shows or in media attention or through fictional reimagining of the experience of rape and a trial from the perspective of the survivor (Serisier 2018a).

In the past decade, #MeToo has been the focal point for cultural attention to survivor narratives that was unimaginable in the 1970s. Survivors who speak out are awarded "women of the year" awards by *Glamour* magazine or made "people of the year" by *Time*; some even receive open letters from the US vice president (Serisier 2018b). Of most relevance here, however, are the discursive shifts themselves. We now live in a culture in which overt laughter or ridicule of survivor stories is largely condemned, even if survivors continue to face significant social stigma and opposition to their stories (Gilmore 2017). But in mainstream discourse, it has become far less acceptable to subject survivors or their narratives to ridicule, although there remain prominent exceptions, such as the online ridicule directed toward Amber Heard, as mentioned above. However, the willingness to ridicule Heard is based on the premise that she is not a legitimate survivor. Overall, this shift reflects the success of survivors and feminists in claiming discursive and cultural space to ensure that survivor narratives are heard and responded to.

Recognizing Other Gifts: Beyond Good Storytelling

There is an important broad narrative of progress to be told here. This narrative is a good feminist story of good stories supplanting bad ones and improving our understanding of sexual violence, shifting it slowly but inexorably to a social understanding grounded in women's experience rather than patriarchal rape myths. In this section, however, I consider another angle on how that story has come to be, looking at the ways in which feminists and survivors have made use of existing narrative conventions to have stories told and heard. Thinking about the relationship of feminist storytelling to dominant notions of good stories can help us to identify some of the stories and modes of storytelling that continue to be rendered untellable.

As noted above, the treatment of rape, in Western cultures at least, has been that of "obsessive erasure" of the reality of rape, accompanied by "obsessive inscription" of sensationalist and victim-blaming accounts of rape (Higgins and Silver 1991: 2). Both news and fictional storytelling have long been fascinated with tropes of sex and violence, particularly when they include stories of victimized and violated women. Debates within feminism about the recuperation, commodification, and exploitation of survivor narratives have recognized these tendencies, noting the always-present risk that, rather than the personal being politicized, the political point of these narratives can be rendered purely personal or spectacular (e.g., Alcoff and Gray-Rosendale 1993; Armstrong 1994; Naples 2003; Horeck 2004).

It is for this reason that Tanya Horeck (2004: vi) argues that feminists need to consider the conditions and effects of rape's "public volubility" as well as the silence and taboo that have surrounded it. Rather than continuing to focus solely on the "conspiracy of silence" identified by 1970s feminists such as Brownmiller and Griffin, we need to consider the intense publicity given to sexual violence. This includes paying more attention to the preconditions and effects of survivor speech and feminist stories. It also means acknowledging that counter-narratives, such as those produced by feminists and survivors, must make use of some elements of existing dominant narratives in order to be hearable and tellable (Bamberg 2004). In the case of stories of sexual violence, these have tended to be narratives that fit existing ideas of criminal strangers and innocent victims. This is what Susan Estrich (1987) has described as archetypal "real rape," which approximates a myth of a criminal stranger in the bushes. These stories have also tended to be those involving white, young, successful, famous victims, who are able to successfully demonstrate to the satisfaction of the media and courts that they are not responsible for the violence committed against them. Helen Benedict (1992) has also described how media portrayals of rape tend to bifurcate between a small number of supposedly innocent and blameless "virgins," deserving of sympathy, and a larger pool of "vamps," whose stories are either ignored or reported through victim-blaming tropes.

Stories of "real rape" involving symbolic "virgins" are, in other words, easily recognizable as good stories, even within older, dominant narratives. They have clear victims and villains, climactic moments, and recognizable tropes of dangerous strangers and the risks the public sphere poses for women. As Horeck and others have argued, these narratives also rely on, and potentially reinforce, cultural desires for stories of violated and victimized women. They not only fit the criteria for good stories in many conventional ways, but also risk reinforcing dangerous misapprehensions about what rape really looks like and feeding demands for victims to demonstrate their innocence or blamelessness.

Recent years have seen changes to the cultural standards for recognizing good stories of sexual violence. So, where Benedict, writing in the early 1990s, focused on the consumption of alcohol as a narrative element likely to preclude a survivor from being granted victim status, this is no longer necessarily the case. There are several examples of prominent survivor narratives that have achieved large amounts of public sympathy involving consumption of alcohol, the most notable of which is the case of Chanel Miller, previously known by the pseudonym Emily Doe. Miller told her story publicly following a trial in which her assailant, Brock Turner, was convicted, but received a relatively light sentence based on the judge's perception that a harsh sentence would have a "severe impact" on Turner, who was presented as a young athlete with a promising future. Directly contesting both this representation and her own construction within the courtroom as a "vamp," Miller wrote, "I am not just a drunk victim at a frat party found behind a dumpster, while you are the All-American swimmer at a top university, innocent until proven guilty, with so much at stake" (Baker 2016). In the statement, which was read millions of times and prompted an open letter from the then US vice president Joe Biden, Miller was able to assert her innocence, even though she had consumed a great deal of alcohol at the party. She did this by asserting her own youth and innocence, suggesting that her level of intoxication was because she did not have a high alcohol tolerance as she did not usually attend drunken parties, and emphasizing that she was clearly unconscious, rather than simply intoxicated, at the time of the sexual assault. Miller's story demonstrates that there is some flexibility in criteria of innocence, but shows that this innocence must still be demonstrated by survivors in the public sphere as part of efforts to construct an easily accepted and consumed narrative.

Philosopher and survivor Susan Brison (2002: 110) observes that survivor stories receive a far greater hearing when they fit a simple narrative structure, which she labels the "reverse conversion narrative," in which a "perfectly good, intact, life was destroyed, then painstakingly pieced back together again." Such narratives have a linear plot framed around a single climactic event and the heroine's quest to restore order following the chaos it creates. As Kimberlé Crenshaw (1991) has argued, social narratives about justice and injustice tend to be dominated by those that fit what she describes as "single-axis thinking" or a "but for" logic. This logic is essentially a liberal one where there is one identifiable cause of disadvantage "but for" which a particular individual would be able to live a good, socially integrated life. *But for the spectacular single act of sexual violence, my life would be good like yours. Because of that act, I have to make a heroic effort to re-establish a good life, and that is my story.* In the case of rape, this type of narrative also presents the badness of rape in opposition to, and disruptive of, an otherwise benign social order.

The framework of single-axis thinking dominates stories told by feminists and survivor advocates from the 1970s onwards, and contributes to a logic of exceptionalism around narratives of rape. In this understanding, rape is uniquely politically significant, and uniquely traumatizing for those who experience it, because of its centrality in the construction and maintenance of gendered power relations and gendered subjectivities. It is also, by extension, a universal and universalizing experience, that in Brownmiller's famous phrasing, victimizes "all women" and implicates "all men." However, this framing separates rape from other forms of structural and systemic violence. It neglects the ways in which sexual violence sits within intersecting logics of power and marginality, and the ways in which these logics help to perpetuate that violence.

An example of this type of framing is the influential "continuum" model of sexual violence, where rape sits at the far end of a continuum ranging from what is often termed sexist microaggressions through various forms of sexual harassment and assault (Kelly 1988). Karen Boyle (2019) has pointed out that the continuum model is influential in feminist narrative practices such as #MeToo, which link sexual assault to milder forms of sexual violence and harassment. Boyle suggests that what she terms "continuum thinking" continues to offer a useful model of thinking about the interconnectedness of sexual violence. However, the continuum operates along a single axis, largely omitting connections with other types of structural and systemic violence. Ultimately, this can work to perpetuate the dominance of the "but for" logic and the reverse conversion narrative.

An example of single-axis narratives can be seen in Brownmiller's account of changing her mind about rape and its impacts on her thinking about gender and race. Angela Davis (1983) offers one of the original and lasting critiques of Brownmiller's overarching narrative. She argues that Brownmiller had to blind herself to ways that both rape and accusations of rape were used as tools of racial power and violence, in order to advance her thesis of rape as a tool of men, united as a class, to oppress women, united as a class. She draws attention to Brownmiller's discussion of Emmett Till, a young boy brutally murdered because, it was claimed, he had whistled at a white woman. While Brownmiller (1976: 247) declared that people are "rightfully aghast" at the murder, she did, as Davis points out, also describe the whistle itself as "just short of physical assault" and a "reminder" to the woman involved that fourteen-year-old Till "had in mind to possess her." Brownmiller here is unable to take account of the gendered violence of rape while also recognizing the racial violence inherent in what Davis labels the "myth of the black rapist" and so, ultimately, reinforces this myth.

The lure of single-axis thinking and narrative structures like the reverse conversion narrative is that they offer dramatic stories with clear morals. There is a climactic moment of harm and a gradual redemptive arc with identifiable individuals in the role of heroes, villains, and victims. Ironically, feminist attempts to politicize rape by relating it to structures of gendered power have, by focusing on men and women, frequently not only failed to operate intersectionally, but also struggled to tell stories that locate rape within institutional failings and a framework of structural harm. Instead, the problem is articulated through reference to individual victims and perpetrators. This model can explain why male-dominated legal systems deny and delegitimize the voices and perspectives of survivors. But it cannot enable understanding of the ways that sexual violence is used to justify extreme forms of violence perpetrated against Black men and boys like Emmett Till. It also does not adequately explain the prevalence of sexualized forms of violence within the carceral system, and the ways in which criminal justice institutions like prisons function through officially sanctioned forms of sexualized violence such as strip searches and invasive body cavity searches, and failures to protect incarcerated individuals from sexual violence from both staff and other incarcerated people.

A fuller and more nuanced story of sexual violence is one in which some men are also victimized by sexually violent practices, and in which the policing of or failure to police certain types of sexual violence can foster its own sexualized forms of violence. Rather than a continuum stretching along a single axis of gendered violence, it is a complex nodal system about which it might be impossible to tell a single story with a clear moral message. It requires being alive not only to the damage of acts of violence and social indifference to them, but also to the violence that enables these acts, and the systems of state and institutional violence that themselves impact violently marginalized subjects and bodies.

There are alternative ways of thinking about the harms of rape, but they do not fit as easily within the constraints of what makes a "good story." As Jamie Kalven (1999: 291) notes in his discussion of the experience of his family following the rape of his wife, there are clear "conventions by which we recognize and understand stories." It is difficult to resist these conventions even where they are "poorly adapted to the task of rendering that which is strenuously ongoing." Specifically, Kalven recounts his concerns that the conventions of storytelling will be unable to offer an authentic account of the uneven, interminable process of his family's adaptation to life after violence.

These conventions are similarly ill-adapted to telling stories in which life is not "perfectly good" before rape (Brison 2002). For many, the harm and significance of rape do not necessarily lie in its exceptionality but in its relationship and interplay with other forms of structural violence and suffering. Indeed, it is the fact that life is not perfectly good that renders them vulnerable to sexual violence and within which sexual violence may not be experienced as a uniquely damaging trauma, "but for" which my life would be as good as yours. It remains very difficult to tell stories that do not present rape as a singularly or uniquely traumatizing event where, for instance, sexual violence is part of an ongoing experience of incarceration, slavery, or domestic abuse.

Seeing these kinds of stories as gifts presents a particular challenge for the version of narrative politics that feminists have constructed in relation to sexual violence (Serisier 2018b). As already discussed, there is a long history of criticism of dominant, and white-dominated, feminist single-axis thinking around rape by scholars such as Crenshaw (1991) and Davis (1983). Sara Ahmed (2000) too has argued that white feminists particularly struggle to see interventions by women of color that challenge single-axis thinking as a gift rather than a threat. Where feminists have insisted on the value of more straightforward survivor narratives that emphasize the gendered dimensions of rape, we have frequently failed to emphasize the necessity of understanding rape as always possessing multifaceted and intersectional meanings. Ahmed was writing about a conflict in Australia in the 1990s between white feminists and

Indigenous women about the understanding and representation of rape in Indigenous communities. A white feminist anthropologist, Diane Bell (1996), had written several articles asserting her right to speak about sexual violence within Australian Indigenous communities as a purely gendered issue. A group of Indigenous women, led by historian Jackie Huggins (1991), insisted that any discussion of rape in Indigenous communities had to be mindful of the ongoing colonial violence, which structures and limits the possibilities of life within those communities. Speaking of the intervention by Indigenous academics, Ahmed writes, "If white feminism could begin to receive that gift and speak to those others who will not be assimilated into an epistemic community, then a dialogue may yet take place" (Ahmed 2000: 64).

Questions around the possibility of such a dialogue have reopened in Australia in recent years as the issue of gendered violence has once again achieved cultural prominence. In 2021 feminist organizations and individuals organized a set of protests under the banner of "March 4 Justice" in response to the narrative of Brittany Higgins, a government staff member who described being sexually assaulted by another staff member at Parliament House and to the revelation of a historic allegation of sexual assault against the then Australian attorney general by a woman who had subsequently committed suicide (Nelson 2021). Indigenous advocates and journalists, however, questioned why similar mobilization was not happening for Australia's missing and murdered Indigenous women, despite the fact that, according to an investigative report by First Nations journalists, over three hundred Aboriginal women have died or gone missing in mysterious circumstances since 2000 (Carlson 2021). Families, friends, and advocates for these women speak of the indifference they face as they seek to have their demands for justice heard in a context in which gendered and sexual violence cannot be separated from the racism of state services and criminal justice institutions, and the ongoing effects of colonization on Australian First Nations communities and lives. They continue to seek an adequate reception for their stories and other discursive interventions, and they continue to find this reception lacking, as instead they are faced with indifference or relentless demands to frame their interventions through recognizable and palatable narrative forms (McQuire 2022). These interventions are still not understood as a gift in the same way as the survivor narratives discussed above, and they represent a fundamental challenge to dominant models of good stories.

The example of missing and murdered Indigenous women also points to the link between the reverse conversion narrative and the trope of "survival" that dominates much feminist discourse on sexual violence. Survival of any structural violence is not a guarantee, nor is it evidence of individual merit. But it is much more difficult to survive violence that is entrenched within a complex array of social marginalization and harm. It is also much harder to tell stories in which sexual violence is part of what cultural theorist Lauren Berlant (2011) has described as the experience of "slow death," or having life chipped away by complex, repeated, and intersecting experiences of violence, which characterizes many lives under neoliberal capitalism. Or indeed, it is far harder to tell stories with no resolution or even plot developments, but where missing Indigenous women exist in "a state of ambiguity between life and death," as they continue to fail to be found or even searched for by a state machinery marked by indifference (McQuire 2022). In fact, part of the injustice of the experience of slow death is that it is not easily narratable in the sense Kalven describes, and so it is far harder to achieve recognition of pain, suffering, and trauma. Stories of slow death might speak of sexual violence alongside the violence of the carceral state, the violence of poverty, and the violence of systemic pollution. These are often not good stories with easily identifiable individual villains or clearly innocent victims; they do not portray lives that are good "but for" the problem of a single instance of direct violence; and they do not offer the promise of simple or easy resolution, particularly through the criminal justice system.

The issue here is not that the stories that have been produced and promoted by feminists are bad as such. Rather, it is that the reliance on relatively simple narratives can function to limit the stories that are told and the kinds of solutions that they produce. Focusing, however, on the need to generally expand the kinds of stories that are considered good and tellable may help to shift this, and to build on the political efficacy and achievements of the feminist stories that have been told over the last half century. It may also be, however, that the model of individualized narratives of victimization and survival is itself not adequate to this task, and that other discursive forms are needed that are more able to communicate the political urgency of responding to the multiple forms of structural and systemic violence that shape and limit the lives of Indigenous Australians and other socially marginalized communities.

Conclusion

In this chapter I have argued that feminists have engaged in an epistemological repositioning of survivor narratives of sexual violence, insisting that they be seen as a gift that offers insight into the realities of gendered oppression and structural violence. Combating historical tendencies to ignore women's testimonies of this violence, feminists have insisted that they are valuable narratives that can lead to political change, even as they tell bad stories of traumatic events that should not occur. In order to enact change, these stories have had to be heard and received. Therefore, feminists in the 1970s and beyond have created themselves as a "counter-public" who can offer an "adequate witness" to narratives of sexual violence, by hearing them, believing them, and condemning the sexual violence that they speak of (Gilmore 2017; Salter 2013). Perhaps most importantly, feminists and survivor activists have insisted on a wider acknowledgment of the value of these narratives, and the truth they reveal about the problem of sexual violence.

Garnering this wider reception, however, has required engaging with the conventions of good storytelling more generally, producing and prioritizing stories that have a clear narrative arc, convey a moral, and, at least in some ways, resonate with existing tropes such as criminality and innocence. Rape narratives tend to center on rape as a singular, climactic event, rather than engaging with the systemic nature of violence and the enduring nature of its effects, especially in situations where sexual violence is repeated and endemic, such as family violence, slavery, or detention. In seeking to highlight the harms of sexual violence, feminist stories have tended to rely on "single-axis thinking," which, in making rape exceptional, fails to locate it within wider social conditions that both make this violence more common and exacerbate the harms that it causes (Crenshaw 1991).

Feminists and survivor advocates must, therefore, consider moving beyond the domain of good and easily narratable stories, seeking ways to communicate and hear the ordinariness, tedium, and repetition of sexual violence, and its links with other forms of structural and systemic harm. It may be that this involves not merely an expansion of stories told but a reconsideration of what I have elsewhere described as the "narrative politics" of feminism, a belief in the transformational political potential of survivor narratives in and of themselves (Serisier 2018b). Such a shift cannot focus simply on the production of new or more complex narratives, as important as these are. This is because there will always be stories that are more or less tellable within a public sphere structured through relations of social power and marginality. Rather, the focus must be on, as Sara Ahmed (2000) notes, continually seeking to receive the gifts offered by those who are not currently incorporated within dominant epistemic communities, whether that be in the public sphere more broadly, or within dominant strands of feminism. The project of learning to receive the gift of challenging and unexpected narrative, testimony, complaint, and other forms of political speech is, of necessity, an ongoing one for feminists and others interested in social justice.

REFERENCES

Ahmed, Sara. 2000. "Who Knows? Knowing Strangers and Strangerness." *Australian Feminist Studies* 15 (31): 49–68.

Alcoff, Linda M., and Laura Gray-Rosendale. 1993. "Survivor Discourse: Transgression or Recuperation?" *Signs: Journal of Women in Culture and Society* 18 (2): 260–90.

Armstrong, Louise. 1994. *Rocking the Cradle of Family Politics: What Happened When Women Said Incest*. Reading, MA: Addison-Wesley.

Baker, Katie J. M. 2016. "Here's the Powerful Letter the Stanford Victim Read Aloud to Her Attacker." *Buzzfeed*, June 3. www.buzzfeednews.com.

Bamberg, Michael. 2004. "Considering Counter Narratives." In *Considering Counter-Narratives: Narrating, Resisting, Making Sense*, edited by Michael Bamberg and Molly Andrews, 351–71. Amsterdam: John Benjamins.

Bell, Diane. 1996. "Speaking of Things That Shouldn't Be Written: Cross-Cultural Excursions into the Land of Misrepresentations." In *Radically Speaking: Feminism Reclaimed*, edited by Renate Klein and Diane Bell, 247–53. Melbourne: Spinifex.

Benedict, Helen. 1992. *Virgin or Vamp: How the Press Covers Sex Crimes*. New York: Oxford University Press.

Benjamin, Walter. 2002. "The Storyteller: Observations on the Works of Nikolai Leskov." In *Walter Benjamin: Selected Writings*, vol. 3, *1935–1938*, edited by Howard Eiland and Marcus W. Jennings, 143–66. Cambridge, MA: Belknap.

Berlant, Lauren. 2011. *Cruel Optimism*. Durham: Duke University Press.

Boyle, Karen. 2019. *#MeToo, Weinstein and Feminism*. New York: Palgrave Macmillan.

Brison, Susan J. 2002. *Aftermath: Violence and the Remaking of a Self*. Princeton: Princeton University Press.

Brownmiller, Susan. 1976. *Against Our Will: Men, Women and Rape*. Melbourne: Penguin.
Brownmiller, Susan. 1999. *In Our Time: Memoir of a Revolution*. New York: Dial.
Campbell, Joseph. 2008. *The Hero with a Thousand Faces*. Novato, CA: New World Library.
Carlson, Bronwyn. 2021. "No Public Outrage, No Vigils: Australia's Silence at Violence against Indigenous Women." *Conversation*, April 16. https://theconversation.com.
Connell, Noreen, and Cassandra Wilson. 1974. *Rape: The First Sourcebook for Women, by New York Radical Feminists*. New York: Plume.
Crenshaw, Kimberlé. 1991. "Mapping the Margins: Intersectionality, Identity Politics, and Violence against Women of Colour." *Stanford Law Review* 43 (6): 1241–99.
Davis, Angela. 1983. *Women, Race and Class*. New York: Vintage.
Duru, N. Jeremi. 2004. "The Central Park Five, the Scottsboro Boys, and the Myth of the Bestial Black Man." *Cardozo Law Review* 25: 1315–56.
Estrich, Susan. 1987. *Real Rape: How the Legal System Victimizes Women Who Say No*. Cambridge, MA: Harvard University Press.
Ferguson, Frances. 1987. "Rape and the Rise of the Novel." *Representations* 20: 88–112.
Fraser, Nancy. 1990. "Rethinking the Public Sphere: A Contribution to the Critique of Actually Existing Democracy." *Social Text* 25/26: 56–80.
Gilmore, Leigh. 2017. *Tainted Witness: Why We Doubt What Women Say about Their Lives*. New York: Columbia University Press.
Griffin, Susan. 1979. *Rape: The Power of Consciousness*. San Francisco: Harper and Row.
Higgins, Lynn A., and Brenda R. Silver. 1991. "Introduction: Rereading Rape." In *Rape and Representation*, edited by Lynn A. Higgins and Brenda R. Silver, 1–11. New York: Columbia University Press.
Horeck, Tanya. 2004. *Public Rape: Representing Violation in Fiction and Film*. New York: Routledge.
Huggins, Jackie, et al. 1991. Letter to the editor. *Women's Studies International Forum* 14 (5): 506–7.
Jacobs, Harriet. 2000. *Incidents in the Life of a Slave Girl: Written by Herself*. New York: Oxford University Press.
Kalven, Jamie. 1999. *Working with Available Light: A Family's World after Violence*. New York: Norton.
Kelly, Liz. 1988. *Surviving Sexual Violence*. Cambridge: Polity.
Lacey, Kate. 2013. *Listening Publics: The Politics and Experience of Listening in the Media Age*. Cambridge: Polity.
Lee, Harper. 2010. *To Kill a Mockingbird*. New York: Arrow.
Lejeune, Phillippe. 1989. *On Autobiography*. Minneapolis: University of Minnesota Press.
McGuire, Danielle L. 2010. *At the Dark End of the Street: Black Women, Rape and Resistance—A New History of the Civil Rights Movement from Rosa Parks to the Rise of Black Power*. New York: Vintage.
McKay, Nellie V. 1991. "Alice Walker's 'Advancing Luna—and Ida B. Wells': A Struggle toward Sisterhood." In *Rape and Representation*, edited by Lynn A. Higgins and Brenda R. Silver, 248–60. New York: Columbia University Press.

McQuire, Amy. 2022. "The Act of Disappearing." *Meanjin Quarterly* (Summer). https://meanjin.com.au.

Mendes, Kaitlynn. 2016. "Discursive Activism and Counter-Memories of SlutWalk." In *The Past in Visual Culture: Essays on Memory, Nostalgia and the Media*, edited by Jilly Boyce Kay, Cat Mahoney, and Caitlin Shaw, 101–18: London: MacFarland.

Naples, Nancy A. 2003. "Deconstructing and Locating Survivor Discourse: Dynamics of Narrative, Empowerment and Resistance for Survivors of Childhood Sexual Abuse." *Signs: Journal of Women in Culture and Society* 28 (4): 1151–87.

Nelson, Camilla. 2021. "'What Are You Afraid of ScoMo?': Australian Women Are Angry—and the Morrison Government Needs to Listen." *Conversation*, March 15. https://theconversation.com.

Plummer, Ken. 1995. *Telling Sexual Stories: Power, Change and Social Worlds*. London: Routledge.

Salter, Michael. 2013. "Justice and Revenge in Online Counter-Publics: Emerging Responses to Sexual Violence in the Age of Social Media." *Crime, Media, Culture* 9 (3): 225–42.

Serisier, Tanya. 2018a. "Speaking Out, and Beginning to Be Heard: Feminism, Survivor Narratives and Representations of Rape in the 1980s." *Continuum* 32 (1): 52–61.

Serisier, Tanya. 2018b. *Speaking Out: Feminism, Rape and Narrative Politics*. London: Palgrave Macmillan.

Serisier, Tanya. 2022. "What Does It Mean to #BelieveWomen? Popular Feminism and Survivor Narratives." In *The Routledge Companion to Narrative Theory*, edited by Paul Dawson and Maria Mäkelä, 342–53. New York: Routledge.

Whiting, Jason B., Rachael Dansby Olufuwote, Jaclyn D. Cravens-Pickens, and Alyssa Banford Witting. 2019. "Online Blaming and Intimate Partner Violence: A Content Analysis of Social Media Comments." *Qualitative Report* 24 (1): 78–94.

10

Mandela and Luzira Prison

A Mother-Daughter Story

CHARLOTTE ANDREWS-BRISCOE AND MOLLY ANDREWS

We sit across the kitchen table from one another, mother and daughter, casting our memories back a few years ago, to a place and time remote from our London home. Luzira Prison, Kampala, Uganda, April 2019. This chapter focuses on two days we spent teaching together in the prison, combining Molly's background as a narrative scholar with Charlotte's legal training. Through this lens, we seek to address questions such as, What good can stories do, and do those stories themselves need to be "good stories"? What is the relationship between stories and social change? If some stories help to promote social justice, how does that happen? How do narratives operate as a relational tool, serving as a ligament between differently located persons? Can they help traverse difference?

There has long been an understanding that somehow stories can, and often do, promote social change, and there has been increasing scholarship investigating this (Davis 2002; Poletta 2006; Selbin 2010; Squire 2021). Corinne Squire's *Stories Changing Lives: Narratives and Paths toward Social Change* takes this purported relationship as its central focus. Squire explains that the book is called *Stories Changing Lives* rather than *Stories Changing Society* "because it focuses on the effects of personal narratives, which must always include, although they may not be limited to, those narratives' impact on narrators' own internal social worlds" (2021: xiii). Elaborating on this, she writes,

> Social change happens at a micro level through remakings of the everyday social worlds that surround the subject, as well as at larger, social and

political levels. The "social" does not just exist in a sphere beyond the personal, but also "inside" it, in the very constitution of the subject. (xiv)

This chapter employs the use of multiple and multiply layered stories in precisely this way—from a launchpad that extends from the personal, but reaches out to that which is deeply social and political. People's lives, and our lives, are transformed not only by the stories we see and tell, but by the stories we live. This has a particularly powerful potential in the context of prisoners, whose existences are confined even while their "internal social worlds" (Squire 2021: xiii) can be transformed. This chapter first addresses in brief the transformative potential of legal education in prisons, before focusing in detail on the specific example of two days' teaching to explore how that potential can be realized through the medium of stories.

Identity Transformation and Legal Education in Prison: "What Would Lord Denning Do?"

Justice Defenders equips prisoners and prison staff with law degrees or in some cases other, more rudimentary legal training.[1] These students then become paralegals in clinics that operate from within the prison walls and provide legal representation for much of their respective prison populations.[2] The benefits of this program are often evaluated in terms of increasing access to legal representation within the prison and beyond (once the paralegals are released back into their communities). However, Charlotte conducted some research in 2016 and found that, in addition, the program as it operated in Kenya did a lot to transform many of the prisoners' sense of self.

In Charlotte's interviews, many of the prisoners discussed the ways in which, through their legal training, they had come to see themselves as people who may have done wrong but who are capable of making a significant contribution to society.[3] For example, Pauline said that while in her cell, she "began thinking about the magnitude of what had happened to my life." She began to see herself in a different way, as a capable person who helps others, which was "an indescribable feeling . . . a terrific feeling of joy." Pauline found that being able to offer legal assistance to other prisoners was psychologically beneficial:

Helping the other person helps me to really come to terms with, I am touching the problem, and I am touching the same problem I might be in, so it releases me, the feeling is of true release. . . . It has made me know that I am a very good person. . . . It taught me that I had many other gifts inside myself and I have the capability, if groomed, I can do tremendously a lot for the society.

Others likewise reported a significantly enhanced sense of their own capabilities:

First I saw myself like, "Oh, I am nothing, something good cannot come out of me," but through the training I was like, "OK, I can be somebody, something good can come out of me, I can help somebody to go through their case." . . . It has really helped me from low self-esteem to high. . . . Now people see you as somebody who can do something, and they say, "OK, we can respect this person because when we have a problem and we go to her, she is able to help us." (Conceptah)

Knowledge is power and if I have power, I do not live in fear. . . . I was empowered. . . . I can make it. I used to assume that I don't have the capability, I cannot make it, I am weak. . . . [Studying law] really motivated me. . . . It brought strength in my life. (Sara)

I really don't know the words that can describe the transformation. . . . I'm really humbled when I stand before people and am able to show them something I learnt. . . . [The training] really changed my perception of life. . . . I'm not fearful, I know that I have what it takes to argue my case in court, so empowering other prisoners. . . . It will make people to get the justice that they have always been craving for. (Phillip)

What was it that had helped these prisoners see themselves as agents of change? Sara reported that it was the knowledge that, in many respects, her life story wasn't that different from those of the people she was helping, and that she had the power and the knowledge to change their stories:

It is a shoe that I have already worn, I know how it fits me, I know how I am meant to walk with it, I know how to be called a prisoner, I have experienced the rejection from the society, and it is my passion to find that finally women are no longer convicted under those harsh sentences.

Others reported that this proximity to their clients in fact made them better legal advocates:

> [Prisoners think,] "These are our own, these are people who do not want me to suffer, so whatever advice they give me must be the best advice." A lawyer can go and give advice to an inmate, but that inmate might think, "Is this lawyer aware that today I have slept without eating?" Because they feel that maybe a lawyer can never understand what happens in prison. (Hamisi)

Morris, on the other hand, offered a different explanation as to how his legal education had changed him. He recalled a time when he was asked to mediate a conflict between prisoners in his ward and a welfare officer who had appropriated some of their belongings. When Morris arrived, he found that the conflict

> was very similar to a case I was studying just that day, so I pretended to be Lord Denning ["the most celebrated English judge of the 20th century," according to Dyer 1999], and I tried to think like him in the situation that was before me, and at the end of the day I made a decision that was really appreciated by almost everyone. I handled it like a contract case, and the officer agreed he had breached the contract with the people.

In Morris's words, we can hear the importance of being able to identify a legal mentor, and the effect of Morris's prospective role taking, asking himself, "What would Lord Denning do?" and thereby creating for himself a pathway to successfully resolving the conflict.

These interview excerpts provide some context on the Justice Defenders program, and people's reported experiences of the impact of that program. In the rest of the chapter, we look specifically at two classes to assess how stories in this context—particularly a story by and about a possible moral mentor—might contribute to social transformation, both internal and external.[4]

Situating This Story

In April 2019, Charlotte was a legal officer for Justice Defenders (then African Prisons Project) in Kampala, Uganda, helping to run two legal clinics that operate in, respectively, Luzira Women's Prison and Luzira Upper Prison (which holds men). Molly, Charlotte's mother, had come to visit her. A university professor, Molly was a narrative scholar who had spent many years thinking about how stories function. Charlotte—who was in charge of legal training at the clinics—wanted her students to use stories as a way to promote their own learning, and so asked Molly whether they could teach a class together.

They—that is, we—decided to focus the class on an in-depth reading that we would choose together, based on several criteria. First, we had a clear educational agenda. The students' law exams were looming, and Charlotte wanted them to develop their textual analysis skills. Our second goal was more amorphous. Morale at the clinics, particularly the men's, was at a low point. One of the clients in the men's clinic had died while on remand, following a drawn-out and painful illness, after four years awaiting trial. The students were aching with the injustice of it all, and many were struggling with direction and motivation. We wanted the text we chose, whatever it would be, to offer some glimmer of hope.

In hindsight, perhaps there was also a third goal: to traverse the differences between us, Charlotte and Molly, and the prisoners—to choose a story that might bring to the fore our disparate experiences of life and give us a mechanism with which to discuss those. Our students were all incarcerated for capital offenses; some were on remand (awaiting trial), but most had been convicted. They were all at this point well educated, but for some their entire schooling had been done from within prison. Their socioeconomic backgrounds varied, but most came from poverty. Some were arguably political prisoners; some had been or were on death row. They all knew what it meant to be behind bars in extremely harsh conditions.

We shared very little experientially with our students. We were privileged white people from the United Kingdom and United States. In "Upper" (the men's prison), we were also some of the only women, among roughly three thousand men. Charlotte was significantly younger than most of the students. We were acutely aware of those differences, most especially our whiteness, given the postcolonial context in which we were operating. Luzira Prison was built in 1927 by the British, at the time when Uganda was a British protectorate. The penal regime under the British was brutal, and they largely used the prison to house nationalists and political dissidents. The harsh governance introduced by the British had continued well into the Idi Amin era, and traces of it remain evident today. We wanted the text that we chose to speak to those underlying dynamics and make space to address the operation of white privilege.

Given all of these considerations, Nelson Mandela's autobiography seemed like a promising choice. Mandela was a hero for the students. These men and women share with Mandela a knowledge of what it means to be imprisoned. The key international legal instrument that governs the treatment of prisoners is known as "The Mandela Rules" (UNODC 2016) and, as such, Mandela's name is a part of legal discourse within the prison. The name Mandela therefore has a profound resonance with the people incarcerated in Luzira Prison, because of who he was as a person and the journey he traveled, as well as what his name has come to symbolize. Mandela, like many of our students, acquired a University of London law degree while incarcerated.[5] For Mandela, law—among other things—was a weapon of change. Our students were familiar with these facts, and a number had read *Long Walk to Freedom*, which they had nicknamed "the prisoner's Bible." Many of them, however, were not familiar with the details of Mandela's days as a young lawyer, when he and Oliver Tambo set up Mandela and Tambo Attorneys, one of the first Black-owned law firms in South Africa.

We selected a passage of about 1,500 words from a portion of Mandela's autobiography, hoping it would give the students a sense of the experiences he endured as a young lawyer, his response to those experiences, and how he found the fortitude to persevere, regardless of the injustices he suffered.

In Ken Plummer's classic *Telling Sexual Stories* (1995), he addressed the dynamics of what he called "storytelling in the stream of power" (26). He constructed what he termed "a political model of the contingencies of constructing stories," which had five phases:

- Imagining—visualizing—empathizing
- Articulating—vocalizing—announcing

- Inventing identities—becoming storytellers
- Creating social worlds/communities of support
- Creating a culture of public problems

In 2017, reflecting on that seminal work, Plummer added a few more "critical moments" to this "life story of stories," summarized as the "birth, institutionalization, re-negotiation and ultimate entropy of stories" (283). Each of these moments is pregnant with questions "about the role of narrative power and narrative empathy being transformed; how the capacity to speak and develop dialogues and understanding are constantly transformed, alongside how empathy is being developed" (283).[6] Plummer's analytic framework is useful for the present discussion, as its insistent focus on power and power relations in narrative storytelling (and silencing) is particularly germane to the context of prisons and our evaluation of who can say what to whom.

While an appreciation of different locations between teachers and their students is always an important component of effective teaching, this is particularly so in the context of prisons. We were always highly aware that this was a world that we could enter and leave at will (and Molly was aware of her status as an outside visitor whom the students may never meet again). Moreover, it was entirely at our discretion what we would select as the focus for the classes. We specifically searched for a text that might shine a light on a world beyond the psychological and physical confines of the prison. Our hope was that Mandela's compelling storytelling about his life before prison would function as a vehicle to motivate the storytelling of our own students—through analyzing his accounts, they were invited to articulate their own experiences. The collective identity of the classroom, of students with different but shared experiences, also enhanced the sense of the group as a "community of support."

Hannah Arendt has written that "storytelling is the bridge by which we transform that which is private and individual into that which is public, and in this capacity, it is one of the key components of social life.... What makes mass society so difficult to bear is... the fact that the world has lost its power to gather [people] together, to relate and to separate them" (Arendt 1958: 50–51). While of course it is imperative to remember that the prisoners were not gathered together in the prison by choice, they were enrolled for their law degree by their own volition, and our classroom was a space in which their private narratives found a space for public articulation. And Mandela's story, with all that it held, was an affirmation of themselves. "The presence of others who see what we see and hear what we hear assures us of the reality of the world and ourselves" (Arendt 1958: 50). It was our sincere hope that the choice of this particular text would serve as a means to encourage articulation of related narratives and help to provide the assurance of the world and of themselves of which Arendt speaks. Arendt argues that

> even the greatest forces of intimate life—passions of the heart, the thoughts of the mind, the delights of the senses—lead to an uncertain, shadowy kind of existence unless and until they are transformed, deprivatized and deindividualized, as it were, into a shape to fit them for public appearance. The most current of such transformations occurs in storytelling. (Arendt 1958: 50)

It was our intention and our hope that the choice of the extract from Mandela's *Long Walk to Freedom* would help the students to analyze not only the text but even their own life experiences in the broader context in which they occurred. This in fact proved to be the case.

The Extract as "the Story"

The passage we selected offers a lively demonstration of the power of small stories. Within narrative research, debates surrounding the identification and analysis of small stories has attracted much attention in the past two decades. Bamberg and Georgakopoulou (2008) argue that small stories represent an altogether new perspective in narrative and identity analysis "navigating between the two extreme ends of fine-grained micro analysis and macro accounts." Here we do not strictly adopt this framework, but rather use the discrete accounts to reveal something larger about the storyteller. In just a few pages, Mandela (1994: 173–77) tells five different stories, each with a distinctive central theme that we have identified, and it is to these that we now turn our attention.

Identity: The "Certificate"

In the first of these small stories, Mandela tells the story of being asked at the outset of a trial for his law diploma, proving his right to practice law. "The magistrate said, 'I don't know you. Where is your certificate?'" Mandela writes. The magistrate refused to hear the case unless Mandela could produce his diploma on the spot, and rather than allowing the trial to proceed, requested that Mandela be evicted from the court. Eventually the violation of court practice was considered by the Supreme Court, and the magistrate was reprimanded.

(Dis)respect: "Thank You John"

The next small story involves the young Mandela trying to help an elderly white woman whose car was stuck between two other cars. He helped to roll one of the cars, and the woman whose car he freed turned to him and said, "Thank you John"—intended as a generic name for any African man—and tried to hand him a sixpence coin. Mandela politely refused the money. The woman then pushed the money toward him, which Mandela again refused. In exasperation, the woman then exclaims, "'You refuse a sixpence. You must want a shilling, but you shall not have it!' and then threw the coin at me, and drove off."

"Fighting for Justice in an Unjust System": Sloping Shoulders

In this portion of the extract, Mandela addresses the complexity of the moral terrain in which he was practicing law. The client whom he was representing was a Coloured man who had been reclassified as an African. Even while Mandela clearly did not support the principles of the Population Registration Act, the misclassification of his client had concrete adverse implications. Here, though, rather than listening to Mandela's evidence, the magistrate asked Mandela's client to turn around so that he could see his shoulders—sloping shoulders were a stereotype of Coloured bodies—and on this alone decided that the man was indeed Coloured. Mandela offers the summary: "And so it came about that the course of this man's life was decided purely on a magistrate's opinion about the structure of his shoulders."

Preconceptions and the Magical Sneeze

In the fourth small story, Mandela is representing a local medicine man, accused of witchcraft. He sets the scene, describing the people in the village who "both worshipped and feared" the medicine man. The courtroom was full, and when his client sneezed, there was "a virtual stampede. . . . Most observers believed he was casting a spell." Mandela reports that the observers from the township most probably attributed the man's acquittal to the power of the herbs he possessed.

Unconventional Defense: Brandishing Panties

In the final story, Mandela is defending a domestic worker who is accused of stealing her employer's clothes. He opens his cross-examination of the employer by walking over to the table on which the items were exhibited, and using his pencil, picked up a pair of women's underwear. "I slowly turned to the witness box brandishing the panties and simply asked, 'Madam, are these . . . yours?' 'No,' she replied quickly, too embarrassed to admit that they were hers." The case was dismissed.

In this cluster of five small tales, Mandela powerfully and graphically communicates what it meant to be a Black lawyer in South Africa in the 1950s. These stories, with all their concrete detail, tell the reader volumes about Mandela's early challenges to devote himself to the practice of law, demonstrating what it means to practice law in an unjust system. He also shows that he himself is not above resorting to prejudice if it might serve his client's case, as he explains that he "often played on racial tension." Mandela uses the term "moral jigsaw" to describe the terrain in which he operated. For him, the experience of working as a lawyer in South Africa "meant operating under a debased system of justice, a code of law that did not enshrine equality but its opposite." In these pages, Mandela details his efforts to pursue justice, operating within such a corrupt system.

We selected this extract from Mandela's autobiography, focusing on his early years as a lawyer and his troubled encounters with authority, thinking that it addressed some of the issues with which we knew our students were grappling at the time. In this extract, Mandela refrains from offering a clear pathway to resolution. In fact, read in isolation, these stories are just—well, depressing. Mandela is operating in a racist, corrupt system. But his story does not end there. We thought that there might be something here to get the students speaking. And we were right.

The Class

The first time we were to teach together was in the Women's Prison. The women here had known Charlotte for many years and were extremely excited to meet Molly. We were also aware that our mere presence was itself significant to the women, most of whom were themselves mothers and were touched by the visit of this mother and daughter. The overwhelming majority of the women in the class had experienced sexual violence in their lives, and for some it provided the motivation for their crimes: a number had killed partners who they allege had abused them. This context is ever-present in any class with the women—earlier in the day they had devised the debating motion "This house believes that battered women should not be prosecuted for killing their husbands"—and so, too, was their analysis of the *Long Walk to Freedom* extract framed by their experiences of gender-based violence.

In the extract, Mandela notes that "police assaults were always difficult to prove. . . . Often it was simply the word of a policeman against our client." The women reflected on how this resonated with their experience, and shared their views that, often, where legal structures purport to engage in fact-finding, what they often do is entrench the position of the powerful party. The women also commented on Mandela's decidedly optimistic outlook, even at this early stage in his career, and his determination to overcome victimization. When the class ended, there was a shared sense of gratitude for the hours we had spent together, and the mood was joyous. Before we parted ways, the women sang a song they had composed, and we left the prison with that harmony in our ears.

That night, while decompressing at a live music venue, Charlotte put her arms around Molly and said, "I will tell the story of this day at your funeral." It was a beautiful moment, one of those rare occasions when you are aware at the time that a most special memory is in the making.

The next day, we were at the men's prison, where the atmosphere was palpably different. As Molly read the Mandela excerpt aloud, the men were entirely focused, barely moving in their chairs. The reading ended and immediately the room came alive in a most animated discussion, which lasted the entire morning. As we left the room together, one of the prisoners said to us, in a matter-of-fact way, "The next Mandela will come from this class!" Now, more than three years later, some of the students from those classes still recount to Charlotte how meaningful they found it.

What was it about this story that had spoken to the men and women in these classes? Mandela had been terribly treated, and the discrimination that he suffered was followed by twenty-seven years in prison. What was uplifting about this story? Why was this a "good story"?

In addition to those previously mentioned, there were similar themes that came up in both classrooms. First, our discussions centered a great deal on the use of law as both an oppressive and a liberational tool. Mandela's extract is evidently about his capacity as a lawyer to change people's lives for the better. But at the same time, it is about maneuvering within legal structures that oppress him. He describes how he and Tambo "occupied our premises illegally" because their offices weren't in an "African location" and, further, how "whenever I had a case outside of Johannesburg, I applied to have my bans temporarily lifted." Our students were prisoners in Yoweri Museveni's Uganda, where he has ruled the country with an iron fist for more than thirty-five years, having eliminated presidential term limits in 2005. Most of them waited years without trial before being convicted (or are still not convicted). They all have experience of law as an oppressive tool. Equally, they all dedicate their time to law in its liberational capacity, by representing other prisoners. Further, on a deeply personal level, they live and breathe law's liberational value: it is only by operation of law that they can be given their own freedom.

Second, the students noted that Mandela, as a Black man, was never expected to be a lawyer; he writes that people "never considered me anything other than a 'kaffir lawyer.'" As prisoners, our students are also not expected to be lawyers. People regularly doubt their intellect and their competence, before assessing the quality of their work. The students readily shared such experiences in the classes, describing how they had been ridiculed for their supposedly lofty desire to become lawyers. Reflecting on this now, one of the participants in the men's class, Canaan Nkamuhabwa, writes, "We were empowered by a desire to prove them all wrong, just as it was with Mandela." Mandela experienced practical barriers to his lawyering because of his "otherness." He explains, "We frequently encountered prejudice in the court itself. White witnesses often refused to answer questions from a black attorney." Our students also experience such practical barriers—for example, through regulations that prohibit people with a criminal record from acting in certain legal capacities. Mandela suggests that, for him, much of the work of *belonging* as a lawyer was psychological: "I did not act as though I were a black man in a white man's court, but as if everyone else—white and black—was a guest in my court."

Finally, Mandela writes about the importance of being Black to his clients:

> I realized quickly what Mandela and Tambo meant to ordinary Africans. It was a place where they could come and find a sympathetic ear and a competent ally, a place where they would not be either turned away or cheated, a place where they might actually feel proud to be represented by men of their own skin color. (Mandela 1994: 173)

This sentiment resonated profoundly with our students. Many of them had firsthand experience of poor legal representation (state-appointed lawyers are grossly overworked and underpaid).[7] If they didn't have personal experience, all had heard horror stories. At the time, they knew what it would mean to their fellow prisoners to have competent legal representation from people who understood them. Indeed, years later, in many cases this has proven to be true. Nkamuhabwa further writes that "I still have a line of prisoners who followed [me] to the outside, wishing that me, and not any [not formerly incarcerated] lawyer works on their case." Mandela's words echo Sara's (above): she felt that she was a better lawyer because of her shared experience with her clients; theirs is a "shoe [she] ha[s] already worn."

Good Stories

In the opening lines to this volume, the editors write that even in the context of great suffering and hardship, sometimes "good stories" can emerge "in the shadow of . . . troubles." Narratives, and stories more generally, exist only in context; they are made and remade by people, as we try to create and find meaning in the worlds in which we live. In the introduction, the editors pose a series of related questions, inviting the reader to engage with the meaning and potential of "good stories":

- What kind of narratives can make harms and threats thereof endurable?
- What kinds of narratives might effectively produce social change?
- What does it take to tell good stories?

Before addressing these questions, we first direct the reader's attention to the three different stories that we are considering.

- First, there is the excerpt from Mandela's autobiography. Although, as already highlighted above, this brief extract encompasses five stories, for our purposes here we shall consider them together as "Mandela's story."
- Second, there is the story of the classes that we, Charlotte and Molly, shared together with the prisoners.
- Third, there is the story of the mother and daughter—we, the authors of this chapter—who have chosen Mandela's story as a reading for a legal clinic in two maximum-security prisons, and have chosen the story of that experience as a focus for our contribution to this book.

An analysis of each of these three stories invariably involves the other two: this essay is an analysis about the intersection of these three stories. Stories never stand alone, and a key challenge of interpretation is insight into which stories (articulated, unsaid, and/or silenced) are impacting upon what is told. While recognizing the interrelatedness of the stories as they function in this chapter, we will now look briefly at each on its own.

Let us deal first with Mandela's story/stories, as it appears in his autobiography. Critically—and obviously—it is important to know who this speaker is. Mandela's journey is a well-known one, and his name associated with these stories imbues them with a significance that they might otherwise lack. In a sense, these early days of being a lawyer in South Africa are about Mandela before he was Mandela. Not only does he represent the long and bloody fight against apartheid in his own country, but for the rest of the world he has become a symbol of the triumph of good against evil—David against Goliath, someone who stood up against injustice, and remained standing, even when the personal cost to him was great. Often his efforts have been individualized, minimizing the crucial role of others in his journey, the political struggle of which he was but a part. When one reads these stories of racist abuse, one knows in advance that Mandela will triumph, despite all odds. The stories, in that sense, derive much of their meaning from the context of Mandela's life, of which they are but a stop on his journey to achieving his goals. But the stories are exemplary, not unique: even were the details of the speaker's biography less well-known than Mandela's, one could proceed to make the linkages between the smaller stories of the legal encounters and the larger story of the person—who they were, and who they were to become.

The second story is that of our class. Our students told us contemporaneously (and still now, years later) that Mandela's story and our discussion of it re-motivated them, and reminded them of the importance and possibilities of their work. In many ways, being "Nelson Mandela" is unattainable; only the most arrogant person could equate themselves to such a name. But in other ways, Mandela's extract from his time as a young lawyer, before he was *the* Mandela, offered our students an "adjacent possible" (Unger cited in Loader and Sparks 2022). They could see themselves in the barriers he faced. They could relate to the tools he employed—pretending that everyone was a guest in his court—to remind himself that he belonged. They could see that, at one point, his vision seemed impossible, too.

Further, they could relate to the urgency with which Mandela and Tambo experienced their clients' cases. Mandela describes Tambo as being "touched by the plight of the masses as a whole and by each and every individual." One of our students, Pascal Kakuru, completed a fourteen-year prison sentence shortly after we had our class together. Having left prison with a law degree, and determined to fight for justice on behalf of others, he said,

> In my time in prison, I have not been blind to the injustice of others around me. Poverty does not allow efficient legal representation, causing the poor to be convicted on the strength of evidence they failed to adequately challenge. This problem is larger than Uganda and is prevalent wherever poverty, disadvantage and marginalization are found. (Kakuru 2019)

One can hear in Pascal's words his commitment to fight not only for his own freedom but for those who are disadvantaged by poverty everywhere. It is not difficult to see why Mandela's story—of discrimination, resilience, and inspiration—would have such a compelling attraction for the students in our classes.

Now we come to the third story, that of this mother and daughter—our story—what we learned from one another being in this context together, and what this experience has come to mean to us over time (at the time of this writing, more than three years ago). It has already been recounted that the night after our first class of teaching at the prison, Charlotte had commented that the story of this day would be included in her version of Molly's life—at her funeral. Both of us knew at the time that we had shared something very special. Molly had been teaching life history work for nearly three decades, but she had never been in a prison before. In contrast, this was Charlotte's third time living in Uganda, and she knew and was well known in the prison, but Molly had never seen her teach. Somehow these two days signified a meeting of their two intellectual worlds, in a practical way that had not happened before.

Molly's experience was colored by the fact that in Ugandan culture, parents are highly honored, and the prisoners were noticeably very touched that Charlotte's mother would pay them a visit. One of them had a very special gift made for her—a carved wooden tray, painted with "Professor Molly" on its surface. Another prisoner arranged to have extra food available during lunch, and he laid out a veritable feast between lessons. Molly was told that Charlotte was not hers, that she "belonged to the whole of the world." When they went to death row, one of the most grim places Molly had ever seen, she had to fight against the inclination to emotionally withdraw. But when they turned the corner, and the prisoners on death row saw Charlotte, they shouted out her name with great enthusiasm and hurried toward her. Suddenly this transformed the place in Molly's eyes—here was a place, so far removed from anything that she had ever known or experienced, but a world where her daughter had clearly made an impact. Young though she was, Charlotte had touched the hearts of these men and women, who had been rejected by so many in their lives. For Charlotte, the act of welcoming her mother into this world that she had become a part of, was a gift; the men and women who were our students on those days meant a lot to her and had contributed significantly to her emotional and intellectual development.

It was through the teaching of this class together, thousands of miles from the home they had shared for so many years, that new bonds were created, that Charlotte could experience Molly not only as her mother but also as someone who was open to a world that was unknown to her, and Molly could have a glimpse into Charlotte's work in the prison that words could not convey. For Charlotte and Molly, this was a "good story" because it allowed them to create an environment together in which they could not only collaborate, but also come to have a fuller appreciation of who each other was. We are mother and daughter—but that is not all we are. Or perhaps it is more accurate to say that that relationship took on a new dimension through that shared experience. The story of those two days has, in time, become a springboard for our story of our evolving relationship and appreciation of one another and of the work we do.

Mark Freeman argues that "narratives, as sense-making tools, inevitably do things—for people, for social institutions, for culture, and more" (Freeman 2002: 9). Similarly, Catherine Kohler Riessman states, "Narratives are strategic, functional, and purposeful" (Riessman 2008: 8). We have argued that doing a close reading of the extract from Mandela's life as a lawyer before he was incarcerated is a "good story" because of the rippling effects that it had, within the classroom and beyond, both for our students and for ourselves. We can see that the three stories all "do" something on their own; however, it is only by recognizing the ligaments that hold them together—their fundamental interconnectedness—that we can fully appreciate Ken Plummer's compelling argument in *Narrative Power*, which concludes,

> And so, once again, we have the stories of power and the power of stories. The power to remind of the inequalities of narrative: of who gets routinely heard and who does not. . . . And of the ultimate need for daily narrative acts questioning what it all means to be a human—of the storied values humanity must cherish and help to survive in the face of storied monstrous cruelties and adversities. Living actively, creatively and positively with the power of our sustainable stories of hope is what helps make us truly human. (Plummer 2019: 162–63)

Our classroom encounter cannot erase the inequalities that are inherent in the context in which we find ourselves. Nonetheless, these "narrative acts"—of Mandela, the students, and ourselves—help us to find "sustainable stories of hope" not just in the text but within ourselves and between and with one another.

Conclusion

It is evident that the teaching of Mandela's autobiographical extract not only engaged the prisoners of Luzira Prison, but even created a small space for inspiration and hope. The claim that "the next Mandela will come from this class" indicated to us that, at least for that brief moment, the speaker had come to see himself and his classmates as capable of effecting social transformation. Mandela's story shows that social change can happen. His accounts of discrimination and abuse derive much of their power from the fact that his audience all know that he will go on to become the first democratically elected president of South Africa. And the question of tellability—What does it take to tell good stories?—cannot be disentangled from that of audience: if there is no one willing to listen, there is unlikely to be anyone to tell. In the context of legal training in Luzira Prison, our preparations focused not so much on finding a story that was good, as finding a story that did good. Encouraging the students to think about Mandela's early days as a lawyer, knowing that he would go on to become a moral icon for the world, opened up space for us to talk together about pursuing justice in an unjust world.

NOTES

With special thanks to Canaan Nkamuhabwa and Pascal Kakuru for their insightful feedback on this chapter.

1 Many of the paralegals are enrolled in the distance-learning University of London Bachelor of Laws (LL.B.) program.
2 Justice Defenders works in Gambia, Kenya, and Uganda across thirty-four prisons in total.
3 Although Charlotte's interviews were with a range of people connected to the legal education provided in the prison, in this chapter we focus on what she heard from the prisoners. However, it is noteworthy that an important aspect of the legal training is that both prison guards and prisoners are students in the same class.
4 While the interviews were conducted in Kenya in 2016, the two classes that are the focus of the chapter were held in Uganda in 2019.

5 For Mandela, this was an additional legal qualification.
6 Plummer's subsequent book, *Narrative Power: The Struggle for Human Value* (2019) is entirely devoted to fleshing out this model of narrative movement and represents this outstanding narrative scholar's final contribution on this topic.
7 In Uganda 79 percent of prisoners have had no legal representation (Human Rights Watch 2011). However, if a person is charged with a capital crime—which all of our students were—then they are afforded free representation by the state.

REFERENCES

Andrews-Briscoe, Charlotte. 2018. "Legal Education in Kenyan Prisons: What Is the Impact on the Right to Legal Assistance?" Queen Mary University. August. Unpublished dissertation.

Arendt, Hannah. 1958. *The Human Condition*. Chicago: University of Chicago Press.

Bamberg, Michael, and Alexandra Georgakopoulou. 2008. "Small Stories as a New Perspective in Narrative and Identity Analysis." *Text & Talk* 28 (3): 377–96.

Davis, Joseph, ed. 2002. *Stories of Change: Narrative and Social Movements*. Albany: State University of New York Press.

Dyer, Clare. 1999. "Lord Denning, Controversial 'People's Judge,' Dies Aged 100." *Guardian*, March 5. www.theguardian.com.

Freeman, Mark. 2002. "The Burden of Truth: Psychoanalytic *Poiesis* and Narrative Understanding." In *Strategic Narrative: New Perspectives on the Power of Personal and Cultural Stories*, edited by Wendy Patterson, 9–27. Lanham, MD: Lexington Books.

Human Rights Watch. 2011. *Even Dead Bodies Must Work: Health, Hard Labor, and Abuse in Ugandan Prisons*. July 14. www.hrw.org.

Kakuru, Pascal. 2019. "Pascal Kakuru: In His Own Words." *Justice Defenders Blog*, August 15. www.justice-defenders.org.

Loader, Ian, and Richard Sparks. 2022. "Reasonable Hopes: Social Theory, Critique and Reconstruction in Contemporary Criminology." In *Crime, Justice and Social Order: Essays in Honour of A. E. Bottoms*, edited by Alison Liebling, Joanna Shapland, Richard Sparks, and Justice Tankebe, 100–125. Oxford: Oxford University Press.

Mandela, Nelson. 1994. *Long Walk to Freedom*. London: Abacus.

Plummer, Ken. 1995. *Telling Sexual Stories: Power, Change and Social Worlds*. London: Routledge.

Plummer, Ken. 2017. "Narrative Power, Sexual Stories and the Politics of Story Telling." In *The Routledge International Handbook on Narrative and Life History*, edited by Ivor Goodson, Ari Antikainen, Pat Sikes, and Molly Andrews, 280–92. London: Routledge.

Plummer, Ken. 2019. *Narrative Power: The Struggle for Human Value*. Cambridge: Polity.

Polletta, Francesca. 2006. *It Was Like a Fever: Storytelling in Protest and Politics*. Chicago: University of Chicago Press.
Riessman, Catherine Kohler. 2008. *Narrative Methods for the Human Sciences*. London: Sage.
Selbin, Eric. 2010. *Revolution, Rebellion, Resistance: The Power of Story*. London: Zed.
Squire, Corinne, ed. 2021. *Stories Changing Lives: Narratives and Paths toward Social Change*. New York: Oxford University Press.
United Nations Office on Drugs and Crime (UNODC). 2016. UN Standard Minimum Rules for the Treatment of Prisoners (Nelson Mandela Rules). www.unodc.org.

ACKNOWLEDGMENTS

We are grateful to our visionary contributors and reviewers, and to our institutional supporters.

ABOUT THE CONTRIBUTORS

MOLLY ANDREWS is Honorary Professor of Political Psychology at the Social Research Institute at University College London, Adjunct Professor at the Graduate Center at the City University of New York, and the codirector of the Association for Narrative Research and Practice, UK.

CHARLOTTE ANDREWS-BRISCOE is currently a Lawyer at the Global Legal Action Network, UK, and formerly a Legal Officer at African Prisons Project (now Justice Defenders), Uganda.

ROBIN KUNDIS CRAIG is the Robert C. Robert A. Schroeder Distinguished Professor and Professor of Law at the University of Kansas School of Law.

TANIA DOCARMO is Assistant Professor of Legal Studies at University of Massachusetts Amherst, USA.

CHRISTINA ERGAS is Associate Professor in the Department of Sociology, University of Tennessee, Knoxville, USA.

JONATHAN ILAN is Assistant Professor of Criminology at the Sutherland School of Law, University College Dublin, Ireland.

PAUL JOOSSE is Associate Professor in the Department of Sociology, University of Hong Kong, Hong Kong.

VANESSA LYNN is Assistant Professor in the Department of Criminal Justice, Marist College, Poughkeepsie, New York, USA.

SHADD MARUNA is Professor of Criminology, Queen's University Belfast, Northern Ireland.

FERGUS MCNEILL is Professor of Criminology and Social Work at the University of Glasgow, Scotland, where he works in the Scottish Centre for Crime and Justice Research and in the Division of Sociological and Cultural Studies.

FRANCESCA POLLETTA is Chancellor's Professor of Sociology at the University of California, Irvine, USA.

TANYA SERISIER is Reader in Feminist Theory, School of Social Sciences Birkbeck, University of London, UK.

SÉBASTIEN TUTENGES is Professor at the Danish School of Education (DPU), Aarhus University, Denmark.

KELLY MARIE WARD is Assistant Professor of Sociology and Gender and Women's Studies at the University of Wisconsin–Madison, USA.

ABOUT THE EDITORS

JENNIFER FLEETWOOD is Senior Lecturer in Criminology in the School of Law and Criminology, University of Greenwich, London, UK.

LOIS PRESSER is Distinguished Professor in the Humanities in the Department of Sociology, University of Tennessee, Knoxville, Tennessee, USA.

SVEINUNG SANDBERG is Professor in the Department of Criminology and Sociology of Law, University of Oslo, Norway.

INDEX

Abdi (former gang member), 19–20, 22; as storyteller, 25–27, 29–30
abolition, 42
Aboriginal women, 225
abortion rights, 165–66, 174
addiction, ix
adequate witness, 227
advocacy storytelling, 164; agency promoted in, 172–73; agenda-building in, 177–81; authenticity in, 170–71, 175–76; crafting stories in, 171; creation of empathy in, 168–69; discourse of, 166–67; empowerment in, 168, 173, 176; intimate relationships in, 170–73; in nonprofit organizations, 166; online videos in, 167; personal, 180; political messaging in, 177–81; professionalized, 165–67; reciprocal relationships in, 169–70; relationship building in, 167–69; suffering modulated by, 173–75
agency, 168–69, 171; actualizing, 58–59; advocacy storytelling promoting, 172–73; defining, 52; regaining of, 61–62; temporal, 51, 57–58
agenda-building, in advocacy storytelling, 177–81
Ahmed, Sara, 216, 224, 228
AIDS, 182
Alabama, 31
algorithmic marketing, 163
allegory, 119, 124, 126–27, 132, 136
Alternative to Violence Program (AVP), 51
Altieri, Miguel, 107
American exceptionalism, 95

Amnesty International, 200
analytical philosophy, 122–23
Andrews, Molly, 12, 231–32, 235, 241, 246–47
Andrews-Briscoe, Charlotte, 12, 231–32, 235, 241, 246–47
anthropocentrism, 122
anti-trafficking movement, 172–73
apocalypse: climate change and, 91–92; defining, 92, 112n1
Arendt, Hannah, 237–38
Asaṅga, 93, 98, 103
Asperger's Syndrome, 193
asthma, 202
Australia, 224–27
Australian First Nations, 225
authenticity, 68, 74, 181–82; in advocacy storytelling, 170–71, 175–76; in UK rap, 76, 83
autism, 193
automaticity, 135
AVP. *See* Alternative to Violence Program

bad stories, 140–50
bad trip stories, 21
Bahamas, 51
Bakhtin, Mikhail, 123
Basic Units of Cooperative Production (UBPCs), 107
Bauman, 26
benefactors, 168
Biblical narratives, 3, 126–28
Biden, Joe, 221
biodiversity, 100–101

biotic community, 120
Black Lives Matter, 204
Blackness, 45; Mandela on, 243
Black Panthers, 51
Black people, 45; marginalization of, 72; in UK, 71
"Blankface," 140
Bourdieu, Pierre, 76, 83–84
Brison, Susan, 4, 221
Brownmiller, Susan, 216, 217, 220; Davis, A., critiquing, 222–23
Buddha, 3
Bush, George W., 95
"but for" logic, 221–23

cannabis, 21
Caribbean African Unity (CAU), 51
Carswell, Grace, 153; Mary and, 151–52, 155, 156, 158–60
categorical imperative, 120
category expansion, 118; King using, 134–37; in moral philosophy, 119–22; suffrage and, 122
CAU. *See* Caribbean African Unity
CBOs. *See* Criminal Behaviour Orders
Center for Reproductive Rights, 174
certificates, 239
chauvinism, 122
Chernaik v. Kitzhaber/Brown, 195, 196
child psychologists, 189
Children's Panel, 143
child-saving movement, 153
Chip, 83
Christianity, 126–27
civil rights, 133, 165, 204
CliFi, 91, 202
climate change: apocalypse and, 91–92; colonialism linked to, 92; cultural meaning of, 190; denialism, 94–95, 112; depression linked to, 193; empowerment and, 189–90; good stories of survival of, 94; harms from, 202; hope and, 96; inaction, 94–95; individualism and, 95–96; narratives of, 187, 188–89, 201–4; policy, 189; in popular media, 91–92; scope of, 91; social psychology of, 94–98; Thunberg on, 186–87; victimization and, 189; young people and, 188–91; youth climate narratives as good stories, 201–4
co-construction of narratives, 8–9, 145, 160
code of the street, 46–47, 74
collectivism, 93, 96
colonialism: climate change linked to, 92; sexual violence linked with, 225
comic correctives, 5
commodification, of storytelling, 163–64
common ground, 131
common ownership, elitism vs., 124–25, 131–32
community: in El Organopónico, 106; of support, 237
community cultural wealth framework, 44
compañeros, 94, 106–7, 109
complicating actions, good stories and, 8
conformity, 7
Connell, Noreen, 211, 215
consciousness-raising, 215–17
consensus, 99; defining, 101; in ecovillages, 101–3
Constitution, US, 196
continuum model of sexual violence, 222
continuum thinking, 222
control theory, 7
COP26, 186
counternarratives, 6, 86–87; feminist, 214–15
counter-publics, 215–19, 227
crack epidemic, 48, 52, 59; trauma from, 55
Crenshaw, Kimberlé, 221, 224
Criminal Behaviour Orders (CBOs), 75–76

criminalization, 72
criminalized storytelling, 19–20
criminology, 3, 36; cultural, 67–68. *See also* narrative criminology
critical race theory, 44
crowdsourcing, 166
crying, 173
Cuba, 93; race in, 112n2
Cuban revolution, 104–5; changes in, 105–6, 107; economic hardship in, 110
cultural criminology, 67–68
culture, defining, 68

dancehall, 72
Davis, Angela, 222, 224
Depp, Johnny, 215
depression, climate change linked to, 193
deprivation model, 42
Descartes, René, 123
Deschênes, Olivier, 187–88
desistance, 45, 73; in fresh home rap, 76; imaginative storytelling and, 34–35
dialogical narrative analysis, 145, 159
didacticism, 118–19; polysemy vs., 122–24, 132–34
digital natives, 191–92
discourse: of advocacy storytelling, 166–67; construction of, 9; feminist, 209–10; risks of, 175–76; of storytelling, 164–65
Discourse on Method (Descartes), 123
disrespect, 239
Djinn, 21
domestic violence, 215
double entendres, 75–76
Dreamer movement, 179–80
drinking stories, 28–29, 30
drug dealing, 22–23, 49, 72, 74; entrepreneurship in, 78
Duarte Agostinho and Others v. Portugal and Others, 199
Durkheim, Émile, 27, 132
dystopia, 110

ecovillages, 93; consensus in, 101–3; permaculture in, 99–101
ECtHR. *See* European Court of Human Rights
elitism, 118–19; common ownership vs., 124–25, 131–32; King on, 136–37
Emancipation Proclamation, 128
embodied stories, 29
Emirbayer, Mustafa, 52
empathy, creation of, in advocacy storytelling, 168–69
empowerment, 164, 181–82, 242–43; in advocacy storytelling, 168, 173, 176; climate change and, 189–90; of young people, 189–90
entrepreneurship, 82; in drug dealing, 78
environmental ethics, 120
envisioning, 10–11, 92, 97–98, 110
ethical storytelling, 174–75
ethnography, narrative, 145
European Center for Constitutional and Human Rights, 200
European Commissioner for Human Rights, 200
European Convention on Human Rights, 199
European Court of Human Rights (ECtHR), 199–201
event stories, 144
everyday, 2–3, 5–6, 61, 71, 79, 86–87, 212
evil, xi; defining, 35
excuses, 24
Exodus, 126, 138n12
extracts, 238–41
extremism, 31–32

Facebook, 163
faith-based organizing, 178
family support, 49–50
fascism, 2
fathers, in prison, 24
Federal Constitutional Court, 199

feminism, 12, 165, 214; counternarratives, 214–15; as counter-public to sexual violence, 217–18; discursive activism, 209–10; narrative politics of, 227–28; second wave, 209
Flaherty, Michael G., 51
Fleetwood, Jennifer, 7, 10, 29, 34, 87
food: in fresh home rap, 79–80; in prison, 80–81
formerly incarcerated men, 45–53
foster care, 56
Foucault, Michel, 140
Frank, Arthur, 4
Fraser, Nancy, 218
freedom, 242
freestyling, 77
Freire, Paolo, 177, 180
"Fresh Home," 68, 78
fresh home narratives, 34–35
fresh home rap, 10, 34–35; defining, 69–70; desistance narratives in, 76; food in, 79–80; as good story, 72–73, 85; habitus and, 83–84; lyrics of, 73–74; marginality and, 71–72; in music industry, 81–83; narrative resistance in, 79–81; narratives in, 67; paradoxes in, 81–82; personal narratives in, 83–84; as resistance, 86–87; street narratives in, 74–75, 77–79; survival and, 71–72; themes of, 74, 87; women in, 74–75, 86
Frye, Northrop, 102

gangs, 56–57
gangster stories, 26
GED, 50–51
gender, 122; confinement and, 154–55; violence and, 217. *See also specific topics*
Georgakopoulou, Alexandra, 238
Germany, 199, 202
GHGs. *See* greenhouse gases
Gilman, Robert, 93
Gilmore, Leigh, 216
Ginnungagap, 4

Global South, 190
Goffman, Erving, 42
the good: defining, 35–36, 118–19; King storying, 125–30
good-making, 117, 134
goodness, xi, 44
good stories, 1, 3–5, 10–13; of climate change survival, 94; complicating actions and, 8; creation of, 181–82; critiques of, 227–28; defining, 35; fresh home rap as, 72–73, 85; of Mandela, 243–48; of probation, 143; types of, 20; youth climate narratives as, 201–4
Gordon, Avery F., 45
grand narratives, 4
grassroots movements, 182n1
greenhouse gases (GHGs), 91, 92
Griffin, Susan, 211, 214, 217, 220
grime music, 72; defining, 87n4; marginalization resisted through, 85–86
Grounded Solutions Network, 169
group homes, 56
group values, 183n2
Gubrium, Jaber F., 145
guns, 49
Guterres, António, 192

habitus, 76; fresh home rap and, 83–84; of storytellers, 29; storytelling structured by, 9
happiness, 35
Harari, Yuval Noah, 4
hard life stories, 23
harm: from climate change, 202; in probation, 142
harm-limiting storytelling, 29–32
healing storytelling, 21–25; humor in, 23–24; transcendence through, 22
Heard, Amber, 215, 219
Hegel, G. W. F., 124
hepatitis C, 178–79
Heystoun Hospital, 150
Hieroces, 120

Hollaback London, 7
Holmgren, David: on permaculture, 100; on sustainability, 100–101
Holstein, James A., 145
homosexuality, 166, 182
hope, x, 172; climate change, 96
hopelessness, 95
human rights, 12, 118, 172
humor: in healing storytelling, 23–24; trauma alleviated by, 48

Ibsen, Henrik, 34
identity, in prison, 42, 232–34
ignorance, veil of, 121
"I Have a Dream" speech, 134–35
"I Have Been to the Mountaintop" speech, 11, 125–30
illness, 21, 179, 235
imaginative storytelling, 32–33; desistance and, 34–35
immigration, 179
immorality, 31
Indigenous peoples, 197–98, 225–27
individualism, 91–92; climate change and, 95–96; defining, 95
intentional communities, 93–94
intimate relationships, in advocacy storytelling, 170–73
ISIS, 31–32
Islam, 31–32, 33, 52

Jim Crow, 214
Johannesburg, 242
joint fantasizing, 33
Juliana v. United States, 194, 195, 196
justice, 127; Mandela fighting for, 239; racial, 135–36
Justice Defenders, 248n2
Justice Social Work, 141

Kalven, Jamie, 224, 226
Kampala, 235
Kant, Immanuel, 120

Kenya, 232, 248n4
Kierkegaard, Soren, 137n1
King, Martin Luther, Jr., 119, 137n9, 138n11; assassination of, 125; category expansion used by, 134–37; on elitism, 136–37; the good storied by, 125–30; as leader, 131–32; as storyteller, 126
Kinsey, Alfred, 213
Kirke, Jemima, 174
Kuranko people, 21

Latin America, 110
laughter, 48; resilience and, 62
law, as oppressive tool, 242
Lefebvre, Henri, 6
legal education, in prison, 232–34
Leopold, Aldo, 120, 137n2
life stories, 144
Lincoln, Abraham, 128
logocentrism, 69
Long Walk to Freedom (Mandela), 13, 236, 238, 241
Luzira Upper Prison, 12–13
Lyotard, Jean-François, 4
lyrics, 69; of fresh home rap, 73–74; violence in, 74–75

Machiguenga, 4
Making Good (Maruna), 34
Malcolm X, 41
Malopticon, 140, 156
Mandela, Nelson, 13, 236, 237, 238; on Blackness, 243; good stories of, 243–48; on justice, 239; on police, 241; as storyteller, 238–41
"The Mandela Rules," 236
marginality: advanced, 71; of Black people, 72; fresh home rap and, 71–72; grime music resisting, 85–86; of UK rap music, 72
Marshall Islands, 198
Marshall Project, 41, 62
Maruna, Shadd, 34, 73

Mary (probationer), 144, 146–47; Carswell and, 151–52, 155, 156, 158–60; mobility in story of, 154–55; rites and recognition in story of, 155–57; silencing in story of, 157–59; social class in story of, 152–54; on supervision, 149; upbringing of, 152–53
mass incarceration, 10, 45, 62
maturity, 59
McNeill, Fergus, 6, 11, 160n2
meaning-making: narratives and, 247; storytelling and, 22–23
mental flight, 128
methamphetamine, 31
#MeToo, 215, 216, 218–19, 222
microaggressions, 222
microtargeting, 163
moral jigsaw, 240
moral philosophy: actualization of, 134–35; category expansion in, 119–22; narrative in, 117–18; rhetorical tendencies in, 118–19
Moses (Biblical figure), 130, 131–32, 138n12
mothers, in prison, 24
munpain, 71
music: in prison, 77–78; resistance and, 86; social change and, 85–86; women in, 86
music industry, fresh home rap in, 81–83
mutual aid, 11
myths, 4

narrative analysis, 145; dialogical, 145, 159; in moral philosophy, 117–18; types of, 145
narrative consultants, 163
narrative criminology, 6–8, 45, 61, 67–68; foundational concerns of, 20; oral history and, 144–46; political change investigated in, 86–87; Presser on, 144
narrative ethnography, 145
narrative labor, 45

narrative persuasion, philosophical persuasion compared with, 122–25
Narrative Power (Plummer), 247–48
narrative psychology, storytelling in, 3–4
narrative resistance, 6–8; in fresh home rap, 79–81
narratives: of climate change, 187, 188–89; co-construction of, 8–9, 145, 160; constitution of, 9; of crises, 3; criticisms of, 2–3; in fresh home rap, 67; grand, 4; meaning-making and, 247; personal, 5; portraiture methodology and, 44–45; progressive, 3; reform, 3; in resistance to oppression, 5. *See also specific topics*
narratology, 8; sociology and, 9
Navajo Reservations, 196
neoliberalism, 85, 226
neoliberal subject, xi
Netherlands, 198, 202
New Deal, 128
New York, 48; violence in, 49–51
New York Radical Feminists, 211, 216
New Zealand, 203
Nietzsche, Friedrich, 35, 124
nonprofit organizations, 46; advocacy storytelling in, 166; storytelling by, 163–64
Nonprofit Quarterly, 174–75
Norgaard, Kari Marie, 95, 96
Norway, 198

OCT. *See* Our Children's Trust
Open Society Foundations, 182
oppression: law as tool of, 242; narratives and resistance to, 5
oral history, narrative criminology and, 144–46
Oregon, 195
organic urban agriculture, 107–8
El Organopónico, 93–94, 104–10; community in, 106; *compañeros* in, 106–7; organic urban agriculture, 107–8; worker cooperatives in, 108–10
orphans, ix

Oslo, 19, 22, 28, 34
otherness, 243
Our Children's Trust (OCT), 195–97

Pakistan, 198–99
Palau, 198
panopticon, 140
participant observation, 94
participatory learning, 177
past, speaking, 157–59
pedagogy, 177, 180, 237, 246–47
penal supervision, 140
performance, 25–29, 145, 158, 173
permaculture: defining, 100; in ecovillages, 99–101; Holmgren on, 100
personal narratives, 5; in fresh home rap, 83–84; political change and, 86–87; in prison, 61–62; social change and, 231–32
personal storytelling, 164; in advocacy, 180
phenomenology, 44
philosophical persuasion, 135; narrative persuasion compared with, 122–25
Plato, 124, 137n1
plea deals, 54–55
Plummer, Ken, 9, 236–37, 247
police, 241
political consciousness, 177–81
political messaging, 163; in advocacy storytelling, 177–81
Polletta, Francesca, 9, 12, 202
polysemy, didacticism vs., 122–24, 132–34
Population Registration Act, 239
portraiture methodology: narratives and, 44–45; prison and, 44–45
Portugal, 199–200
post-incarceration life, 42–43
poverty, 24
preppers, 91
Presser, Lois, 7, 34, 62, 97; on narrative criminology, 144

prison, xi, 10, 34, 245–46; education in, 241–43; fathers in, 24; food in, 80–81; identity in, 42, 232–34; legal education in, 232–34; mothers in, 24; music in, 77–78; networking in, 78–79; personal narratives in, 61–62; portraiture and, 44–45; positive change in, 41; privations in, 80–81; reflection in, 77; rehabilitation in, 52, 61; research on, 61; sexual violence and, 223; street narratives in, 76; theorization of, 42; violence in, 80–81. *See also* formerly incarcerated men
Prison, Luzira, 231
prison paradox, 42–45
probation, 157–58; good stories of, 143; harm in, 142; impacts of, 147; oral history on Scottish, 141–43; study on, 142, 143–44; surveillance in, 142
professionalization, 182n1
progressive narratives, 3
Promised Land, 126, 130
provident cheques, 160n5
psychedelic drugs, 21
psychotherapy, 8
public narrative, 183n2

quest narratives, 212

race: in Cuba, 112n2; sexual violence and discourse on, 213–14; in United States, 130, 132. *See also* Blackness
racial justice, 135–36
radicalization, 32
rags to riches narratives, 81–82, 87, 154, 159
rape, 211; narratives of, 213–14, 227; as oppressive tool, 214; as political act, 213–14, 216–18; real rape, 220; single-axis thinking about, 222, 223; as social problem, 217
Rawls, John, 121, 136
reaction videos, 69
Reagan, Ronald, 59–60, 95

real rape, 220
reciprocal relationships, 181; in advocacy storytelling, 169–70
recognition, 159; in Mary's story, 155–57
recovery, ix, 2–3
redemption, 2, 172
reentry, 42–43
reform, 163; narratives, 3, 34–35
rehabilitation, 42, 46; in prison, 52, 61; Schinkel on, 53
relationship building: in advocacy storytelling, 167–69; intimate, 170–73; reciprocal, 169–70
religion, 3, 4, 36, 119, 126–28, 178. *See also specific topics*
research methods, 93–94, 140, 144–46. *See also specific topics*
resilience, laughter and, 62
resistance: fresh home rap as, 86–87; to marginalization through grime music, 85–86; music and, 86; to oppression, 5. *See also* narrative resistance
reverse conversion narratives, 221, 223, 226
rhyme, 125
Ricoeur, Paul, 5
Riessman, Catherine Kohler, 145, 247
rites, in Mary's story, 155–57
road, 87n3

same-sex marriage, 166, 196
Sandberg, Sveinung, 6, 8, 10, 86–87; on tropes, 144
Save the Polar Bear campaigns, 190
Schinkel, Marguerite, on rehabilitation, 53
sci-fi, 91
Scottish Children's Hearings system, 160n3
Scottsboro Nine, 214
self-actualization, 165
self-defence, 7
self-help, 165

selfishness, 120
sexual violence, 209; colonialism linked with, 225; continuum model of, 222; feminists as counter-public to, 217–18; Indigenous representation and understanding of, 225–27; as nodal system, 223–24; prison and, 223; race and discourse on, 213–14; slow death by, 226; structural violence linked with, 223–24. *See also* rape; survivor narratives
sex work, 24
Al-Shabaab, 31
shame, 47, 73, 85, 148, 172, 182, 209, 212
Sierra Leone, 21
silencing, in Mary's story, 157–58
Singer, Peter, 120
single-axis narratives, 221, 227; critiques of, 224; about rape, 222, 223
slavery, 126
slow death, 226
small stories, 238–40
Smith-Pennick, Jy'Aire, 41, 62
social change: music and, 85–86; personal narratives and, 231–32
social class, 154–55; Mary and, 152–54
social media, 163, 203, 215
social psychology, of climate change, 94–98
Social Work Act 1968, 141
sociology, 36; narratology and, 9
Socrates, 117
solitary confinement, 50
South Africa, 166, 240
South Bronx, 48, 49
speaking out, 86
Special Period in the Time of Peace, 104, 111; changes in, 107; economic hardship in, 110
speciesism, 120
Squire, Corinne, 231
stereotypes, 6
stigma, 182, 209, 212

stoicism, 120
stories, x–xi; criticisms of, 2; extracts as, 238–41; good, 1; interrelatedness of, 244; scholarly attention to, 2; small, 238–40. *See also specific topics*
story banks, 163
story-critical narratology, 2
storytelling, ix–x; of Abdi, 25–27, 29–30; commodification of, 163–64; egalitarian, 169; habitus and, 29; habitus structuring, 9; harm-limiting, 29; healing, 21–25; humanity and, 169; imaginative, 32–35; of King, 126; of Mandela, 238–41; meaning-making and, 22–23; in narrative psychology, 3–4; by nonprofits, 163–64; professionalized, 4; transactional, 163; uplifting, 25–29. *See also specific topics*
Strawson, Galen, 2, 3–4
street narratives: in fresh home rap, 74–75, 77–79; in prison, 76; reaffirming, 73–77; reflection through, 77–79
strip searches, 223
structural violence, sexual violence linked with, 223–24
struggle, 135
success, 85
suffering, modulation of, 173–75
suffrage, 122
suicide, 225
surveillance, 140–41; in probation, 142
survival, fresh home rap and, 71–72
survivor narratives, 209–10, 228; audience of, 212; erasure of, 213, 219; as gifts, 212–13; as quest narratives, 212
survivor stories, 12
sustainability: Holmgren on, 100–101; modeling, 103–4; necessity of, 98–99; paths to, 111–12; as practice, 99
Sweden, 203
Sykes, Gresham M., 42, 43
syllogistic argumentation, 122–23
Syria, 174

Tambo, Oliver, 236, 242, 245
teaching, 237
temporal agency, 51, 57–58
terrorism, 31
Thatcher, Margaret, 95
thematic analysis, 145
Thunberg, Greta, 190, 197, 202–3, 204; on climate change, 186–87; youth-led climate politics and, 191–94
Till, Emmett, 223
Time (magazine), 219
To Kill a Mockingbird, 214
townships, 240
tragedy, 19
transactional storytelling, 163–64, 169
the trap, 71–72
trauma, 5, 36–37, 171, 212–13, 224; from crack epidemic, 55; humor alleviating, 48; uplifting storytelling dealing with, 28–29
tribalism, 2
tropes, 226; Sandberg on, 144
Truth and Reconciliation Commission, 166
Tuck, Eve, 44
turning points, 157
Tutenges, Sébastien, 10

UBPCs. *See* Basic Units of Cooperative Production
Uganda, 12–13, 242, 246, 248n4, 249n7
Ugelvik, Thomas, 160
UK drill, 76
UK rap music, 67, 68; authenticity in, 76, 83; marginalization of, 72
undocumented students, 179–80
Union of Concerned Scientists, 200
United Nations Committee on the Rights of the Child, 197–98
United Nations Convention on the Rights of the Child, 190, 197, 201, 202
United States: portrayals of, 133; race in, 130, 132

the unsaid, 80–81, 144–45, 152–54, 157–60
uplifting storytelling, trauma processing via, 28–29
urban agriculture, 107–8
urban farmers, 93
Urgenda case, 198
utopian stories, 96–98, 110

veil of ignorance, 121
victim-blaming, 219, 226–27
victimization, 5, 81, 165–66, 175–76; climate change and, 189
violence: gender and, 217; in lyrics, 74–75; in New York, 49–51; in prison, 80–81; structural, 223–24. *See also* sexual violence

walking probes, 46
Warr, Jason, 45, 76
whiteness, 45, 112n2
white supremacists, 213–14
wildfires, 200
Wilson, Cassandra, 211, 215
women: in fresh home rap, 74–75, 86; in music, 86. *See also* gender
worker cooperatives, 108–10
Wright, Erik Olin, 97–98

young people: climate change and, 188–91; climate litigation led by, 194–201; climate narratives of, as good stories, 201–4; empowerment of, 189–90; Thunberg and climate politics, 191–94
YouTube, 163, 170, 173–74

www.ingramcontent.com/pod-product-compliance
Lightning Source LLC
Chambersburg PA
CBHW031144020426
42333CB00013B/500